INTRODUCTION

SPINECHILLER is a unique collection of true, authentic ghost stories, the experiences of ordinary people from all over the country, also some from overseas.

The stories have been collected over many years, mainly as a result of radio phone-in programmes where listeners have responded, in writing and over the air, to Mary's request for unexplained experiences. One of the most influential sources of material has been the regular MYSTERIES PHONE-IN with Pete Murray on LBC (London Talkback Radio). Mary has been the psychic researcher on this programme for over three years and has received a wealth of intriguing stories from listeners.

It is interesting to note that within the vast weekly mailbag a high percentage of letters start with the words: "Now I don't believe in ghosts, but . . ." Then the writer goes on to tell his or her ghost story! This shows that although people are often hesitant to divulge their experiences for fear of being ridiculed, the effect of what has occurred in their lives has been so overwhelming that they feel compelled to share their stories with others. Most of the stories in the book have been first time encounters and the people have gone to great lengths to emphasize that they have not dabbled in the occult.

PETER & MARY HARRISON

A Sinclair Book

First published in Great Britain in 1990
Reprinted 1990
by Sinclair Publishing Ltd.

Typeset by Metropress (Type) Ltd, Wellingborough
Printed and bound in Great Britain by
Cox & Wyman Ltd, Reading

BRITISH LIBRARY CATALOGUING IN
PUBLICATION DATA
Harrison, Peter
    Spinechiller.
    1. Great Britain. Ghosts. Claimed observations, history
    1. Title II. Harrson, Mary
    133.1'02941

    ISBN 1-872149-03-0

Sinclair Publishing Ltd.,
26 Silver Street, Wellingborough,
Northants, NN8 1AY, U.K.

SPINECHILLER

by
PETER & MARY HARRISON

We would like to thank all the people who took the time and trouble to share their unexplained experiences with us. To all of the people featured in this book we are forever grateful.

SPINECHILLER

CONTENTS

Chapter One
THE SOUTH OF ENGLAND

LUTON, the industrial town set in the heart of the Chilterns, is the home of Gary Eldridge whose story began when he left school at the age of 16 in 1974.

'I did not know what I wanted to do for a living but after answering a few advertisements I went for an interview for a job as a trainee baker. The bakery was in Salisbury Road in the older part of the town. The owner lived in a flat above the bakehouse and there was a shop at the front of the premises from which the sales were conducted. The baker was married and had five children. Even at my tender age when I first met the man I had a feeling that all was not quite right. I could not put my finger on it and looking back I suppose he might be described as being mildly eccentric.

'Anyway, the job consisted of learning the bakery trade which I was looking forward to and I was offered a reasonable pay packet, mainly because of the unsociable hours that had to be worked; 3.30 a.m. until the work was finished from Monday to Thursday and on Fridays I had to work from 11.00 p.m. until 9.30 a.m.

'I was shown around the bakehouse which consisted of a medium sized room in which wedding and birthday cakes were made; down some old wooden steps into the old kitchen which had been turned into the frying room; the main bakehouse which had two large mixers and two very large old fashioned wooden benches and two ancient provers.

'So my first morning of work arrived and off I went slightly apprehensive as any young boy would be on his first day at a job. At that time the business was being run just by Colin the baker and his wife who ran the shop. I was shown some of the things that I was expected to do.

'On that very first day Colin called me over and asked me something that I will always remember simply because it seemed so strange at the time. He asked me if I scared easily! I said, "No". Nothing more was said which made me wonder even more.

'After I had worked there for about six months, one morning I was just getting on with my chores as usual. I had grown to enjoy the job very much and I was fond of the owner and his wife. I remember I was dividing dough into two pound lumps ready for proving. After a while at the job I'd found that I did not need to keep putting the knife down to add bits of dough to the lump to ensure that the specified weight was maintained. Anyway on this occasion I stuck my knife into the dough to add a small piece to the lump on the scales. I only turned around for a matter of seconds but when I turned back the knife had been moved away out of my reach.

'At the time, although I was puzzled, it never really occurred to me to say anything to Colin as to me it was insignificant. However when the same kept happening about four or five times that week I thought that I'd better mention it to Colin.

'I will always remember the look on his face. His mouth opened and he said, "Oh no. Here we go again." He then surprised me by telling me that if I wanted to leave he would understand. I assured him that I was very happy in the job and I was sorry that I'd even mentioned the incident to him as I did not want to cause a fuss over nothing. No more was said and although I probed him to tell me why he seemed so concerned he refused to say a single word on the matter.

'Shortly after that I was in the bakehouse on my own. I needed to go into the loft to collect a sack of flour. I had done this many times before so it was just part of the normal proceedings. I was in the loft picking up the sack of flour when the only window in the room slammed shut with such a force that one of the glass panes smashed to smithereens. I felt all the hairs on the back of my neck stand up. It had suddenly turned freezing cold. I kept thinking that the loft was always the warmest place in the whole building, the temperature kept at approx. 30° C, so I could not understand why the atmosphere had gone frigid. It was a scorching sunny day so even though the window was broken no cold could have come from outside.

'Something told me to get down the stairs as quickly as I could so I grabbed the big bag of flour and charged down the steps. Halfway down, a box of wafers came toppling down on me making me lose my balance and trip over. The flour bag burst and I found myself almost smothering in clouds of flour.

'I went up to Colin's flat to report what had happened. He saw that I'd had a fright and I was covered in flour so he immediately told me to go home and get changed and that I could take the rest of the day off. I washed my face and hands and brushed down my clothes as best I could, and then I thought I'd better just call back to the bakeroom where Colin was to tell him that I was off home.

'I heard terrible shouting as I approached the bakehouse and when I entered I found Colin on the floor shouting and cursing at something which seemed to be holding him down. When he saw me he shouted over at me to get out quickly but there was no way that I could have left him like that. I made myself walk over towards him. It crossed my mind that perhaps he was having some kind of fit. I was not quite sure what to do so I reached down to grab his arms to try to help him up on to his feet.

'As I reached out for his arms I again felt a blast of cold air and again, unaccountably, I felt the hairs on the back of my neck rise up. Try as I would I could not grasp his arms even though they were only inches away from me. Something solid, but invisible, was preventing me like a barrier. We were both in a state of terror and felt completely helpless. It was as if we were battling with a tremendous unseen force.

'I don't know if Colin had experienced anything like that before but he suddenly seemed to get the upper hand and he roared – and I mean really bellowed at this thing to go away (although his language was somewhat stronger!) The thing, whatever it was, seemed to get the message because suddenly whatever barrier had been preventing me from grabbing Colin's arms had gone. I helped him up off the floor and I noticed that the icy feeling had also gone and the room temperature was back to normal.

'Although everything was back to normal we were both very shaken up and he was flinching as if he was in physical pain. He rolled up the sleeve of his shirt and I was appalled to see three large scratch marks on his arm. They were not bleeding but raised up like weals and they looked extremely painful. I knew that I couldn't have made those marks on his arm as by the time I was able to grasp hold of him he was already starting to get up himself so all I did was to take a hold of his right arm, more to steady him than anything. The marks were on his other arm. (I have given this incident

9

much thought over the years since then and I have always come to the same conclusion: there is no way that he could have made those marks himself.)

'I went home and had the rest of that day off as was arranged. The following morning I reported for work as usual. Each of our baking racks consisted of about 25 heavy steel trays full of bread tins. I had filled up one of the trays with the tins when for no reason that I could think of, the tins started to move around by themselves. They moved only a few inches but the peculiar thing was that they had moved in all different directions so it's not as if the tray was on a slant or anything like that. As I walked out to the retarder room I heard a few loud clicks. By the time I got to the room all the retarder doors were wide open.

'Being a practical person I was getting a bit sick of all the nonsense that appeared to be going on and this was the last straw. I stomped over to the retarders, slammed the doors shut and in my mind I kept repeating Colin's words of the previous day when he had suggested that the entity should "go away". Only I didn't just suggest, I downright ordered the thing to depart from us.

'Just as I turned round from the retarders, out of the corner of my eye something grey caught my attention. I looked round and at the entrance by the doorway there was a cloud of greyish smoke hanging in mid air. I looked hard at this and slowly the sting of coldness permeated the room. I quickly lost my spirit of bravado and started to feel the fear creeping over me.

'In a panic I ran straight for the door thinking that I could maybe just barge through and get out of that place. As I braced myself to pass through the cloud of smoke I suddenly was hurled straight back into the small room with such force that I actually hit the back wall opposite the doorway. I was stunned. Not daring to move again I stood leaning against the wall staring at the smoke. It started to swirl around, at first quite slowly then as it gathered momentum it was moving in a furious circular motion.

'It seemed to work itself into a spiral then it promptly shot upwards and in a flash it was out of sight. I gave a heavy sigh of relief but still did not move – just in case. A bit gingerly I walked across towards the open door and went out of that room never to return.

'I reluctantly left the bakery as I had come to the end of my tether. I remained friends with Colin for a couple of years after I left until he also decided that the time had come to move on.

'One day he had been working in the outhouse by one of the retarders and he also was confronted by the grey cloud of smoke. I had never told him the exact details of what had happened to me in that room because at the time I was only interested in leaving with the minimum of fuss – also I did not want to worry Colin unduly.

'Like me, he saw the smoke in the open doorway. He also tried to get out and he felt himself catapulted back. He had started verbalizing at the smoke in his characteristic vocabulary but this did nothing to help his situation. He heard the sound of mocking laughter, quietly at first, but then it grew louder and louder until he thought that his eardrums would burst. It was harsh and malicious and really terrifying. As he watched, the smoke started swirling again and formed itself into a spiral but instead of just moving upwards and away as it had done when I had seen it, it turned on its side and shot into the room towards him. He buried his face in his hands and cowered down in the corner all the time hearing this fearsome outlandish laughter. He could also hear a swishing sound as this spiral kept swooping around the room.

'With all the courage he could muster he got up on his feet and when the spiral was in the opposite corner he ran out of the room and across the yard. He looked over his shoulder just in time to see the column of swirling smoke whizz upwards towards the sky, the laughter fading as the entity eventually evaporated.'

∞

JOAN Read, a lady from Lewisham, was carrying out a photographic survey of Deptford in South London in 1962 and she had decided to work on Deptford High Street. "Despite the cloud, the light was still good enough to get the detail that I needed. As I worked steadily along the street, the sun came out and the breeze died down.

'By the time I reached St. Paul's churchyard, I was very hot and one of my cameras needed reloading. I mingled through the crowds that always crammed the street on a Saturday, and then I remembered that Saturday was the only morning that I would be able to get into St Nicholas' church. The vicar had explained to me that other than for services the gates would only be opened for about a couple of hours while the flower lady was busy inside.

'I decided that it would be nice to go into the cool church where I could take my coat off and reload the camera then take some interior shots. Five minutes or so later I arrived at the church gates which were surmounted on either side by the figures of Adam and Eve which had looked down on generations of parishioners.

'The gates were unlocked so I went into the churchyard where the air was very hot and still. I made my way to the main doors of the church but found them locked, yet I could hear the organ being played inside. I thought that perhaps the organist was practising, so hoping that he would not mind me sitting in the church I walked round to the vestry door. I was thankful to find that it was slightly ajar. I pushed the door open and walked inside, finding the vestry empty. There was another door on the far wall which obviously led into the main church.

'It was quiet. The music had stopped. I then heard the sound of a door banging loudly in front of me. I wondered if the organist was just leaving, in which case he or she would hardly want to see me hanging around. I paused where I was in the vestry but I heard nothing more. I gently pushed the door to the church open and went inside. There was a lady busy arranging flowers on a small table behind the pews near the door.

'I said that I hoped I would not be disturbing her and I explained that the vicar had invited me to take some photographs of the church. She said that she would not be disturbed and that I was just to carry on as if she wasn't there. She said that she was usually there on her own at that time on a Saturday morning.

'I took my coat off, folded it and reloaded my camera. The church had been badly damaged during the war, but the restoration work had been extremely well done, using many pieces of masonary from the old building. I admired the Grinling Gibbons carving "The Valley of the Dry Bones", which then, in 1962, was not covered by protective glass as it is today.

'The church is a very old one, originally built on

Deptford Green in Saxon times. It was rebuilt in the 12th century and consisted of a chancel, nave and two aisles. In 1630 it was repaired and considerably enlarged. In 1697, due to a big increase in the population, the whole church was pulled down, with the exception of the tower, and rebuilt to a larger scale. The architect did his work so badly that the church had to be fully repaired in 1716. Other repairs followed and during the First World War it was closed for three years. It was bombed in the Second World War and restored in 1958. From early in the 12th century the church tower, with its beacon, guided ships round that bend of the River Thames. This association with seafarers led to the annual gathering on Trinity Monday of the Corporation of Trinity House.

'Just to make conversation I asked the flower lady if she played the organ as well, mentioning that I'd heard the music as I'd walked along the path outside. She looked puzzled as she told me that I must have been mistaken. She had not played the organ and certainly no one else had been in the church as she had been there on her own.

I did not say anything because I was so surprised. The music was so loud that she couldn't have avoided hearing it and it definitely was organ music coming from inside the church. She however was so adamant that there had been no music that I just didn't know what to think but I knew that I had heard it loud and clear.

'This incident made me start to wonder so much that I thought I'd better mention it to the vicar. Not wishing to make too much of it I started by asking him general questions about the church then I just asked casually about the organ. He told me that the original organ had been a 'Father Smith' built in 1697, but this had been destroyed by fire and rebuilt by Hunter in 1868. Further damage was done which was repaired by Bevington in 1876. When the restoration of the church took place in 1958 a new organ was built by N.P. Mander, installed and then decorated with the gilt carvings from the original organ casing.

'He told me something else that really made me think. He said that the day before, he had been busy supervising the reburying of bones which had been left out from the last time that the two large crypt chambers had been tidied up.

'He then went on to tell me that during the last war, a gang set up a workshop in the crypt to steal lead. The coffins were opened, the occupants tipped out and the lead cut up for removal. Later, when the rebuilding of the bombed church commenced, mountains of human remains were found in various stages of decomposition. The corpses had been covered with plenty of lime and left beneath the pews. Perhaps one of the poor wandering souls was an organist. It gave me the shivers to think that only I had heard that music.'

∞

BRENDA Whincup of Shropshire married in January 1961. Her husband is a northerner who at that time was serving in the Metropolitan Police and he wanted to transfer back up north.

'It meant that I was going to have to leave my mother, my one living relative, all alone. However she was only 52 at the time and said that she would consider moving north to live with us if my husband got his transfer.

'We moved north as planned, but my mother remained in London with promises of joining us very soon. Came that

Christmas though, she was still down south so we went down to London to spend the holiday with her. She couldn't come to us as she worked in a local hospital, in catering, and was working an early shift on Christmas Day.

'Our journey south on Christmas Eve, in our old car, was slow and grinding and we did not arrive until very late in the evening. My husband wanted to be up early the next morning to drive my mother to work – they thought the world of each other. She however would not hear of him getting up early after such a long gruelling drive so she insisted that he should have a rest the following morning and I agreed with her. My plan was to be up early myself and walk with her to her place of work.

'She was not pleased to see me up and ready to go out early the following morning and said that she wanted me to have a rest. I argued that I needed cigarettes and so we reached a compromise. I would keep her company part of the way to where there was a vending machine from where I'd let her continue on her own and I would return home with my cigarettes.

'We left the house so early that it was still dark. There was a glorious golden moon and the stars were sharp and bright. We walked hand in hand like a couple of excited children singing carols along the road. When we reached the vending machine, as promised, I let my mother go on alone and watched her go out of sight.

'I did not return to the house by the way we'd come. By taking a right hand turn I could go home by walking around the block which I did listening to my own footsteps echoing loud and lonely. Reaching the end of this road and taking another right hand turn, the last 200 yards to the corner of our road stretched before me.

'Here, with such a short way to go, everything seemed to wind down and go into slow motion. I'd never experienced anything like that ever before and I was most confused and somewhat alarmed. I remember very slowly almost floating up in the air between my steps as I moved along the left hand pavement. Then, from my right, on the other side of the road, the shape of a woman appeared from between a row of parked cars. I was certain that no one had turned into the road from the other end and there had been no sound of any door opening or any cars. She was just all at once there, crossing over towards me.

'My first impulse was to laugh. I had done a lot of amateur drama and here seemed to be someone over-playing a part. She was tall, well-built, wearing a coat so unfashionably long that it was almost down to her ankles. She was leaning heavily on a stick and sort of lumbered forward. Suddenly it was no longer funny and I became aware of the first feelings of fear sweeping over me

'As I moved on she came right up to me face to face. She asked me if I had a cigarette. With my new unopened packet burning a hole in my pocket, I said "No" and tried to hurry past but the slow motion was holding me back. Try as I would I could not move my feet at normal speed. She called after me, "Do you know how late it is?" I turned around and there was no one there. I found that I was walking at normal speed, in fact slightly faster than my usual pace.

'All over the Christmas period the incident was upper-most in my thoughts and I felt very worried by it. I felt an overwhelming guilt about my own meanness in refusing to give that woman a cigarette. I could have spared one easily. I hadn't even offered her a kind word. My actions worried me and I also had a nagging feeling at the back of my mind that I should have recognized this woman. I felt that I should know who she was yet at the same time I knew that I'd never seen her before.

'In the New Year, as other matters took over, I forgot about the incident. We discovered that my mother was seriously ill. She did, at last, come north to live with us for what turned out to be the last few months of her life.

'It was after my mother's death, when we were sorting out her things, that we came across some old photographs. There was one of me as a small girl taken in a garden, where I was standing beside my maternal grandmother who had been dead for some 20-odd years. She had been a big woman, and sturdily built. In the picture she wore a coat which came almost down to her ankles and she was leaning heavily on a stick.

'With great pain, I recognized her as the woman I'd met that last Christmas morning when, I believe, she had tried to warn me just how late it was and how little time I had left with my mother.'

∞

PETER Knights of Wisbech, Cambridgeshire, purchased a run-down property with a business partner in 1971. It was a corner shop with three floors and a cellar. It was situated in London's Fulham Road. 'The idea was to renovate the property and then let it out as flats and a lock-up shop.

'In order to keep the costs down I decided to do most of the interior decorating myself. At that time I was living in Surrey and in order to avoid the double journey each day I would often sleep on the premises in one of the bedrooms on the second floor which I had made habitable.

'I was wakened up one morning at 2.00 a.m. by the sound of glass breaking. My first thought was that a car must have crashed on the main road outside the shop. I looked out of the window onto the road below. The street lights remained on all night and I could see that there was no sign of any accident.

'I then thought that it must have been a passing drunk who had smashed the window of the shop, so I went down to the ground floor with some trepidation. The previous occupiers of the shop had been newsagents and confectioners and they had gone out of business and had done a moonlight flit leaving all the shop fittings, and display stands, behind them. These were all still in the shop as I had not got round to starting the renovations on the ground floor.

'There was a half glazed door leading into the back of the shop so I peered through this to take an initial look at the damage which I was sure must have been done to the large plate glass shop window.

'I was immediately aware that something was different about the shop. Instead of the outline of the counters and newspaper racks, greetings cards display stands, etc., I saw along one wall a number of tall mirrors with basins in front of them and a row of old-fashioned barbers chairs. An old fashioned gas fitting hung from the ceiling and there was a smell of cheap perfume.

'A figure was sitting slumped forward in the chair farthest from me. There were slivers of broken glass all around the place. My first reaction was that a drunken yob had broken into the shop and fallen asleep in the chair. The

19

different appearance of the shop had somehow not completely registered in my brain.

'I quietly opened the door and reached for the light switch, getting ready to run if the figure sprang up at me. I turned on the light. The shop was instantly back as it should have been with the old counters, display stands etc. all in place. No mirrors on the wall, no basins or barbers chairs and no slumped figure. Nor was there any sign of any attempted break-in or any splinters of broken glass anywhere.

'The next morning I visited a nearby hardware store to make a few purchases. It was a traditional old type of shop which had been in the same hands for several generations. I told the elderly proprietor about my experience the previous night. He said that his father had once told him that at the early part of the century my shop had been a barbers, and the owner, returning from the First World War in 1918, had found that his wife had been unfaithful to him. He had gone straight down into the shop and cut his throat with one of his razors. His body had slumped forward smashing one of the wall mirrors as it did so. The time of his death was reported to have been around 2.00 a.m. I shivered as I returned to the shop resolving never to stay overnight in that flat again.'

∞

IN the late 1920s Verity Blake won a scholarship to a grammar school in South London. 'It has never been fashionable to actually like school but I have always cherished happy memories of mine – although I cannot say that I was one of its brighter lights.

'On leaving school I joined the Old Girls' Association. I was most active in the drama section the founder of which was an old teacher whom we all called Miss Dorothy. Seeing that I was keen, she took me under her wing. It was a joke between us that she had left school in the year of my birth.

'The play we were working on was *Viceroy Sarah* based on the relationship of Queen Anne and Sarah, Duchess of Marlborough. I had the part of the eldest Marlborough daughter, and Dorothy played Prince George, the Queen's consort. One tiny cameo remains with me. As the prince, Dorothy took leave of the two ladies announcing that 'he' would take a little nap. "And stay out of the pantry" was Queen Anne's reply. Putting his head round the curtain the prince answered with immense dignity: "I may have my little peculiarities, Annie, but I do not sleep in the pantry." This line always brought the house down.

'The war came and Dorothy went to the Midlands and I did not see her for many years. The end of the war found me with a husband and a family of little daughters, whose care precluded Old Girls' membership so I let my subscription lapse.

'Some years later, when the girls were growing up and becoming reliable, I did temporary secretarial work for an agency in London. One day I met another ex-schoolfellow with whom I had corresponded over the years. She told me that the school Christmas reunion was soon to be held so I decided to go along for old time's sake.

'The first person I saw in the well-remembered school hall was Dorothy. She came forward to welcome me and she introduced me to the school's new headmistress. There were several members of staff whom I had known in my schooldays – most of them long since retired but they all still came along to the reunions. They all remembered me and were glad to see me. I decided to renew my subscription and to attend meetings and functions whenever possible.

'In time, I was voted onto the committee and later I became the secretary for my own age group, so I saw Dorothy more often. She had been retired for several years and lived in a pleasant flat in South London. She used to have open house to her own ex-pupils. Now and then I would telephone her and arrange an evening together. By this time, we had moved to Surrey and all but one of our girls were married. Gradually I realized that Dorothy was looking older and more frail. After all she was into her seventies, but her interest in people was as keen as ever.

'On our Christmas reunions, refreshments were provided and served by committee members. On one such occasion Dorothy and I were dispensing tea and coffee from the refectory. We reminisced about the old Drama Section, which had never been revived since the war. Slyly I quoted: "I may have my little peculiarities, Annie, but I do not sleep in the pantry." Dorothy beamed with pleasure. "Fancy you remembering that, after all these years," she said, and I could see that she was touched.

'The next year, I was discussing herbs and herbal emollients and remedies with the botany mistress, who invited me to the staff table for refreshments. I followed her up to the top table instead of taking my food at the committee table where I generally sat. I could see Dorothy sitting alone at one end of it. I waved and she lifted her hand and smiled, but she looked far from being well.

'Refreshments over, it fell to me to collect money for the school's charity. Rattling my box at my fellow-committee

22

members, I asked: "Where's Dorothy? I thought she looked rather ill."

'There was a shocked silence – then someone said: "Didn't you know? Dorothy died last Easter."

∞

JEREMY of Frome in Somerset used to live on a council estate in 1963. One of his school friends, Gareth Lewis, lived in Styles Avenue which bordered the grounds of an old house called Easthill House.

'The house had been derelict for a number of years and I understand that it had been requisitioned in the war by the army for the use of officers (Americans, I think). An old caretaker lived nearby in the early 1960s. Easthill House was uninhabited but stood in a lovely setting surrounded by trees. In the grounds there was a lodge, and strangely, a mortuary. In the bad weather of 1963, Gareth and I were playing, as we often did, in the grounds. That was a winter of extremely heavy snow that stayed until March or April.

'I must, at this point, mention that we were only ten years old at the time and when an old ambulance appeared on the drive outside the mortuary our only concern was to hide behind a hedge from where we had a clear view of the happenings.

'The ambulance looked new but old fashioned and had a red cross on the side of it. Gareth and I had been chased many times by the caretaker but we were prepared to risk this as we were so curious to watch, whilst hidden from view.

'The driver and his mate got out of the ambulance and went to the back of it, opened up the back doors and brought out a body on a stretcher. They went into the mortuary and came out again several minutes later without the body but carrying the empty stretcher. They both got back into the ambulance. Suddenly it disappeared.

'Gareth and I were shocked but finally plucked up enough courage to creep over to the mortuary, some 30 yards away. The snow showed no tyre marks and in actual fact the snow was about two feet thick, sufficient enough to deter most vehicles. The only prints in the snow that day were the ones we made as we dashed home in terror.'

∞

REG of Peacehaven in Sussex got the sad news one day from his wife that her friend's husband had suddenly died at the wheel of his car at the age of 42.

'The following evening my wife and myself called to the lady's home to see if we could help in any way. We had been there on only one other occasion when I had met her husband for the first time. When I met him he seemed rather reserved and his wife explained to us later that he was not keen on having visitors in the house.

'On the evening after he had died, his widow was understandably still in state of shock. After about half-an-hour I had to go outside to fetch something from my car. I let myself out by the front door which opened very easily, but on my return, after only a few minutes, if that, I found the door very hard to push open. It was as if someone was behind the door trying to force it closed on me.

'I was just about to ring the doorbell when the door swung wide open, as if of its own accord. No one was behind the door when I stepped into the house. I did not say

24

anything at that stage as I did not want to distress the lady needlessly.

'We stayed in the house for about an hour and in that time I had the constant feeling that the dead husband was trying to tell me something. It was like someone talking to me from another room. I knew I was being addressed but I just could not make out what the message was.

'On returning home, approximately eight miles away, I suddenly said to my wife to telephone the lady and ask her to pull back the corners of her fitted carpet in the dining room as there would be some money there. My wife was most hesitant to do such a thing in case her friend might feel that it was some kind of practical joke. I had no idea why I had asked her to do this but the feeling was so strong that I was convinced that she should make the telephone call. She did so very reluctantly, and held on whilst the widow turned up the corners of the living room carpet only to find that there was nothing there. My wife was most apologetic to her friend, and what she said to me will remain undisclosed.

'For some days after this I still kept getting that voice in my head over and over again instructing me to make the lady look under the carpet again, and there was something about a blue book to do with the Royal Navy. None of this made any sense to me whatsoever and after my wife being told by the woman that there was nothing under the carpet I thought that I'd better keep my thoughts to myself.

'About five weeks later the lady had to call in some workmen to her house to carry out some repairs. They pulled back the dining room carpet to get underneath the floorboards, and there, just a bit further in from where the lady had first looked, was a large envelope with £200 in it.

'On thinking back to the time I had tried to re-enter that

woman's house, I can't help thinking that the lady's husband had not realized that he was dead as it had happened so suddenly. I feel that he was still around the house that day and he looked upon me as an intruder trying to enter his home.'

∞

MR. Rudland, a Sussex man, like all grandfathers, thinks the world of his first little grandchild, Kirsty. 'When our daughter used to come to visit us when Kirsty was a baby we would put the little one in her carry-cot and put this on the lounge floor or sometimes in one of the bedrooms.

'When Kirsty was about four months old we noticed that after a while she would get very excited and her eyes seemed to be following something around the room. At first we thought that she was just interested in the new surroundings but even when she was left in the dark she would sometimes just stare at one spot without blinking but her arms and legs would be thrashing around in great jubilation. She would then suddenly stop as if someone had left the room, but after looking around the room she would start again, this time laughing and becoming very excited.

'Just before Kirsty's first birthday I was sitting in the lounge with her as she tried to climb up on my lap. She suddenly turned round and started to giggle. She stretched out her arms towards the other side of the room. As I looked up and tried to stop her from falling over, there, on the other side of the room about ten feet away from us, was an elderly man with a kind smiling face.

'Before I could call my wife and daughter he just faded away. When I looked down at Kirsty she was looking at me but pointing to the spot where the man had been standing. At that stage she had not started to speak but I can't help thinking that she had her own means of communication unknown to the adult world.'

∞

JACK Read of Lewisham, South London, remembers when London was still enduring the nightly bombing raids in late 1940. He had come home for a week's leave from his ship.

'I arrived at Kings Cross station many hours late, the train having been delayed by air-raids. I made my way to the underground. What a sight met my eyes! The platforms were crowded with sleeping figures spending the night down there, safely but most uncomfortably. Yet, despite all of the inconvenience, there was little grumbling, just the good old Cockney humour and a hope that their homes would still be standing in the morning.

'When the "all-clear" sounded, I made my way to London Bridge station where I was lucky to catch a train straight away to Forest Hill. Shortly after leaving the station at Forest Hill to walk home, the air-raid warning sounded. It didn't seem long before I heard the drone of enemy planes overhead.

'I became aware of some footsteps just behind me and then I heard a voice call out, "Hello Jack." It was pitch black and I couldn't make out who was calling to me. I then heard the words, "Don't say you've forgotten me – it's Marjorie."

27

'I peered into the darkness and recognized her. She was one of the sisters of my best friend. We passed a few words of general conversation until we arrived at the swimming baths where Marjorie left to cross over the road to her home in the street opposite. However, just before she left me, she made me promise that I would go home the long way round by the old pub called The Woodman and not up Thorpewood Avenue as I normally would have done.

'On reaching the start of Thorpewood Avenue I was in two minds about which way to go, but there was something about Marjorie's insistent manner that made me carry on via The Woodman.

'Some minutes later the sound of a plane's engines grew louder. Here it comes, I thought. Suddenly there were three thundering crunching sounds followed by a violent explosion which made the ground shake under my feet. The explosion was in the immediate vicinity so I started running towards my home to see if the house was still safe.

'I was relieved to see that there was no damage in our street but within minutes the whole area was in a frenzy of activity. Thorpewood Avenue had come under direct fire and three bombs had fallen across the road wrecking nearly all of the houses. My mind immediately flashed to Marjorie and how she had made me promise not to walk up that road. I would most definitely been hit had I gone that way.

'A devastating thought then shot through my mind and I just rushed straight out of our house without taking the time to say a word to anyone. Marjorie lived on one of the small streets branching off from Thorpewood Avenue.

'I raced all the way down the road past the uproar of rescue vehicles and the hundreds of people who were milling around outside, some of them screaming, some very badly injured and some in a complete state of shock. I got to Marjorie's road and to my horror I saw that the whole area – her small street plus a similar one – was demolished.

'I just stood there staring, not quite taking it all in. That was my first night back home after being away on active service for the best part of a year and I was still getting aclimatized to the real effects of war in our ordinary communities.

'I was the only person standing in that devastated road. It then occurred to me that although the houses had been obliterated, everything seemed to have been tidied up in a rough sort of way, but I still couldn't understand why there were no rescue teams bothering to attend to the area.

'While I was still standing there in a dazed condition, a couple of young lads walked by. I asked them if they had seen what had happened. They told me that a land mine had fallen on Marjorie's small road of just ten houses in the middle of the night some weeks previously. Marjorie and all of her family had been killed.'

∞

PATRICIA Ambler of Marlborough in Wiltshire sat one day with her mother in a pleasant room by a large open window. 'It was during the very unhappy early period of the Second World War. Norway had fallen and news from all fronts was discouraging. A large liner had just been sunk carrying hundreds of children to safe keeping in America. We had just heard about this earlier in the day.

'My mother had a few sisters and although great affection certainly existed between them, the distance separating their homes was such that it prevented much in

29

the way of visiting. I always regretted this as I would have welcomed the intervention of my aunts to help me look after my mother. My father, who had always been so full of vigour, and who always knew how to handle every situation, had died suddenly the year before.

'The strain of just trying to survive in those days was beginning to tell on both of us and we had been arguing quite a lot. This particular day I had been trying to read a book but my mother just kept interrupting me constantly. On looking back I can now see that it was her way of telling me that she was feeling insecure and needed attention.

'Suddenly there was silence. After a few moments I looked over at my mother who was sitting bolt upright on her chair, staring into space. She then pointed over and said, "It's Lally. What's she doing here?" I looked all around the room but I could see no one. My aunt Lally was mother's sister.

'The next moment my mother turned a ghastly shade of white and collapsed back in her chair. I thought she was going to faint. All she kept saying was "She's gone. Lally's gone. She's gone." After a few minutes when her colour had slowly returned she told me that she had just seen Lally in the middle of our room, then she had suddenly vanished.

'My mother was a thorough realist and she would not speak further about what she saw. Slightly embarrassed, she fobbed off the incident by saying that she must have been imagining things.

'Early the following morning one of mother's other sisters telephoned us. Lally had been a passenger in a ship called the Simon Bolivar. It had been torpedoed the day before. She had been killed with her children.'

FOR ten years Frank used to be the landlord of the Star public house in a certain Hertfordshire village. 'It had been a fairly busy summer night and I made my usual check on the premises before retiring to bed. On my left was the fireplace with its usual quota of cigarette ends and empty crisp packets which I decided I would clear up the following morning.

'The front wall was at right angles to the fireplace wall and contained the front window, and at the far end, the front door and porch. The serving counter was about six or seven feet long and curled round onto the back wall where there was a small window. That window, with its four panes of glass, was very handy for my customers to look through and watch their children sipping soft drinks and eating crisps in the conservatory type lean-to. The ladies' room was at the far end of the lean-to. I had already switched off the lights but I could still see quite clearly as a very bright moon illuminated the room. I turned to leave the bar, closing the sliding door behind me, turned right and went up the stairs to bed.

'I woke up in the middle of the night in answer to a call of nature. As was my habit, I looked at my wrist watch to check the time. It was only 3.00 a.m. All of the toilets were on the ground floor so I got out of bed and made my way downstairs, thinking to myself that I would just slip into the ladies' room since that was less of a walk. On my way back upstairs I was walking through the conservatory and came to the little window. I just casually glanced towards it and for a few seconds I was rooted to the spot. I'd seen a glimpse of someone in the main bar. My first thought was that burglars had entered the building. I approached the window to get a better look.

31

'Something was dreadfully wrong. The bar looked very different. An almost white solid table stretched for most of the distance between the front and back walls and around it were seated about a dozen or so figures. They were all dressed in a similar fashion with very wide lapelled coats of grey, some with grey or dark blue edging. All of them looked happy and were drinking from large earthenware tankards.

'Some of these figures wore three-cornered shaped hats and I noticed that on a small table in the corner there were more of these hats. Far away in the background I could hear music and singing although I could not see anyone playing a musical instrument. The music sounded as if it was being played on a lute or some such stringed instrument. The figures at the long table were swaying with the music.

'Bizarre as it seems, I was not in the least bit afraid at the time. In fact I was rather annoyed that these people were in my pub drinking without my permission. I walked straight over to the sliding door all set to have a confrontation and walked into the bar. It was empty.

'I must have stood in that room for a good five minutes trying to think of a logical explanation for what I had just seen. I scrutinized every part of the room almost refusing to believe what had happened. Everything was normal, just as I had left it before I had gone to bed. Not knowing what to make of it all I went back out of the room and closed the sliding door behind me.

'I put my foot on the first stair to go back to the bedroom then hesitated. Just to keep myself sane I went back to the little window to have one more look to convince myself that this really hadn't happened to me. Somehow or other I must have misread the scene.

'I pressed my face against the cold glass window pane and

looked through into the bar. They were back! My heart almost leapt out of my body when I saw them. Their faces were quite clear, the tankards, the hats, the long white table, and I could even hear the distant music. They were people, not illusions. Two or three of the men had unbuttoned their coats and then I noticed that amongst them sat a buxom looking lady. All of them had long hair, some tied into a sort of pigtail style at the back. The tankards were quite large and some of the contents had spilled onto the table, which, apart from these stains, looked to be habitually scrubbed white.

'It suddenly struck me that although my face was pressed very close to the window, not one of the revellers had seen me. I stepped sideways away from the window and quietly moved again to the sliding bar door and this time, very gently and as silently as possible, I eased it open. The bar was again empty.

'For ages I stared into that moonlit bar trying to see something of what I had seen through the window but there was nothing unusual there. Leaving the door open this time I quickly moved back to the window. There they were again – the people swaying to the music and quaffing their ale around the white table. I gazed for a few more seconds, and realizing that my door opening and window watching could go on for the rest of the night, I left the window, closed the door on the empty bar, and went to bed, a rather frightened and confused man.

'My wife was fast asleep so I did not wake her. I now regret this as a witness on that night would have been a great consolation to me. I just lay in bed wide awake for the rest of that night bewildered by what I had seen. Being the landlord of a public house I realized that it would be futile to try to explain what had happened to anyone because they would invariably assume that I must have had a bit too much to drink. Only another publican would understand that serving behind a bar on a busy night, single handed, means a minimum of drinks for the barman. I myself knew however that I had only had one pint of my mildest ale. I resolved that I would tell no one about the night's encounters and thus I would retain my reputation for being a sensible, sober landlord of the Star. In common with most people, I do not enjoy being ridiculed.

'It was three or four months later that my wife and I went out for an evening with friends for a meal in a restaurant 50 miles away from the Star. Towards the end of the meal our friend mentioned that he had been reading a book about ghosts in old houses. Because they were long standing friends and I knew that they would not scoff spitefully, I mentioned what I had seen that night in the bar.

'My story provoked a fair amount of laughter from our friends. My wife however, was not so amused. This was the first time that she'd heard of the night merry-makers and she kept giving me knowing looks except I didn't know what the knowing looks were meant to mean.

'On our way home in the car she admitted to me that she too had, as she put it, felt funny things, when she had been alone in the pub. She had once seen a pocket of dense mist on the landing and upstairs passage on a bright clear evening. She had never mentioned it to me as she just didn't think that I would believe her. She added that our two pub dogs had backed away trembling with fright from this mist, which vanished a few seconds later.

'About five or six months later, on a Saturday, I had to go to London for an association meeting. I left my wife to open up the pub for the evening trade and to await the arrival of our barmaid. My wife had been busying herself dusting around the bar when two women entered. One was about 65 and the other about 20 years younger. Both of them were dressed in the quiet, rather old fashioned way, of country folk. My wife bade them a cheery good-evening as they sat down and they replied to her in like vein. They asked her for a fruit juice each which she got them. They explained to her that they were not really drinkers but that they had called into the Star out of curiosity.

'It came out that the older one had lived in the Star many years ago, in fact she had spent her childhood and teenage years there. She told my wife all about the various tenancy changes she had seen and the little alterations that had been made since her father's days. A short time after her marriage, she and her new husband moved north because of his work. She had only come back on a few occasions to relatives' weddings and funerals. Then, without any preamble, she asked my wife, "Have you seen or heard the ghosts around here?"

'Being on the cautious side my wife replied that she had not seen any ghosts but she'd heard some funny noises. The woman looked straight at my wife as if weighing her up, probably trying to establish whether my wife would ridicule her, and subsequently went on to tell her story: It seems that all those years ago there had not been a convservatory behind the bar, and the little four paned window had looked out onto the street. The woman had returned from a very late party and had to get into the building by the back door. As she had passed the little window she'd got the impression that something was not quite right. She stopped and looked into the bar through the window. She went on to describe in explicit detail the exact scene which I myself had witnessed.'

∞

MRS. Seddon from Hertfordshire was on holiday in Devon with her husband about eight years ago. They stayed near the famous Buckfast Abbey.

'We are interested in old churches and so one evening we decided to walk over to Buckfastleigh Parish Church which is very ancient. When we arrived the light was just beginning to fail but we decided to go in anyway.

'The entrance door was made of heavy wood and it required some force to open it. When we entered, the door creaked noisily and when we closed it it slammed shut with a resounding thud. We walked down the right hand side of the church and proceeded towards the altar. As we walked down the length of the building we saw a man walking away from the altar on the opposite side to ourselves. He was dressed in trousers and a woollen jumper. We noticed that he had a bad limp and was using a walking stick. We spoke to him across the building but he took no notice of us and continued to walk past us.

'We reached the altar and both noticed that it had gone extremely cold. I was actually shivering. We turned to walk back and immediately noticed that the man, who had been there only a few moments earlier, was no longer to be seen.

'He couldn't have gone out through the door or we would most certainly have heard him depart what with the creaking and banging of that door. We decided that there must be another exit. There was another door towards the bell tower but that was padlocked. There was no other way out except by the way that we had come in. We tried the door but it was impossible to open or close it without making a great deal of noise.

'We found out later that there used to be a robber roaming Dartmoor with two savage dogs. He was eventually caught and hanged and his dogs were destroyed but initially he was not buried on consecrated ground. It was not until much later that his remains were buried in the Buckfastleigh church graveyard. The ghost of that robber can still be seen roaming in search of his dogs.'

∞

R. HAYTER of Dorset had been working on the Wiltshire Downs in a large sloping field one hot summer's day. 'I had gone there with two friends to help clear ragwort from the field.

'We each had a supply of dustbin bags and set to work. The others had moved into the middle of the field in the hollow of the Down and I worked along the outer raised bank. It was very pleasant in the sunshine just pulling away at the ragwort and not thinking about anything in particular, and filling my dustbin liner with the fruits of my labour.

'I had ambled out of sight of the others and was just putting a handful into the sack when I happened to look up. I saw a man, a soldier or a traveller, sitting under an old thorn tree. He was hunched up with his knees pulled up to his chin. He was dressed in a wine coloured cloak which was wrapped around him tightly. Sticking out from under the cloak was a pair of soft leather boots. On his head was a leather helmet with flaps on it. He looked very dejected and forlorn.

'Beside the man, tied to the thorn tree, was a black mule. It had a soft leather harness on it and a cloth saddle. There were two large soft looking bags tied on either side of the saddle. The mule had its back hunched. What really frightened me about the whole scene was that it was pouring rain over the man and the mule but the rest of the field was bathed in brilliant sunshine. I wiped my eyes to make sure that they were not playing tricks on me, but the man and the animal were still there. The mule streamed with the rain and the man was trying to shelter under the tree, yet I could feel the hot sun burning into my skin.

'I ran, leaving the sack which I had been working with, to find my friends. They remarked that I looked as if I had had a fright, but not wishing to tell them what I had seen, I just remarked that I was a bit worried because I thought that I had lost them.'

∞

MR. E.A. Mead of Gloucestershire was employed as a chain examiner some years ago in a large railway works. 'We formed a gang of about a dozen men and one evening when we were about to go home, one of our mates said that he would not be coming in to work the following day because he would be celebrating the day that he made the best decision of his life.

'Naturally curious we asked him what he meant. Taffy replied, "The day I decided to join the British Army." He went on to say that although he had joined up exactly 30 years ago he felt just the same as he had done on that day – just as fit and the same weight.

'The next day, as expected, Taffy was absent. He did not

come into work on the following day either, nor the day after that. The next day, however, he returned and as he walked down the middle of the workshop all the lads began to send him up, banging their hammers on steel plates and calling out "Taffy you drunken old man" (or words to that effect).

'He had his usual lop-sided grin on his face and yelled over at the micky-takers, "It's grand to be dead." They roared back accusing him of having been stewing in drink the whole week and they jested about the hangover that he must have had. He did not respond to this banter but just walked over to the office to report to the boss, opened the door and went in, closing it behind him.

'After some time when there was no sign of Taffy coming back out of the office the shop steward remarked that the boss must be giving him a right going over so he suggested that he would go in on some other pretext to get Taffy out. The shop steward went into the office but was surprised to see that the boss was just sitting there on his own quietly working away as usual.

'When the boss was asked where Taffy had gone he assumed that the shop steward had been referring to the recent absence of Taffy from work. The steward said that Taffy was back and everyone had seen him walk into the office. There was no other way in or out of that office and the boss swore that he had not set eyes on Taffy since before his absence.

'Later that afternoon the boss received a message to say that Taffy had died in his bed several nights previously.'

∞

A LUTON man, Robert Judge, was walking his dog one

morning in late July 1983. 'It was usual for me to walk the dog over the open land at the back of my home as it is a lovely walk with trees, flowers and wild life.

'I left my home at 6.00 a.m. and after walking for about a mile I sat down on the grass to roll a cigarette. As I was doing so, two magpies flew down in front of us about 40 yards away, fighting over some scrap or other which one of them had been carrying. My dog decided to go over and settle the dispute but I grabbed hold of his collar to prevent him.

'As my dog and I were watching the antics of the birds, I noticed a woman immediately to my right, walking from a narrow trackway between the hedgerows. My initial reaction was to wonder what on earth she was doing walking along in such a deserted place at that hour of the morning. I remember thinking that I would not want my wife doing such a foolish thing.

'As she emerged from the bushes into the open, the magpies took fright and flew off, although she appeared not to have noticed them. She was looking down all the time I was observing her so I thought perhaps she had lost something earlier and was retracing her steps to search for it. She then stopped and stood staring down at one particular spot.

'I got a perfectly clear view of her and saw that she was about 5ft 6ins tall, very slim with a roundish face and light brown hair which was quite long. She wore a pink cardigan with long sleeves, a white blouse with the collar turned out over the cardigan, and a pale blue pleated skirt which reached to just below her knees. She had a crepe bandage over her left ankle and I also noticed what looked like a green stain on the skirt on the left side which I first thought

40

was paint but then thought that perhaps it could be a grass stain.

'At this point my dog, who had been watching her, started to whine and to become very agitated. This was not a bit like his normal character so I was patting him and talking to him just to try to calm him down a bit. I remember my words; "Don't be daft, she's not going to hurt you, whatever's the matter with you?" Looking back over at the woman I started to feel sorry for her and I thought that I'd better go over to see if I could help her in any way. I stood up and was about to walk across to her, at the same time beckoning to my dog to follow me, but he would not move, and just continued to whimper. I tugged on his lead and he took one reluctant step forward and then pulled back. He normally runs to greet people wagging his tale as he enjoys being made a fuss of.

'Leaving my dog where he was, I approached the woman and stood about five or six feet away from her, and as I got closer I could smell her perfume. I asked her if she had lost something. I stood there waiting for her to answer but she just ignored me completely and kept looking down at the ground. I wondered if she might be deaf or if she had some mental illness. By this time I had started to feel uneasy about the situation and decided to leave her to it.

'I was just about to turn away to return to my dog when to my astonishment she completely disappeared just as quick as you would flick a light switch off. There was absolutely no way I will ever understand that, as there was nowhere she could have gone and anyway it happened so fast – one second she was standing there looking down at the ground and the next she was gone, and besides I had not taken my eyes off her, even for a moment. I looked over at my dog. He was still where I had left him so I called to him but he refused to come to heel. He was always the most obedient animal to me but it was obvious that he was frightened out of his wits.

'I stepped over a pace or two to where the woman had been standing to see if there was anything on the ground at that spot. All I could see was vegetation, then something blue caught my eye. I stooped down to get a closer look and there in the long grass was a hair-slide made in the fashion of a bow. I picked it up to examine it and noticed that the clip part had become rusty so I figured that it must have been lying there for some time.

'I moved away from that spot to again call my dog to come to me. Although I was calling him all the time he would not budge until I walked about 20 feet or so away from where the woman had been standing. He then raced up to me and jumped up to greet me nearly knocking me over in the process. I threw the hair-slide for him to retrieve and he ran after it, tail wagging. When he reached the object however, he hesitated, then backed off and came running back to me minus the hair-slide. Now I'd had that dog for 12 years and being a labrador he liked nothing better than retrieving objects that I would throw for him. Never once in all the time I'd had him had he refused to bring back any article I had ever thrown for him.

'I kept thinking about that woman and wondering if I had seen what people call ghosts, but she was as solid as I was and I genuinely thought that I had been talking to a real person. I then remembered that when I had picked up the hair-slide from where the woman had been standing, I had felt extremely cold. At the time I hadn't given too much importance to this as I was more interested in seeing what the blue object was.

'Just to satisfy my own curiosity I walked back to that same spot again and sure enough, at the precise spot where she had been standing, it was still freezing cold. Could it be my imagination, I wondered, so I stepped away from that spot and the air was distinctly warmer. Again I moved to the spot where the hair-slide had been and again I could feel the drastic change of temperature, so much so that it sent a shiver all though me.'

∞

MR. Pengilly of Southampton remembers a story which his late father had related to him. 'My father was born in the Whitechurch area of Hampshire in the late 1800s. When he was in his teens he used to deliver groceries for his father's shop to all of the houses in the vicinity and he became friends with a man called Joe Lloyd.

'Joe lived in the old mill in Whitechurch which is mentioned in the Domesday Book. It seems that many years previously an abnormal child had been born to the miller. In those days this was looked upon as a terrible disgrace and so the practice was that such children would be hidden from public view. The miller and his wife, being ignorant and illiterate, were so swayed by the terror of public ridicule that they pretended that their child had died. The poor child in fact had been locked away in chains in a dark shed and treated like an animal. Food and water was delivered daily, then the door to the shed would be slammed shut and the child would be left in darkness until the following day's rations were delivered. Not once was that child ever allowed out in the sunshine or to meet another living soul.

'Eventually the child was found by a passer-by who had heard screaming and the rattling of chains coming from the shed, but the little boy was in such a neglected state that although he was taken to the shelter of the local vicar's house, he died within a short time.

'One day Joe Lloyd's wife was sitting alone in the parlour when she suddenly heard a violent clanging sound followed by a pathetic wail. She jumped up and searched all over her home and then ran outside to inspect the outbuildings and gardens but there was nothing to be seen. She was just about to go back into the house when she heard it again. It seemed to be coming from somewhere in the back garden. She ran round to the back of the building but there was no one there. She then heard very faint sobbing which only lasted a few seconds.

'She walked around the back garden and noticed that when she passed the corner at the far left end, the air was quite chilled. As she turned to walk back to the house she heard the clanking of chains. She got a severe shock as the sound seemed to come from right under her feet and she even felt the ground vibrate with the noise. She heard the stifled sobbing but did not stay to investigate further being almost frightened to death, but ran back into the house and locked all of the doors and windows. When Joe returned he had to shout and thump on the door before she would open it, he found her in a state of terror.

'Joe got the whole story out of her and it was only after he started asking a few questions around the locality that he learnt the story of the chained up child. Because of the nervous condition of his wife he called in the local vicar to bless the house and the grounds and since then there have been no further disturbances.'

∞

VERA, a Surrey lady, went to bed one night as usual. 'I was in perfectly good health and was not worrying about anything. In fact it was just an ordinary run-of-the-mill night. Something woke me up. I sat bolt upright in bed wondering what had disturbed me. I looked instinctively towards my bedside clock and was quite surprised to find that I could see what the time was without putting the light on. The reason that I noticed this was that I was fully aware that my clock was not luminous.

'I was about to get out of bed to walk over and switch the light on when I found that the room was growing lighter of its own accord. Within a few seconds it was like broad daylight yet I could see that the time on the clock was just after 3.00 a.m. I then noticed that my mother was standing by one of the two windows in my bedroom. I instantly thought that she must have felt unwell in the middle of the night and had come down to tell me although I could not understand why she was fully dressed and not in her nightclothes.

'Just as I was about to call over to her I thought that she looked unusually tall. I opened my mouth to ask her if she was all right and found that I could not speak. I was not afraid or anything but for some reason I could not move a muscle in my body. I just sat there staring. Then I did begin to feel frightened, thinking that I was having a stroke. At that moment the woman turned round to face me and I saw to my utter horror that she was me.'

WHEN Muriel Stevens of Eastbourne in Sussex was on holiday in Devon she was invited to a party. 'We were asked to leave our coats in a bedroom. As I left the room another woman entered who was a stranger to me. I was half way down the stairs when I heard a scream. Several of us rushed back and we saw the woman standing with her hands outstretched as if she was touching something.

'It was some moments before she was able to speak. She said that she had seen her father in that bedroom and she was most upset because she knew that he was gravely ill. She explained that he had been standing in his dressing gown and he appeared to be very wet.

'We later found out that the woman's father had been in great pain with a terminal illness. Not being able to endure the situation any longer he had drowned himself in a stream at the bottom of his garden.'

∞

MRS. Hathaway of Somerset lived for years in a large Georgian property with her husband and two teenage daughters. It is now divided into two shops with living accommodation above. 'One winter morning my husband and I were unpacking pottery at the bottom of the staircase which spiralled up two floors to a kitchen and lounge on the first floor and bedrooms on the top floor.

'We were very busy and engrossed in what we were doing when suddenly I remembered that I hadn't switched the oven on for dinner. I ran up the stairs and as I reached the bend which led to the corridor which ran between the kitchen and the lounge, I was stopped in my tracks by a man staring down at me.

'My first thought was that we had an intruder who must have come in through the kitchen door somehow although I couldn't see how. As I stood there trying to sort things out in my mind, he disappeared from the head down. He was wearing heavy tweed trousers with turn-ups at the bottom of the legs.

'I ran back down the stairs to my husband and breathlessly told him what I had seen. He told me then that he had also seen a man in the very same place but had not mentioned this to me for fear of frightening me. My mind then went back to two times when I had been working in the kitchen and had felt that someone was looking over my shoulder, but when I had turned round I had been most surprised to find nobody there.

'A few weeks later I was speaking to an elderly lady from our village who told me that there had been two grown up sons living in our house at one time about the turn of the century and that one of them had died by falling down the stairs.

'Nothing would put it out of my head that the man I saw looking down at me was the person who pushed that other poor man to his death.'

∞

A LADY from Kent reports that when she was doing a teacher training course in Bristol she had the most unusual dream. 'I am not an over-imaginative or superstitious person nor am I highly strung. I am a graduate teacher of modern languages, married with three children and am a practising Christian.

'One night I dreamt about a fellow-linguist from Oxford. I had had no contact with him for a couple of years or so, therefore there was no particular reason for me to suddenly dream about him. His French wife, whom I had never met, was also featured in the dream. The very next morning a letter arrived from them informing me that their first child had just been born.

'One other such thing happened in the first year of my own marriage. My husband, who commuted from near Sevenoaks to London, had a peculiar dream about eating glass from a broken light tube. No breakages or such had taken place. That morning, when he got on the train, he sat on some sharp glass that some vandal had left wedged, concealed between the cushions. He suffered deep cuts and had to be stitched up at a local hospital.'

∞

MR. Tony Stokes of Bristol tells about the time in 1973 when he had just moved house. 'The house we had been living in was a semi-detached, three bedroomed property only about four years old. The reason we decided to move was that my wife wanted to live in a small village and the house in question was beautifully situated in the heart of an idyllic little village.

'We had been living in the new house for about a month when one evening all of the family were in the living room watching television and I thought that I heard the sound of laughter coming from upstairs. I assumed that my ears were playing tricks on me or perhaps it was in the background on the television. About a minute or so later I heard the laughter again and this time I was sure that it had come from upstairs in the house. I then heard the chatter of children, again as if it was coming from one of the bedrooms on the first floor.

'Without saying anything to the family, I got up, turned the television sound down and walked out of the room to the foot of the stairs. All the time I could hear the chatter and laughter coming from upstairs. By now my wife and children were all curious as to what was going on so I asked them if any of them could hear anything. None of them could. I went back into the living room thinking perhaps that I must have imagined it after all.

'No sooner had we all settled back down to watch the television when I again heard the excited chatter. I can only describe it as that because I could not distinguish any of the words and the children sounded as if they were talking quite fast in an animated way. Again I asked everyone present if they had heard anything but they all said that they hadn't. I then turned the television off, deciding to investigate, and promptly left the room and proceeded up the stairs.

'As I walked up the stairs it began to feel warmer but the voices had stopped. When I reached the top of the stairs I found that the landing was quite warm. I put this down to warm air rising from below and did not give it another thought. As I could no longer hear any unusual sounds I went back downstairs. By now I had become a good-humoured joke with the children who took great delight in teasing me with remarks like "Dad's been on the bottle," and "Dad's gone senile."

'We lived in that house until October of the same year

49

and I heard the chattering and laughter of children almost every single night for those nine months, but neither my wife nor any of my children ever heard a thing unusual. In the early days, or should I say nights, of hearing the voices, I would get up and go upstairs to investigate but always the result was the same. The voices would stop as I climbed the stairs and it always got warmer the higher I climbed.

'I felt no fear at any time during the whole of those nine months, just a naive curiosity. Gradually I got to ignoring the sounds until eventually I more or less accepted things as they were. I think that had one of the other members of the family said that they had heard the chattering I may well have been less than brave.

'I must at this point say that the young couple living next door had no children nor did any children stay there at any period during the nine months, so the voices could not be put down to that. I must also point out that I never once heard the sounds or felt the warmth when I was in bed at night.

'My wife, who was a trained nurse, eventually got herself a night job caring for the elderly in a rest home. In the evenings when she would be working, I would put the children to bed, tell them each a story and see that they were all well, and tucked in for the night. As I have mentioned, I had grown to accept the chatter and got used to the fact that no one else could hear it, so I was not expecting what happened next.

'I had seen the children to bed as usual, my wife was out working at the old folks home and I decided that it was time I went to bed. The bedroom I occupied was just at the top of the stairs to the left. Three of the children, Tony, Karen and Catherine, were in the long bedroom to the right of the stairs, and Neil was in the small bedroom next to mine. When I went to bed I always left the door slightly ajar just in case one or other of the children should get up in the middle of the night, and as I am a fairly light sleeper it would not take too much noise to waken me.

'I had gone to bed at about 11.00 p.m. and had dozed off lying on my right side facing towards the door. For some unknown reason I opened my eyes and there, standing beside my bed, was a small boy with fair curly hair dressed in a long white nightgown, clutching in his right hand a brass candle holder with a burning candle in it. Within a matter of no more than ten seconds I saw him move away toward the door and leave the bedroom.

'My first thought was that it must have been Neil as he was the only one of our children with fair curly hair, although I could not understand where he'd got the candle from or why he should need it. I called quietly, "Neil, are you alright?" There was no reply so I got out of bed and went into his room to see what was the matter with him. I found him in his bed fast asleep just as I had tucked him in earlier. I then went into the long bedroom just to see if any of the other children had been up but they too were all fast asleep and tucked in just as I had left them.

'I went back to bed puzzled and as I lay down I thought about what I had seen. It then struck me that none of our children wore or even possessed a long white nightgown, neither did we own a brass candlestick, nor were there any candles in the house. The most startling thing in my mind at that moment was that I recalled that the figure of the little boy had not opened the bedroom door wide enough to go out, but had simply gone through it. Although I had left the door ajar, it was no more than about five inches open so no

51

one could have got in or out of my bedroom without opening the door properly.

'The next day I did not tell the children what I had seen and I did not tell my wife for some time after. When I eventually did tell her I felt that she did not believe me – in fact there were times when I had began to doubt my own sanity. It would be about September when I saw the child, about a month before we left and during the whole of those last few weeks I never again saw the boy although the voices continued.

'It was 10.30 on a Friday morning in October and the children were all at school. In fact the cul-de-sac was very quiet and there were no children anywhere to be seen. Our neighbours had both gone off to work and I was busy loading the hired van with our possessions.

'I had loaded some packing cases and had just brought the fridge out of the kitchen onto the path outside the house. As I lifted the fridge up to put it into the van I heard, from behind me, the most pitiful cry of a child calling "Mummy, Mummy." I put the fridge back down on the ground and turned around quickly to see who was crying looking directly at the windows of the long bedroom in the house as the cry seemed to come from that direction. I saw nothing. I turned to my wife who was standing near the garage and asked her if she had heard anything. She said, "No, what do you mean?"

'I explained about hearing the child's cry but then, feeling a bit foolish, I turned back to lift the fridge into the van. I then went back into the house and walked upstairs and into the now empty long bedroom which had been occupied by our three children. I just stood there in the middle of the room looking around me. I don't know what I was expecting to see or hear, but nothing happened so I went back outside to continue loading the van.

'When I was lifting the washing machine into the van, again I heard the terrible plaintive cry of a child coming from the same direction as before, calling in a sorrowful voice, "Mummy, Mummy." I turned as quick as a flash but could see nothing. Again I asked my wife if she had heard anything, but again she replied that she had not. Completely convinced that someone was in the house, I rushed up the stairs into the long bedroom but there was nothing there. This time I checked all the other rooms of the house, upstairs and down, but there was nothing to be seen.

'By this time the van was almost loaded with just a few odds and ends still to be put in and then we would be on our way to our new home after picking up the children from school. My wife was standing by the doorway as I was loading the last box into the van. Once more I heard that loud heart-rending cry, "Mummy, Mummy." This time I did not look up at the windows nor did I go into the house, I just looked at Marion my wife and I knew by the look on her face that she too had heard it this time.

'We quickly packed the couple of carrier bags, locked the house door and left. Some months later when we were settled into our new home I did tell my eldest daughter Karen about the cries I had heard on the day we had moved out of our previous house. She made some enquiries with a friend of hers who had lived in that village all of her life.

'She was told that there had been on old farm house on the site of our previous house. There had been a terrible fire and the farm house had been burnt to the ground and three children had been trapped in the top rooms and had died in the flames.'

MR. Young used to be a cycling enthusiast and belonged to a cycling club in Southend. His club used to run time trials whereby a race was set on open roads, limited to 120 riders who started at one-minute intervals. The distances were set at 25, 30, 50 and 100 miles and the time was clocked both on the distance out to a certain point, and then the return journey to the club. The riders who covered the distances in the fastest time would be the winner of that section.

'On a bright sunny Sunday morning in July 1953 I was riding in a 25 mile event on the Southend Arterial Road which was Course E.3, at that time reputed to be the fastest course in the country, being along a dual carriageway over very flat land. The first rider had set off at 6.00 that morning.

'The race starting point was about two miles east of Gallows Corner. The course ran for about five miles and then came to a roundabout at a pub called The Halfway House. A further two and a half miles on the straight road led to another roundabout at a pub called The Fortune of War. After the second roundabout there was quite a steep hill to go down, then onwards for about another five miles to a check point where each rider's number was taken by the marshal on duty. After this the competitors turned back and reversed the journey.

'I started off as number 10, but since number 9 was a non-starter, I had a two minute gap in front of me. The aim was to catch up with the rider in front and keep well ahead of the rider behind. It was a beautiful morning and in those days at that early hour there was hardly a single vehicle on the road. I was cycling along as happy as a sand boy, looking back over my shoulder every now and then just to

54

check if any other rider was catching up on me, but there was not a soul in sight.

'As I got near to the turn marshal at the half-way point of the race, I took another long look back but there was nobody in sight and both ways the road was absolutely empty. I checked in with the marshal, turned around and was on my way back. I had only gone about a couple of hundred yards when a rider overtook me. He was a tallish fellow with all the proper racing kit and a properly equipped bike. He was wearing long white socks which reached his knees. These caught my eye as everyone else wore ankle socks at that time. The rest of his clothes were grey. No word was passed between us but I remember thinking it strange that he had crept up on me so quickly and I had not heard the slightest sound of his wheels on the road. Even as he passed there was complete silence.

'The rider progressed for about 60 yards or so in front of me and then maintained a steady pace, keeping always the same distance between us. I kept wondering where he could have come from because just a few moments earlier I had an unobstructed view of the entire roadway for miles and miles and there certainly was no rider approaching from any direction. I pedalled faster but noticed that each time I made a little ground on him he also progressed by the same distance, so that no matter how I tried he was always the exact same distance ahead of me.

'By this time I was really bewildered because he had not looked back at me even once so I could not fathom how he knew when I was gaining ground on him. He stayed just ahead of me for the entire five miles back to The Fortune of War pub. He went round the roundabout then up the hill and over the top. Within the next moment or so I too was going over the brow of the hill. I nearly fell off my bike with the shock of finding the road ahead of me completely empty. Except for the few moments when he went out of my sight as he went over the top of the hill I had not taken my eyes off him. He had vanished, bike and all. He could not have nipped into a hedge or anything because the grass verges were much too wide for him to have got out of sight in time, and on that part of the road it was so straight and open that I could look ahead and see almost to the next roundabout. The entire length of road was deserted.

'I found out later that rider number ll who was supposed to start one minute after me did not turn up; therefore there was a two minute gap behind me as well as in front of me. That explains why I could not see any other rider on that stretch of road to and from the check point, except, that is, for the one who did the disappearing trick. When I thought about it afterwards, the greyness of his gear together with the total silence made me shiver. I gave up my membership of the club after that.'

∞

MR. BLETSOE of Hemel Hempstead in Hertfordshire is a widower who remembers that shortly after his wife had died various members of the family had mentioned that they could smell her powder, despite the fact that no one else used that particular brand. It happened at intervals at the most unexpected times and in the most unlikely places, for instance when the Sunday lunch was being cooked in the kitchen and no one in the house was wearing any powder at all. It was even noticed in some of the houses of the other members of the family as well.

'I had a dog at the time and each night I used to take him for a walk past the cemetery gates which are quite near to my house. He always went past without any trouble whatsoever, but one night he refused to pass the gates. No matter what I said or did there was absolutely no way that I could entice him to take even one step.

'At that same time, my son who lives close by happened to be coming up the hill from the other direction. When he reached me his face was grey looking and he was quivering with fright. Just as he had approached the cemetery gates from the other side, he had seen a young girl sitting on the wall against a very thick hedge. He thought nothing of this except for the fact that he thought she had chosen a rather odd place to sit. However as he drew near to her and was just about to pass her he watched her body begin to fade into the hedge until she had vanished.'

∞

YET another story involving a dog comes from Mr. Trueman from Salisbury in Wiltshire. 'Lassie was a German shepherd bitch that I had owned since 1969. She was a very sensitive and gentle creature and had come to me as a rescue when she was about 15 months old. We rapidly became extremely fond of one another. She loved people and other dogs, was a great credit to her often maligned breed, and she provided me with enormous pleasure and endless interest in the canine species all the time she was with me.

'It was part of my daily routine, no matter what the weather, to take Lassie on a reasonably long walk prior to retiring for the night. One night at around 11.00 p.m. we were walking along the Southampton Road out of Salisbury, which was a fairly well lit road. There was a ferocious wind blowing and it was lashing rain.

'Our route on this occasion took us to the end of the commercial buildings on the outskirts of Salisbury, across a narrow bridge, so narrow in fact that no footpath existed on either side of the road. From there we turned off left into a track known as Piggy Lane, an unlit lane that curved round to the left and eventually led us back to the Shady Bower area where I lived.

'On this particular night we had just stepped into the road to cross the narrow bridge when, just ahead of us, I saw a large white horse carrying on its back a young girl of no more than 10 or 11 years of age. She had very long blond hair which streamed out in the wind and rain. The horse turned into Piggy Lane just before we did and I could clearly hear the hoofbeats ahead of us. Then suddenly the hoofbeats stopped. Lassie had always been fascinated by horses so she eagerly walked with me into the lane where I expected to encounter the animal with its rider. When we turned into the lane there was no sign of anything and there was no other means of escape from that narrow passageway.

'It was only then that it dawned on me that at this hour of the night and with the weather being as dreadful as it was, it would be most irregular for such a young girl to be riding alone in the darkness in such a desolated place. Lassie and I walked up and down that stretch of lane looking and listening but there was nothing there.'

∞

NANCY of Swindon remembers one morning during the

last war when she was walking to work. 'It was around 8.30 a.m. and I was walking along a street near to where I live which was lined with very old houses.

'A little old lady came out of the doorway of one of these old houses, walked up the garden path and was about to cross the pavement in front of me. She was wearing a peculiar looking tall black hat. Being polite I stood still to let her pass. She walked into the middle of the road then completely vanished.

'Over the years I've thought about that old lady many many times and the only conclusion I could come to was that behind the house which she had come out of was a complex of very old stone built cottages which had been built in the part of Swindon which had been open fields at the time that the Great Western Railway came to the town. The arrival of the railway attracted a lot of Welsh unemployed people to Swindon to work for G.W.R. The stone houses had been built to accommodate these workers and in fact they all had Welsh stoves in them so that the tenants would feel at home. The little old lady I saw wearing the tall black hat could have been one of the Welsh tenants from all those years ago.'

∞

MR. BRETT, a very down-to-earth Londoner, moved into his house in 1953 and has been living there ever since with his wife and two sons.

'As usual after moving into the new area I was eager to set the large back garden to rights. It had been neglected for some time so I started the first week by clearing the weeds, etc. Eventually, after installing the greenhouse and generally tidying the garden up, it was not looking too bad but as time went on I noticed that the front garden did not respond to my efforts in the same way.

'I tested the soil and it seemed to be of the same quality as that of the back garden. I had great difficulty in getting anything to grow there despite trying various types of fertilisers, top dressings and giving it a lot of care and attention.

'Our two boys occupied the same bedroom for a number of years when they were small. Their bedroom door opened on to the head of the stairs where there is a bend and some wide treads. The nightly routine at that time was that the two youngsters were sent to bed in the evening and allowed to look at their picture books and play for about half-an-hour or so then I would call up to them "teeth time" which was the cue for them to get up, go to the bathroom, and then settle down in their beds ready for me to tuck them in.

'One winter evening in 1961 when I had gone up to see them in their beds the boys told me that they had seen a lady sitting at the top of the stairs watching them as they had gone into the bathroom. They had never ever said anything like that before so I asked them what this lady was like, not sure if it could have been their minds playing tricks on them but both of them were adamant that they had seen her and that she was all in grey. I did not wish to put any ideas into their minds so I let the matter rest at that point but over the next week I asked them very casually at different times when I was speaking to them separately what the woman had been like. Both of the boys seemed certain that the only clear thing about the woman was her face, especially her eyes, and that the rest of her was just a greyish form. Both of the boys remarked at how sad she had looked. The thing that intrigued me most about the whole thing was that neither of the kids seemed to be in the least bit put out by this woman. They both emphasized the fact that she was really sad looking.

'I presume that they never saw the woman again as they never mentioned it to me but there was a nagging feeling at the back of my mind. Neither my wife nor myself had ever seen or heard anything but there was something so convincing in the simple direct way that the children had told me about seeing the woman that I felt compelled to make some enquiries.

'I found out that the site of our house was first built on about 1929. The original house received a direct hit from a bomb on 11 October 1940 and the occupants, a husband, wife and two daughters aged seven and five were all killed. The house had been rebuilt after the war.

'My blood ran cold when I learnt that in the total confusion and devastation caused by the blast which damaged the entire street, the bodies of the two small girls had been laid out in the front garden, covered with a tarpaulin and forgotten about for a couple of days.'

∞

ANN ADAMS of Crowborough, East Sussex, used to work in a residential home for old people in Sanderstead in Surrey.

'I was sitting in the lounge feeding one resident and as I looked across the room I saw a figure standing behind one of the other residents. It was a lady dressed in a bright red dress which had a very full skirt which seemed to billow out. Across her breast was a greyish band like a sash which had what looked like a touch of golden thread running through it which made the sash shine in the sunlight. Her hair was in a bun and I recognized the style of her dress as being Victorian.

'The next instant there was nobody behind the chair at all but the old man who had been sitting there died a few days later. Twice after that I saw the very same woman in the long red dress stand behind chairs of the residents and each time within a few days the person died.'

∞

PATRICIA SLARK of Eltham, London was evacuated during the war – about 1940 – to Hartest in Suffolk with her baby brother, young aunt, mother and grandparents.

'I was only 9 at the time and my aunt was only 15. We had all been sent to a very old large manor house which had fallen into disrepair. An elderly couple owned the house and only part of the building was habitable so we all had to make the most of things. My grandparents had one room and my mother, brother, aunt and I shared another huge bedroom with two large beds in it.

'Set in one wall there was a very deep cupboard secured by a large heavy lock – this was a metal ring type which fastened onto a fitment on the cupboard door something like a padlock. The headboard of the bed which I shared with my aunt was pushed flush back against the door of the cupboard. The first night we slept in that house we were awakened by the sound of the large lock banging on the back of our bed headboard and we found that the cupboard door was ajar. It was then that we discovered that it opened inwards so we reckoned that the cupboard must be big enough to walk into. However, at that time in the middle of the night we did not feel like investigating much further. My mother fastened the lock back again and we all went back to sleep.

'The following night the exact same thing happened. We were quite frightened this time because we knew that the lock had been securely fastened and just before we had gone to sleep my mother checked it to make sure that it could not open and waken us up again. Once more my mother had to get out of bed and fix the lock back in place. By this time we were beginning to get a bit frightened so the following night we swapped beds so that my mother and my baby brother slept in the one where the lock was. On that night the very same thing happened and we were all wakened by the large metal ring clanging back and forward against the head-board.

'The following morning my mother reported the clanging lock to the woman of the house who just refused to believe her, saying that the cupboard in question had not been used for years and years since that lock had been put on the door. No one had even opened the door as the cupboard was no longer required.

'The woman explained that when the house had been originally built over 300 years ago, that cupboard had been built in a particular shape for a very special reason. When any of the family had died they had been placed in their coffins and then left in the cupboard until the funeral – it was a type of chapel of rest.'

∞

MRS. SMITH of Polegate, Sussex, went to bed one night as

usual and woke up in the middle of the night to find a shadowy figure walking round the bed. She was so surprised that next morning, although she remembered waking up and seeing the figure, she convinced herself that it couldn't have really happened therefore it must have been a vivid dream and thought no more about it.

'Quite a time after this incident I again found myself wakened up in the middle of the night but this time there was a man bending over the bed looking down at me. I was absolutely terrified and quickly turned away but he then shook me very hard as if he was trying to get my attention. Then to my horror he took a hold of my head to try to turn me round so that I would be looking at him. Although I was nearly frightened to death I managed to reach out my hand to switch the bedside lamp on. The second the light came on the man disappeared. I sat up in bed trembling. Then my mind went back to the time I had seen the shadowy figure. I realized that it was almost the end of April, a year after I had seen the shadow.

'This April I was again wakened up and saw a light – a sort of glowing candle – with a figure in front of it. I just lay staring at this thing until it vanished. I have since found out that an old man lived here before us and he died in our bedroom in a fire.'

∞

EDDIE of Brighton, Sussex, was brought up solely by his mother after his father died when he was only two years old.

'In January of 1958 when I was eight years of age I was seriously ill with whooping cough over a three week period. I did not respond to medical treatment so the doctor had advised my mother to take me to the beach for the day as the freezing cold sea air might be the only hope of clearing my lungs.

'After spending the day in a shelter on the sea front my mother put me to bed at about five in the evening. There was a roaring coal fire which warmed my bedroom but I was feeling very weak from lack of sleep as well as the effects of the illness and I was crying non-stop. My mother had come into the room to comfort me several times throughout the evening but there was nothing that she could do to help me.

'She had just left me with a promise that she would be back in again to see me in a little while. It was then that my father appeared. He walked in through the door, came to my bedside and put his hand on my shoulder and said, "Don't cry son, you'll feel better soon." He gave me a gentle pat then left the room.

'I called my mother straight away and told her what had happened. I was not frightened or upset by it but more excited over the experience. My mother claimed that it was a dream no matter how many times I told her over and over again that I had not been able to go to sleep and I had been wide awake when I saw him.

'To this day I know that I saw him and felt his touch and I know that I was wide awake at the time. The whooping cough improved from that night onwards and was soon completely gone. Both the doctor and my mother said that the cold sea air had worked but I think that I reached the turning point in life that night between the living and the dead and I am convinced that my father saw me back to the living.'

∞

DAVID RITCHIE of Ashford in Kent used to be an airman

serving with 54 Squadron at RAF Stradishall in Suffolk. 'I had been posted after training and my wife and baby son were still living at my father's house in Ashford.

'After making an appointment I went to see a lady with a view to renting her cottage near the airfield so that my wife and son could join me.

'On meeting the woman and her somewhat older, and unfortunately sick husband, I was shown over the property. As I was leaving she explained that they were moving back to their original home in the Midlands for the sake of her husband's health. When I spoke to the man he said that he was disappointed at not meeting my wife and son.

'By arrangement on the following Monday my family and I moved into the cottage. During the night I was suddenly awakened by my wife who was very frightened. She told me that someone else was in our bedroom. I sat bolt upright, not knowing really what to do because sure enough, standing in our bedroom at the bottom of our bed, was the sick husband.

'He just looked at us. For a few seconds I thought that we must have moved in on the wrong date, but as I was thinking of something to say which would sound reasonable he suddenly vaporized and was gone. My wife and I just dived under the bedclothes.

'Within a few days we received a letter from the landlady to say that the trip to the Midlands had been too much for her husband and that he had died on the Monday. He saw my wife and child after all!'

∞

MRS. CLAYDEN of Southend on Sea, Essex, remembers

when, at the age of 13, she went with her sister to live with her eldest married sister in a very large house. Her sister and brother-in-law were caretakers for the local hospital authority who owned the property.

'This building had been a private school before the war started but at the outbreak of war it had been taken over by the army to house the troops.

'Before and during the two months we stayed with my sister in that house, my brother-in-law had been working night shift at the hospital, so my sister was often alone in this massive house until the time we went to stay with them and again after we left.

'Most of the building was unoccupied except for a few rooms. The room they used as a lounge was very large with a high ceiling and French windows leading out onto a verandah at the side of the house. When it had been a school, this room had been the headmaster's study. At the very beginning of the war the headmaster had been standing out on the verandah and was killed by shrapnel.

'Outside this room to the left were double doors leading to the unoccupied front of the building where nobody ventured. These doors were often found open by my sister who kept locking them but they kept opening again. I was sleeping in the lounge on a put-u-up bed over by the French windows and my sister was in a camp bed in the same room.

'One night we were wakened by the rattling of the door knob. Instinctively we seemed to know that no mortal person was causing this disruption. Our little terrier dog who used to sleep in the corner of the room was positively whimpering with fear. This little dog was hated by the dustman and was the bane of the postman's life, yet here he was, whining in terror.

'I was shivering under the sheets and neither of us would dare to get out of bed to turn on the light because the switch was close to the door which was rattling. Then my sister started to say the Lord's Prayer and after a while the rattling stopped and the dog came over to be stroked. He was quivering with fear.

'My brother-in-law checked the whole building over the next day but everything was secure and just as normal. He said that it could not have been an intruder as there was no sign whatsoever of any break-in. We looked out on the balcony and there was a posy of primroses there. To this day I'll never know where they came from but I can't help wondering if someone somewhere was remembering that schoolmaster who met his death on that verandah.'

∞

JOHN HORSEWOOD of Chatham in Kent used to enjoy hiking when he was a younger man. 'I set out towards Whitestable one day and, realizing that I would not reach the town until very late, I decided to book myself into a small inn and make a bright and early start the following day.

'I found a quaint little pub which had rooms vacant so after a good supper I settled down to sleep. I was wakened up in the middle of the night and as I looked towards the window of the bedroom the complete form of a fully grown man just walked right through the glass window and into my room.

'I was ever so alarmed especially as I knew that the bedroom was on the first floor. I just lay in the bed staring at this fellow who was dressed in an army uniform. It was quite dark but I could see him clearly and I noticed then that it was a German uniform. He had his head bent and he just walked up and down the room muttering away to himself in what I can only imagine must have been German. He had a very bad limp and as he paced up and down he had to drag one of his feet along the floor. I couldn't understand what he was saying but he seemed to be repeating himself over and over again.

'I was so petrified by this man who never once looked in my direction that I did not dare to even move and there was no way that I could bring myself to try to get out of that bed to switch on the light. I never took my eyes off him but I did not say anything to him as I thought that if I spoke it would make him notice me.

'Up and down that room he walked for over an hour by which time I was almost at my wits' end wondering what on earth I should do to get rid of him without attracting any attention to myself.

'I suddenly remembered about my Bible. I always used to sleep with The New Testament under my pillow. I said a prayer first because I was so wary about making any move which might make him turn and look at me. The moment I started to recite the prayer I saw the man move quickly backwards towards the window. It was if someone or something like a magnet was pulling him out of the room backwards. He went straight out through the glass window and that was the last I saw of him.'

∞

MRS. BRICKELL from Blandford Forum relates the story told to her, when she was a child, by her mother: 'My late father was born deaf and dumb. When he and my late mother were courting, they would walk out together in the town. My mother had taken the trouble to learn sign language so that she could communicate with my father.

'When there was no moon they used to keep to the main part of the town so that they could converse on their fingers by the light of the streets or near brightly lit shop windows. When there was a bright moon they would venture beyond the outskirts of the town into the open countryside.

'On such a bright moonlit night they were walking along a lonely country road when suddenly a tall man about eight foot in height loomed up before them on the pathway out of nowhere. He wore a most unusual tall hat. They were both so startled that they just froze to the spot clinging onto each other.

'The man then walked right out into the middle of the road and turned to face them. My father, being deaf, heard nothing but saw the man quite clearly. My mother, however, heard the man say, in a most odd way with a gap after each word: "I – don't – think – we – will – go – this – way – tonight." The man then turned and walked straight through the hedge just melting into the leaves in a swirl of vapour and was gone.

'My parents turned and ran all the way home. When they had recovered their breath they told my grandparents what they had seen and heard. My grandfather said that years ago on that road at the section described by my parents, a sailor and a soldier had a bitter fight with each other and the soldier was killed.'

∞

JEAN MARKS who lives near Yeovil in Somerset used to live

in a 400 year old thatched cottage. 'My younger son, aged two-and-a-half, wakened up, at the same time, in the early hours of the morning for several days on the trot. I would hear him happily laughing and chattering away.

'Bleary-eyed, I would grope my way into his room to quieten him down. Each time I asked him what he was laughing at he always answered that he had been talking to the lady who had come to ask him about his toys. He was very much into combine harvesters and farm vehicles at that time. More just to humour him than anything else I asked him what this lady was like. He replied that she looked like Christopher's teachers.

'Now Christopher is his older brother and at that time attended a convent school and was taught by nuns. I asked my youngest son where the lady went and in a most matter of fact voice he told me that she had gone into the wardrobe. This stood in the corner of his room.

'He never mentioned seeing any lady after that but when the day came for us to leave that house, my mother-in-law had come to help with the move. All of the house had been cleared of furniture and the rooms were completely bare and only the two of us were left in the house to do the last minute clearing up. We were both standing in the kitchen when we heard heavy stomping footsteps move across the room where my youngest son had slept. When they reached the corner area they stopped. Mum-in-law and I just scampered out the front door as fast as we could and drove off never to return to that place. Although I must add that there was no real sense of anything menacing about the property, in fact the house had a happy atmosphere about it, nevertheless we both got the shivers when we heard those footsteps.'

CYRIL ANGEL from Yeovil in Somerset remembers New Year's Eve 1962. 'We had not long moved into our new house in St. James Close and there were a few friends in to celebrate the New Year with us. The bells rang in the New Year and after the noisy well-wishing had subdued we all settled down to watch television.

'All at once the loud thumping of army-type boots could be heard passing down by the side of our house and past the side door. We all heard this at once and wondered if there might be some disturbance or street fight outside so we all rushed out to see what was going on.

'It had been snowing quite heavily all that day and as soon as we went outside we could see that fresh snow had fallen during the evening leaving a smooth surface of about two or three inches. We looked all around the house but there was not one footprint in sight apart from the fresh prints we were making as we searched. The weighty thuds which we all heard could not be accounted for. We then got torches and looked around the back garden to see if there might be prints there but we found none. I later learned that the field in which the houses were built had once been used as a short cut for soldiers walking back to Flouderstone Camp from the Yeovil area.'

∞

ANOTHER story comes from the Shady Bower area of Salisbury. Mr. Simons was out walking with his dog Jasper and they were making their way towards The Hollow which is nothing more than a narrow footpath heavily overgrown with bushes and trees.

'On this particular night, as we reached the start of the footpath, Jasper showed a marked reluctance to leave the lighted street and enter the darkened path. So much so, in fact, that he actually lay down on the ground and firmly refused to budge which was most uncharacteristic of the dog.

'I persisted, however, until eventually Jasper plodded unwillingly behind me for several hundred yards and then he lay down on the ground again. This time no amount of persuasion on my part could get him to move further. At this point I clearly observed on the footpath ahead of us, the figure of a nun, standing quite still in the gloom and looking straight towards us.

'Jasper was clearly petrified but I felt little sense of alarm, mainly, I think, because I was so concerned for my dog and I was doing my best to comfort him. When I next looked up, after only taking my eyes away for a split second, the figure was gone. I had no alternative but to allow Jasper to have his own way and therefore retraced my footsteps to the beginning of the path.

'For months after that, this footpath was taboo and I could not get Jasper to enter it. One night I played a trick on the dog and took him by another route to the far end of The Hollow thinking that we would not know the difference, but the moment we set foot on the actual lane itself he lay down on the ground whining and refused point blank to move.'

∞

ERIC JAMES from Irthlingborough, Northants, happened

to find himself killing time in London in the early hours of a December morning in 1949. 'I was on my way from St. Pancras to Covent Garden hoping to make some purchases at the market which started at 6.00 a.m. and then catch the 8.00 a.m. train back to Wellingborough, the nearest main line station to where I live.

'I made my first call for a cup of tea at one of the all night stalls they had in those days. Just a few old timers were hanging around the stall when a man approached it. He loitered about for a few seconds then he asked if anyone could spare him a cup of tea. Since no one else around looked like volunteering, I handed the man some coins to pay for his tea. He was a tall man, about six feet, unshaven, dressed in an army great coat.

'I drank my own tea and turned to move off when the unshaven man asked me if I would mind if he accompanied me part of my way. I nodded in agreement and the bloke walked along beside me. He did not mention where he was going and I had not said anything about where I was going however he seemed quite happy just tagging along.

'Very little was said until, on reaching the cross roads at Russell Square, he thanked me very kindly for the company and said that he might meet again sometime and thanked me for the tea. I made the usual noises assuring him that it was no trouble.

'He still had not told me where he was bound so out of curiosity I watched him walk into the middle of the road then he simply vanished before my eyes.'

'I've often wondered who this person could have been. I had always believed that ghosts couldn't eat or speak but I know that I shared a cuppa with the one I met.'

∞

DURING the war, Mrs. Betty Cordell of Rayleigh in Essex was evacuated to the village of Offord Cluny in Huntingdonshire. While she was living there she became friendly with an airman called Paul.

'I had agreed to meet Paul the following week on the river bridge near the railway station. I looked forward eagerly to our meeting and when the time came I got myself ready and went to the appointed place. It was a lovely warm sunny summer evening and I remember cycling along in my sleeveless pink print dress full of the joys of life.

'I waited and waited but there was no sign of him. I felt very disappointed as this was most unlike Paul. I was just about to leave the bridge when he suddenly appeared behind me. I was so delighted to see him that I moved towards him but I stopped in my tracks when I saw that he looked absolutely ghastly.

'Paul did not move towards me which I thought was unusual. Instead he said, "Sorry I can't meet you tonight." He then disappeared and I found myself standing on the bridge alone weeping, my emotions in complete turmoil. I walked over and looked from the bridge in every direction but there was no sign of him anywhere.

'With a thumping heart I got on my bike and rode down the short way to the railway crossing. I asked the man in the signal box if he had seen a young airman go past through the gates. The signalman said that he had not noticed the man come by, but he then added, "Do you mean the man you were speaking to on the bridge?" He said he had noticed the man with me on the bridge but did not see where he had gone to.

'The next day the news went round the village that some of our planes had not returned from raids and Paul had been killed in his plane two nights previously.'

∞

A NORTHANTS lady, Mrs. Tomezak, remembers the story told to her by her old friend. 'My friend had to go to view a property which was up for sale called the Round House. Because it was a type of museum there were several people around the building when she arrived.

'She bent down to stroke a cat which had edged up against her and was rubbing against her legs as cats sometimes do. She noticed that one or two people were giving her odd looks but she thought nothing more of it and continued to make a fuss of the cat which was still by her legs. One person actually walked over to her to ask her if she was feeling all right. Quite taken aback she replied, "Of course, why wouldn't I be? I'm only stroking the cat."

'One elderly gentleman then walked over to my friend and whispered, "There is no cat!" She told him not to be silly, of course there is a cat, then looking down, she saw that the cat had gone. She felt icy cold all over. She was visibly shaken, so much so that they had to bring a cup of tea to her to try to revive her.

'Another old gentleman caught her up in the garden and told her that he quite believed her, as he remembered an old lady who used to live there when he was a child and she had kept a houseful of cats.'

∞

MRS. WESTERN of Sidcup, Kent, remembers when her children were small her little son and daughter used to play happily together in the long passage on the ground floor which ran along to the bottom of the stairway.

'I looked along the passage to the end where the children were just to check that they were O.K. and I suddenly saw, at the foot of the stairs, a strange woman dressed in a hat and coat. I was shocked and wondered how she could have got into the house without me hearing her. I ran towards the children and quickly pushed them into the front room and the dog ran in with them.

'I stayed in the passage and walked towards the woman talking to her, asking what she wanted. I looked down at her feet but I could not see them as they were shrouded in mist. This startled me beyond words then I looked at her face which had an appallingly sad expression on it.

'I got very frightened and ran into the front room after the children. We stayed in that room until it was time for the schools to come out and my eldest child, who had come back from school, knocked on the door. I peeped my head round the door of the front room looking up and down the passage but thankfully the woman had gone. I let the oldest child in but all the time kept nervously looking around me.

'In the evening I told my husband what had happened. He asked me what the woman had looked like. I described her hat and coat and, as much as I could, her face and hair. He went very quiet- not the reaction I had expected – and then he told me that he thought that I had seen his dead mother.

'I must explain that she had died long before I met my husband and the few photographs we had of her had been taken in her youth. It was my description of the hat and coat that convinced him because seemingly it fitted exactly the clothes that she had worn quite a lot just prior to her death. My husband felt that these were the clothes that she would feel he would best remember her in. She had died at the age of 32 from blood poisoning leaving her husband to bring up a young family of four children.'

∞

A LADY from Kent was working in a baker's shop with two assistants when the most weird thing happened: 'The windows in the shop had three glass shelves, about five feet in height, on which we displayed bread and cakes. I looked over at the window and I was stunned to see a large loaf of our bread hovering about six feet in the air above the glass shelves in the window.

'I looked at the two assistants who were also staring in disbelief at this loaf of bread dangling in mid air. Suddenly, as if some invisible hand had let go of the loaf, it crashed down onto the display below. A customer came running in from the street to tell us that she had seen the loaf from outside the shop window. She was quite terrified but she calmed down a bit when the three of us told her that we had seen it too. We wondered if it had been my late husband who was always in the shop letting us know that he was still around. He was six feet three inches tall and he could have easily held the bread up at the level we saw it. One lady assistant was extremely worried by the event.

'One evening the shop filled up with the smell of disinfectant. It seemed to be the same smell which had been in the hospital ward where my husband had died. We were just about to lock up the shop so I knew that the time was a minute or so to 5.00 p.m. The telephone rang and I answered it to be told the news that my son had been involved in a serious accident and was fighting for his life in hospital. By the time I put the telephone receiver down the disinfectant smell had vanished.'

∞

MRS. JOAN CALMADY HAMLYN of Okehampton, Devon, has a story which goes back to the first decade of the century: 'Before my father-in-law was married, he was occupying rooms in the bachelor wing of the house and his bedroom overlooked the stableyard. One night he was awakened by the growls of his terrier which slept at the end of his bed.

'He heard the sound of a carriage and four turning in through the gates at the end of the drive. He got out of bed and looked out of the window into the stableyard which was bathed in moonlight. He heard the coach and team approaching up the drive and swirl round the corner into the yard, pass underneath his window and go on round the corner of the coachhouse and fade away into the distance. He saw not a thing.

'It came to light sometime afterwards that a woman servant had been working in the kitchen when the figure of an old time coachman materialized in front of her eyes, stood there for a few seconds and then vanished just as quickly.'

∞

WHEN Cathy Doig of Rochester decided to have an early night for a change something happened which she will always remember: 'I was 18 at the time and I got into bed and settled down. My parents were sitting downstairs watching television and there was no one else in the house.

'As I lay quietly in my bed I became aware of breathing to the right hand side of the bed. I lay and listened for what seemed like ages but I was so petrified I lost track of the time completely. The breathing seemed fairly rhythmical but ever so often it would stop for about five seconds and then a deep breath would come followed by the normal breathing pattern again, and there was the sound of an occasional heavy sign.

'I plucked up courage and shouted loudly for my father who came running up the stairs quickly and put my bedroom light on as he entered the room. I recounted what I had heard and we sat quietly listening but the breathing had stopped.

'The following day my father checked with our next door neighbours who assured us that they had not been in bed at that time. In any case I knew that the breathing had been in my room right beside me. Sadly it turned out that at the time I had heard the laboured breathing my grandmother who lived 70 miles away was dying.'

∞

MRS. WHITE of Eastbourne lives with her husband and two

little girls in a small flat above some garages. 'The property was originally built in 1923 as stables, then in 1940 two flats were built above the stables which were at the same time converted into garages. Our flat therefore was situated where the original hay loft had been.

'One night we were in bed reading when we heard footsteps running across the front room. They stopped outside our bedroom so we naturally thought that it must be one of the girls. I called out, "Lisa – Kelly" but no one came into our room. I got up to find out what they were up to and was surprised to find that there was nobody by our door despite the fact that we had not heard the footsteps retreat. I went straight to the girls' bedroom to find that they were both fast asleep in their bunk beds.

'Shortly after that I was working one evening on the late shift and my husband attended to the girl's nightly routine. He had bathed them and told them that they were allowed to play for a little while before he put them to bed.

'While the girls were playing in the front room, my husband went into the bathroom to have a wash. He left the door open so that he could hear that the children were all right. He looked into the bathroom mirror and caught sight of a small girl running past into our bedroom. He immediately shouted out, "Lisa, Kelly, you know you are not allowed in the big bedroom." As he spoke he walked out of the bathroom to see that both of our girls were still in the living room on the floor playing with some toys.

'Very puzzled he walked into our bedroom and there in the corner stood a small girl dressed in white with long blond hair. He looked at her, completely bewildered. The child just stood there looking equally confused then she disappeared.'

MR. LATTER, a Londoner, and ex-Barnardo boy, worked in a famous hospital in West London. 'I was deputy head porter and once on night shift I was asked to take an oxygen cylinder to the private patients' wing. As I walked along the dimly lit corridor a sister passed me in strange clothing. She wore a long brown uniform which reached her ankles and had a dark blue belt around her waist. She had lace frills at her wrists and on her head she wore a huge white frilled hat.

'I said "Good evening" to her and she said "Good evening" back. She then proceeded to walk straight through the wall. I got the fright of my life and quickly delivered the oxygen which I thought for a moment I would need myself. I went immediately to the night sister and told her what I had seen. She quite casually told me not to worry – it was only the hospital ghost.

'Years and years ago a sister at the hospital had had an unhappy love affair with one of the doctors. She had taken an overdose of drugs and was found dead in one of the side rooms off that corridor where I had seen the vision.'

∞

ESSE from Doncaster remembers clearly the time back in 1946 when his mother and sister-in-law (his youngest brother's wife) were travelling in a train from London to visit his brother who was in hospital in Chatham in Kent.

'Eventually their compartment emptied except for themselves and another lady who was a complete stranger to them. She approached them and said, "I'm glad we are on our own for I have been wanting to talk to you." Then to my mother she said, "You are going to see your son who is dangerously ill. He will have a major operation soon and will only be given a 50/50 chance of recovery but he will recover, and although he will have future set-backs, he will live for a good many years yet."

'My mother and sister-in-law were so completely astonished at the stranger's words that neither of them was able to utter a word. The lady went on to tell them, "At present he is only allowed to have fluids and fresh fruit which he is getting." (At that time fresh fruit was in the way of peaches which were still in short supply but which were kindly sent by my eldest brother who lived in London.) The woman went on to tell my mother, "Don't worry; things look black right now but your son will eventually pull through."

'When my mother got her breath back after the shock of hearing what was the Gospel truth from someone she had never set eyes on before, she asked the lady how she knew all this. The lady replied simply, "Your mother told me."

'My mother's mother died in 1925. My brother had a serious operation to have a greatly enlarged and diseased spleen removed. He had several later haemorrhages which resulted in a further serious and complicated operation. From that date in May 1946 he lived a further 33 years.'

∞

A SHORT story comes from Margaret from Hampshire: 'I was going to an evening class at our local secondary modern school, and being early, I arrived before the school was properly opened and lit. Therefore I decided that I'd better try to get into the building by some way other than the usual entrance.

'The corridor was rather dimly lit and I was sauntering along when I felt a restraining hand on my shoulder. I hesitated and slowly put my foot out for the next step. I found that I was at the top of a small flight of three steps, then there was a small landing and another three steps leading up to the corridor again.

'I felt quite shaken for if I had not been prevented from just walking at my normal pace by that invisible hand, I would have surely fallen down the steps flat on my face and there was no one readily at hand who could have come to my assistance. I suppose I'll never know who saved me that night but all the same I'd like to say a big thank you.'

∞

DOROTHY from Coulsdon in Surrey lived in Victoria, British Columbia, when she was a small child. 'My great-grandparents on my mother's side were living at the Manor House in Buckden, Huntingdonshire, after my great-grandfather had retired from service in the Indian Army.

'When I was quite young my parents brought my elder sister and myself over to England from British Columbia to be introduced to the family, making the Manor House our headquarters. Whilst staying there I complained each morning to my mother that she had wakened me up in the middle of the night by sitting on my bed. She told me that she had done no such thing and put it down to the fact that I was sleeping in a strange bed.

'One morning I was playing about in the rose garden on my own when a woman came over to me and sat down on a garden bench and watched me playing. I did not pay much heed to her as by this time I was used to seeing new people. However I did notice two things about this woman. She was wearing a long cloak which went right down to the ground and she was crying. I thought it odd to have such a heavy cloak on since it was the middle of summer and very warm.

'The following day I was again playing in the rose garden but this time my sister was with me. Again I saw the lady who came from more or less the same direction (up the garden path from the summer house) and again she sat herself on the same bench, and again she was crying. I watched her for a moment and then just went on playing with my sister without saying anything.

'I remember we were playing with a ball. It was a special favourite of mine because it was extra bouncy and would bounce on the lawn. My sister threw the ball to me for me to catch it but I missed it and it went whizzing past me towards the bench where the lady was sitting. I started to giggle and called out to my sister, "I hope it didn't hit the lady." My sister asked me, "What lady?"

'I turned round quickly towards the bench but the lady had gone. She had been sitting there just a second before-hand. I remember feeling so confused that I just went on playing with my sister without making any more reference to the woman.

'One late afternoon I was walking up a narrow stairway at the back section of the house. The stairs led to a long corridor which had several small bedrooms off to each side. This part of the house was known as the children's wing. I loved to go up there because one of the rooms had a great collection of children's picture books and old toys.

'As I walked along the corridor I saw the same lady

coming towards me. She was still wearing her long heavy dark blue cloak but what really attracted my attention was the fact that she was still crying. I couldn't hear any sobs but she had the most sorrowful looking face that I'd ever seen and she kept putting her hands up to her face in the same way that she had done when I saw her sitting on the garden bench. I did not like to say anything, seeing that she was a grown-up, so I just went into the bedroom where the toys were and shut the door.

'After our return to Victoria my great-grandfather decided to have the floor-boards on the stairs and landing taken up in the children's wing. They had become quite creaky with age so he planned to have the area re-laid. During the proceedings the workmen discovered a small storage area the end of the corridor which had been boarded over. No one in the family had ever realized that it had existed because it was behind oak panelling but extended underneath the corridor floor-boards. The workmen had been checking for plumbing piping when they had noticed it.

'Great-grandfather instructed the workmen to take down the panels to check the exact size of the storage area in the hope that it could be put into use. When the outer wood was removed, the workmen found the skeleton of a baby wrapped up in cloth.'

Chapter Two
MIDDLE ENGLAND

ON Sunday 3 March 1782 John Landor, the seven year old son of the Rector of Calton, Rugeley in Staffs. was taken seriously ill at the grammar school at Rugeley.

During the afternoon he was visited by his mother and his aunt. When Mrs. Landor arrived home she reported to the rectory nurse that young John's condition had deteriorated and she asked the nurse to go to the grammar school to sit up with the child all night to comfort him.

Eliza, the nurse, accompanied by a man called William Carser, a groom at the rectory, left for Rugeley at about 8.30 that evening. William carried a lantern to light their way through the dark road. As they drew near to Rugeley parish church a lady in a brown cloak, a stranger to them, approached. She asked Eliza if the rector was at home at Calton.

The nurse replied that the Rector was at home but that he would hardly thank anyone who might disturb him at that time, particularly with his present worries. The woman replied, "I must trouble him for I have a child that I want burying tonight." As the woman said these words she looked down at her cloak, the folds of which Eliza noticed were covering something shaped like a small coffin which the lady was holding under her arm. That instant the woman disappeared.

William held the lantern high in the air while he and Eliza looked all around them but they could see no trace of the woman. They wondered if she could have slipped down the pathway to the canal so they made a thorough search of that area but there was no one to be seen. Both William and Eliza were terrified at the woman's sudden appearance and disappearance and her odd remarks.

When they eventually returned to Calton rectory they found out that no one had called to see the Rector the previous night. Later that same day little John Landor died.

In later years Eliza, a highly respected lady, never liked to refer to this story because of its macabre significance but she was persuaded, in response to repeated requests from those interested in the incident, to make a sworn statement to a solicitor. In this statement she gave the full details as they are recorded here.

∞

YET another story comes from Rugeley, again connected with the canal. John Godwin has been investigating a series of events which started over 150 years ago. He reports:

'On 17 June 1839 drunken boatmen on the Grand Trunk Canal – later to become known as the Trent & Mersey Canal – murdered a helpless female passenger. Two of them were publicly hanged in Stafford and a third was sentenced to transportation for life in Australia. The headstone to the murdered woman's grave – erected by public subscription – still stands in St Augustine's Churchyard, Rugeley, and the poignant inscription is still legible.

'Mrs. Christina Collins, 37 years of age, was the only daughter of Mr. & Mrs. Robert Browne of New Radford, Nottingham. Mr. Browne was the inventor and patentee of a bobbin and carriage design which was used in the Nottingham lace industry. His invention had initially brought him wealth, but it is certain that the family later fell on hard times, and there is reason to believe that Mr. Browne became mentally deranged.

'A local newspaper of the day states that Mrs. Collins had been well educated, of excellent character and was indeed well formed to move in a different sphere, but the unforeseen events which had occurred in Mr. Browne's family when the children were young (Christina had a brother) blighted all their prospects and left them without friends or protectors to guide them in the rugged paths of existence.

'Christina married, firstly, a man some years older than herself, but he died in 1832 in Ireland. After six years of widowhood, Christina married Robert Collins, a stable-man. Both Robert and Christina were desperately poor and at first sought work in Liverpool. Christina obtained a job as a seamstress, but for Robert the outlook was bleak – there was no work to be found.

'He decided to go to London to look for employment and the arrangement was that he would send for Christina when things were more settled. He soon secured work as an ostler and managed to save a guinea from his earnings, which he sent on 9 June 1839 to his wife, with a message that she could now join him.

'Christina, petite and trim in her figured blue silk bonnet and dark coloured gown, and wearing a fawn neckerchief, set off from Liverpool on the morning of Saturday 15 June to travel to London. A rail link (change at Birmingham) between Liverpool and London had been opened a few months earlier, but the fare was more than she could afford, and so was the stage-coach fare. Canal travel offered the cheapest prospect (only 16 shillings) so she made her way across the Mersey to the northern terminus of the Grand Trunk Canal.

'Many boats in those days incorporated a small passenger cabin, and the Pickford's boat which Christina joined had one of these. The Captain of the boat was a man called James Owen, from Brinklow and the crew were George Thomas (alias Dobell) William Ellis (alias Lambert), and a teenager, William Musson from Chilvers Coton, Warwickshire, who was not involved in the subsequent happenings.

'From the moment the boat set off on its journey it was quite clear that Christina was in a potentially dangerous situation, for the crew began to siphon off spirits from the casks in the cargo, and they soon became the worse for drink. Siphoning off spirits was a common practice of boatmen, and the trick was to pilfer it so adroitly – topping up the casks with water – that no one could tell that anyone had tampered with the cargo.

'At most stopping places the boatmen would disappear into the canalside public house, and this naturally added to their drunken state. No approaches were made towards Christina until the boat was passing through Harecastle Tunnel, when one of the crew came and sat by her in the dark, ostensibly to comfort her, but she instinctively sensed that worse was to come.

'As the journey progressed, the boatmen, now completely under the influence of drink, began to take liberties with their female traveller. In an effort to escape the crew's attentions, Christina at times walked along the towing path, keeping abreast of the boat.

'Hoo Mill Lock, near Great Haywood, was reached at midnight on 16 June. By this time Christina was in a frenzy, screaming loudly to the men not to touch her. The lock-keeper's wife stuck her head out of their cottage window and enquired anxiously as to the cause of the noise, but the boatmen assured her saying that their lady passenger had her husband with her.

'This was the last time that Christina was heard or seen alive. At 5.00 a.m. next morning her body was found at Brindley Bank, near Rugeley, only a few yards from the aqueduct which takes the canal over the river Trent. The boat was nowhere in sight but whether or not the boatmen realized at that stage that Christina was dead is not clear.

'By the time the crew reached Woodend Lock, King's Bromley, however, it was obvious that something serious had happened, for the Captain reported to the lock-keeper that a deranged passenger had drowned herself.

'At Fradley Junction the Pickford's clerk became suspicious of the boatmen's behaviour, so he went quickly to Fazeley, the next stop, where the local constable arranged to arrest the men when they arrived. They were all, in the words of the constable, "tipsy and abusive" as he took them into custody. They were cursing Christina as they were led away.

'The inquest was held at the Talbot Inn, Rugeley. The local surgeon declared that death had been due to suffocation and drowning.

'The men were first tried on a charge of rape at Stafford in June 1839 but of this charge they were completely cleared. The trial for murder was delayed until the following year because of the absence of an important witness, and another judge then took charge. The prosecution called numerous people who had seen Christina and the crew as the boat had travelled down the canal. Many testified that the crew were very drunk and that they frequently made disgusting references about their lady passenger. One threatened to "burke" her; that is to smother her in the way that the Scottish criminal Burke had done to his victims a few years earlier.

'The jury found the three boatmen guilty of murder and the judge sentenced them to be publicly hanged in Stafford. At the very last moment, while the final communion service was taking place in prison, a reprieve arrived for Ellis, who, it was felt, was not quite as deeply involved as the other two had been. He was sentenced to be transported to Australia for life.

'A crowd of 10,000 people gathered in Stafford to see the end of the boatmen. A broadsheet, specially printed and giving all the lurid details of the murder, was on sale to the crowd. A copy of this is preserved in the William Salt Library in Stafford to this day.

'There is some uncertainty as to whether Ellis ever went to Australia. He certainly spent a long time in Stafford gaol, but during this time he proved himself to be a model prisoner, learning to read and write. The prison governor, in view of this, made a special plea for clemency, but whether or not this plea was effective is not clear.

'Strong Rugeley tradition says that as the body of Christina Collins was being carried up the flight of steps leading from the spot where she was found to the main road, her blood stained the steps for many years to come. Even today the steps are still known to all old Rugeleians as the "Bloody Steps".

'There is on record a strange incident which happened 50 years ago. A Rugeley lady was walking near the Bloody Steps on a path on the other side of the canal from the towing path on a warm summer's evening when she suddenly heard a scream.

'From the trees near the waterworks she could see the figure of a man advancing towards her. He seemed to glide along and passed through the railings as if they weren't there. He was dressed in black and white with long black hair tied back at the neck. He wore knickerbockers and the lower part of his legs could not be seen for they were shrouded by a mist. He had a sad countenance and did not utter a word.

'Later that day the same lady was impelled by an overwhelming curiosity to look at the inscription on Christina's headstone in St. Augustine's churchyard. A cold chill crept down her spine as she realized that it was a 100 years to the day since Christina was murdered. Who was the ghostly figure? Was it Robert Collins, Christina's beloved husband, returning to haunt the spot where his wife had been so brutally murdered?'

∞

JOAN lives in Heanor, Derbyshire, having moved there with her parents from Leeds just as the last war began. She was the youngest of seven sisters and three brothers.

'We moved when I was about eight years of age. The house we moved into was a strange three storied building with two large bay windows on the second floor. My bedroom was so small that we could only get a tiny wardrobe, a chair and a single bed into it, but it was my very own and I loved it.

'We had only been there for a few weeks when strange things began to happen. First the doors would open and shut on their own, lights would switch off and on, but these things we learnt to live with until one night it happened.

'I was fast asleep when something woke me. I remember opening my eyes and the moonlight was streaming in making the bedroom as bright as day. A tall thin figure of a man stood at the foot of my bed staring at me. I screamed at the top of my voice and pulled the bedclothes over my face. By the time I'd summoned the courage to take another peep he was gone and my parents were entering the room with the rest of the family. I had wakened the entire household with my scream.

'I tried to explain to them what had happened but no one believed me. They said that I must have been dreaming, but my mother let me sleep in her bed for the rest of the night.

'The next day I began to believe myself that it had only been a dream . A few weeks later we had all gone to bed except for my sister Ann who was reading in the lounge waiting for her husband to finish work at the pit. She had our Alsatian, Laddie, sleeping near to her on the floor. He was a big dog who feared nothing.

'The sound of the dog growling made Ann look up. Laddie had got up and was whining at the door leading to the stairs. My sister was terrified. She walked across to the door and just as she put out her hand to reach the handle she could see the doorknob slowly turning. Laddie started to bark furiously and the doorknob sprang back to its original position.

'Taking a deep breath Ann grasped the door handle and flung the door open. The dog rushed through, snarling, then all went quiet. My sister nearly died of fright as she saw Laddie backing into the room, his fur standing up on his back. He was staring into the hallway and whimpering. He was terrified of something out there – something my sister couldn't see.

'Slamming the door shut she screamed and screamed. My father and brothers searched the house from top to bottom but found nothing.

'After that night we all saw the ghost at monthly intervals. We got used to him though we were still scared of being alone in the house. It didn't seem so bad if someone else was present.

'We discovered, in later years, that the house was once a school for Quakers, so maybe one of the teachers was keeping an eye on us. I like to think that.

'We spent many happy years in our house and grew to love its nooks and crannies and dark attics and even the ghost. A few years after my parents died, the house was pulled down and with it our childhood memories. Whenever I pass the site where it once stood I say a quiet prayer for our ghost that he has found at last his resting place and is at peace.'

∞

UTTOXETER is a quaint market town in Staffordshire. Mildred, a lady from that town, will never forget the Saturday afternoon when she went to bed with a headache. 'I suddenly found myself standing by my dressing table mirror, but when I turned back round to face the bed I nearly had a fit when I saw myself still lying in the bed.

'I looked round towards the mirror and saw a wavering column of pale blue energy vaguely in human form and slightly larger than me. It seemed to crackle and sparkle all over. As I stared at this shape I felt a swishing and found myself floating upwards hanging somehow in a peaceful silence. I must have been in mid air but I was still in my bedroom because I could still see my physical body lying on the bed.

'The next thing I knew I was facing a huge gold or brass door – it was certainly not my own bedroom door – at the top of a flight of steps. There was the head of a lion embossed on the door. As I went through this door I found myself in a corridor floating in a lying down position about two or three feet off the ground.

'On my left side stood two young men. One was unworldly in appearance, very handsome with a face so pale the I could hardly see where his skin finished and his whitish golden hair started. He was completely dressed in black. His features were perfect and angelic looking. He seemed to have authority.

'The other man was very ordinary looking with dark hair, earthly features, and sallow skin. He seemed to be under the instructions of the fair haired man.

'The fair man took my left arm and indicated to his companion that he should take my left leg. The dark one did this then both of them began to tug gently. As the tugging started I found myself back in my own bed again, but the two men were still there. I was fully conscious and was lying on my right side.

'I could not move a muscle although I could see the two men hovering above my left side, the fair one holding my left arm and the other one holding my left leg. As they continued the pulling I felt as if my inside was being dragged out of me and there was tremendous pressure on my left arm and leg.

'The most disturbing thing happened then. I felt my

ghost body (or spirit) being gradually dragged forth until it was half in and half out of my physical body. As I glanced to my left, although I could not move my head, I saw myself emerging as a grey shadow. I then felt my right eye go blind as it withdrew from my right side. As this happened I seemed to get a better, clearer view of the two men who appeared to be having a struggle.

'At this point I got very angry, feeling that I was being practised upon. From their gestures it was obvious that the dark young man was there to learn something under the tuition of the fair one.

'I willed myself to return to my body. The moment I had this thought, the pulling stopped. They held a discussion as to whether or not they should continue. It was most strange because I could not hear any spoken words but I seemed to know instinctively what was going on. They made another gentle attempt to pull me away again but I willed further that I would return to my normal physical condition.

'There seemed to be a battle of wills. However, they then decided to abandon the attempt, and the lesson, or whatever it was, was aborted.

'I felt my spirit returning gently into my body again from my left side but it was a very slow process. I couldn't even flicker an eyelid for about four or five minutes.'

∞

LEAMINGTON Spa on the River Leam is well known for its Spa and has been a fashionable health resort ever since Queen Victoria granted the prefix 'Royal' to the town when she visited it in 1838.

When Cyril Carter, a native of the town, was 18 years of

age he had an accident in which he was trapped between a tram and a motor coach. 'I was lucky that I escaped without physical injury but I suffered from delayed shock and I was ill for over 12 months with a nervous condition. At that time I began to notice that I was having premonitions that came true, some pleasant and some not so pleasant. I also noticed that supernatural things began to take on a new meaning, and with understanding came revelation.

'Then one day there was an article in the local newspaper giving details of a house on the mountain side that was supposed to be haunted. The house was vacant because the people who had lived there could no longer stand the hauntings. I then had a feeling that if I could stay one night at the house, I would know the reason for the hauntings.

'After reasoning things out in my mind about making arrangements to gain access to the house for my vigil I went to bed. The upstairs layout of our house was as follows: At the top of the stairs there was a very large bedroom where my mother and father slept. My own bedroom was next to this and then the next room to mine was where my young sisters slept. Exactly opposite my door was the room where my two little brothers slept.

'I woke up just as the dawn was breaking. I had no sooner opened my eyes when I saw a wraith-like mist come through my bedroom door. It was about the size of a tall man but its shape kept changing and all the time it was slowly floating towards my bed. It stopped at the foot of the bed and out of the mist a malevolent face appeared and began to convey to me in unspoken words that I was not to go to the haunted house. I could hear no sound but it was as if the words were being transferred directly to my brain. I got the message that the truth was not to be revealed yet.

'To my absolute horror an arm came out of the mist and stretched out a hand with a long pointed finger, touching me on the chest. The horrible evil face conveyed the message that if I did venture near the house I would be stopped. With that I suffered the most terrible pain that caused me to freeze and groan inwardly. The mist then floated back out through the bedroom door and was gone.

'Three days later I was speaking to my mother and she surprised me by asking if I had seen anything odd in my bedroom. I was very cautious and asked her why she had said such a thing. She told me that my youngest brother, who was then eight years of age, had seen a man come up the stairs and go into my bedroom and then come out again and go downstairs. He had been very frightened. I then told my mother what had happened.

'I did not go to the haunted house because knowing that my previous premonitions had come true I felt that I would not live through the experience.'

∞

YET another story from Royal Leamington Spa comes from Mrs. Barrott of the Whitnash area. One evening last September she had been out visiting a friend at a village near to where she lives. It was getting late – about 11.00 p.m. – so she decided it was time she made a move to go home.

'It was quite a warm evening so when I got into my car I opened the window and set off for home. On passing the village brook I saw a young boy of about 10 or 12 years of age running by the brook. He was all in white with shorts on and I could see in the car lights that he had curly hair. I then got a bit alarmed as he appeared to be running straight towards the road.

'I thought to myself, goodness, fancy letting a boy of his age out at this time of night, his parents must be crazy. He turned sharply and ran right out in front of my car. I had to slam on the brakes. When he got to the other side of the road, he vanished.

'I was quite shocked, never having seen anything like that in my life. I naturally told my husband, my family and a few friends. I'm sure some of them thought that I had just imagined it but I know the boy ran in front of my car and I know I had to make an emergency stop.

'My mother-in-law lived in that same village so I asked her if she knew who the boy could have been but she had no idea. I could not get the incident out of my mind for ages so I went along to the County Council Records Office. When I told the lady in attendance why I wanted to see some books about the village she just burst out laughing so I left straight away feeling very stupid. I was also frightened at the time and I went to see one of our local priests and told him the whole story. He was most sympathetic and gave me a blessing.

'About a year or two after all this my sister was researching our family tree so she had to keep making trips to that same County Council Records Office. I asked her if she could find out anything about the village for me as I was too intimidated to go in and ask for myself. She told me she would do her best.

'After going through lots of books, my sister came across a tragic accident which had happened just by the brook in the village in the 18th century. A young boy of 13 was crushed under a horse and cart. Some time after hearing this I happened to be looking through an old book and I noticed that the same type of shorts were worn by children in the 18th century.'

∞

THERE is a summer school in Swanwick Hayes in Derbyshire which was attended by Hazel Brown on a scholarship.

'It was very exciting and I met many interesting people. There were over 300 pupils there that year. I was allocated a single room in the more modern part of the house, and being very tired I went to bed at about 11.00 p.m. on the first night. In the room there was the minimum of furniture: a bed, a wardrobe, dressing table and a washbowl.

'No sooner had I settled into my bed than I was disturbed by noises coming from the room above me. I thought that someone must be moving furniture about and that they must soon stop as there was so little furniture in the rooms. But the noise did not stop. It went on and on getting louder and louder like a herd of elephants.

'At about 2.00 a.m. I could stand it no longer. I was very upset with tears streaming down my face. I got out of bed, splashed my face with cold water and walked down the corridor. Not a sound could be heard at this point. At the end of the corridor I went through a door and then up some stairs to find myself on a floor exactly the same as the one I had left. It was immediately above my floor. Everywhere was deathly quiet. There was not a murmur from any of the rooms and certainly no loud banging. Feeling embarrassed and pretty sure that I must be on the boys' floor, I retreated and reluctantly returned to my own room. The noises had completely stopped and eventually I fell asleep.

'The next day I asked several people if they had heard the banging but no one had. I just couldn't believe it, as every bed was occupied. Then someone said, "You know this place is haunted, don't you?" Apparently there had been German prisoners in the building during the war. I still couldn't really understand how that could possibly tie up with the terrible thumping and shuffling I had heard.

'Several years later there was a report in the local paper that builders who were excavating in the grounds of the school to build an extension had come across a deep tunnel which had been secretly built by the German prisoners of war for their planned escape.'

∞

A LADY from a Norfolk village had a peculiar thing happen to her when she was a child of about eight or nine years of age. 'I woke up in the middle of the night and was amazed to find that my bedroom had completely changed and it was most beautiful. I could hardly believe my eyes because everything had altered except that the window and the door were in the same place. A gentle golden coloured light seemed to fill the room letting me see everything in perfect detail.

'I had gone to bed in an old iron bedstead but I was now lying in a beautiful brand new greyish coloured bed. Covering me was a most gorgeous patchwork quilt. I sat up in bed and fondled that bedspread it was so delightful. I asked myself wherever did my mother get it from as when I had gone to bed that night my old ordinary cover was over me. In my girlish way I really loved that beautiful bedspread.

'I then had a good look around the bedroom. Over by the side of the bed there was a lovely rug on the floor. When I had gone to bed there had been mats of rushwork spread over the lino. Lovely new fresh curtains hung over the window where mum's shabby old ones had been. The wall paper and paintwork was all fresh and clean looking in lovely light sunshine yellow colour. There had been drab wallpaper with old-fashioned ferns which had been on the walls for years and years.

'There was a large chest of drawers and some quite remarkable looking pictures on the wall of a most unusual shape. There were little shelves on the walls on which stood miniature ornaments made from white china with different painted pictures on them. I was delighted with the way my bedroom looked, so light and lovely, and it made me so happy. I remember pinching myself to make sure that I was really there and not just dreaming.

'I awoke the following morning but all the splendour had gone and I was in my usual dull little room. I lay there for ages and ages trying to figure out what had happened. I was really disappointed and sad. I naturally told my mother all about wakening up in such a lovely bedroom but she just told me not to be silly and that I had just had a nice dream.

'Some time after this a new girl came to our school and she asked me to call for her when I passed her house on the way to school. I did call as I said I would and her mother asked me in to wait for her as she was not quite ready to leave. I was thunderstruck. There on the wall were those same pictures I had seen in my lovely bedroom.

'I must have looked very shocked as the girl's mother actually asked me what the matter was. I just kept staring at the pictures. Trying to make conversation, the woman remarked on how pretty the pictures were. When my friend and I got outside the house and were on our way to school I started to ask questions so furiously that I'm sure the girl must have thought that I'd taken leave of my senses.

'I asked her if her mother had a special patchwork bedspread, describing in detail the bedspread that had been over the new grey bed. I also asked if she had a chest of drawers like the one I had seen in my bedroom. She said yes her mother did own such things and asked me whatever I wanted to know for. "I told her that I had seen those things in my own bedroom when I had wakened up one night. The girl could not understand how her mother's possessions could possibly be in my bedroom. Neither could I.

'The next morning I called for my friend again. She herself opened the door excitedly and pulled me inside to talk to her mother. Her mother told me that she used to live in my house and in fact that had been her very first home as a new bride. She had made that bedspread herself. She asked me to follow her upstairs which I did with my friend. The woman opened a linen cupboard and pulled out the bedspread – the very one that I had seen.'

∞

GALE is now living in Nottingham but at one time she lived in an old house in Ilkeston, Derbyshire. The house was about 120 years old and had originally been a large detatched building but had subsequently been converted into two semi-detatched houses.

'In the back bedroom of the house where my husband and I slept, a lady used to appear almost every night, and sometimes even before we had nodded off to sleep. She would stoop over the bed and arrange the bed covers as if she was tending to someone. When she seemed satisfied that the covers were correctly arranged she would disappear.

'Sometimes when we were in bed reading we would hear the stairs creak and hear footsteps on the landing. We would see the door knob turn, but she would never come into our room until the bedroom light was out. We only saw her in semi-darkness. She was always dressed in an old fashioned style with a bonnet on her head.

'For three years she visited us; then I had the bedroom decorated and altered and we never saw her or felt her presence again.

'I mentioned to my mother-in-law about our night visitor and she thought that it may have been her mother who had passed away about 20 years before. Seemingly her mother had worshipped my husband who had been her favourite grandson. He had been a frail, sickly child and she had always been especially attached to him and had taken great care of him and was incredibly protective towards him. She had lived with my mother-in-law and every single night she used to go up to my husband's room after the light had been turned off to tuck him in.

'The funny thing was that our visitor always came towards us on my side of the bed and then reached over me to adjust the covers around my husband till she was satisfied that the bed was okay. I've often wondered why she just didn't go straight to his side of the bed in the first place. Perhaps she wanted to make sure that I was aware of her presence. She certainly made her point!'

WHEN Stuart Redder of Lincolnshire was quite young he used to sing in the church choir and ring the church bells.

'An elderly lady lived in the town and looked after dogs and cats for people on holiday, and did little gardening jobs. She was quite eccentric but a very lovable and kind person. Every Christmas without fail she used to send a box of fruitgums to us and we always sent her a Christmas card. She always signed her name "Winifred Francis", but we had to put "Miss Francis" on our cards by order of our parents.

'My younger sister was born later, after our choir and bellringing days had been replaced by work and teenage occupations, so she only knew Miss Francis by sight. I'd started work and my younger sister, Elaine, had moved from the infant school to the junior one about five minutes from where I worked for the council cutting grass around the caravan site.

'On Fridays I always had to leave at 3.45 p.m. instead of 4.00 p.m. to go to the council yard and line up for my wages. If I was late I had to do without my wages until the following Monday morning. This system of course changed when local government came into being.

'On one particular Friday I was a bit pushed for time with the grass cutting and I was working to a very fine timetable. I had only the roadside verges to cut in front of the caravan camp before finishing. It was about 3.30 p.m. When I had just about finished I saw Miss Francis coming down the road from where she lived.

'I hated not being able to stop to talk to her. You see it was not easy to have a quick conversation with her as she tended to talk and talk. I just waved up to her, she waved back, and I finished cutting the grass. I put the grass cutter away and locked the shed, then got on my push bike to go for my wages.

'By then, the kiddies were out of school and going home. When I eventually got home I mentioned seeing Miss Francis. My sister told me that she had also seen Miss Francis who had been pushing her pram and that the old woman had said, "Hello, Elaine." Elaine told me that the old woman had been walking up the road by the side of her school. I remarked that I didn't think that Miss Francis knew Elaine to speak to. My sister replied, "Well, she said Hello, Elaine."

'Before I go any further I'd best explain that there is no way in this world that Miss Francis could ever be mistaken for anyone else. Winter and summer she had on an old gabardine raincoat, tied at the waist with string. She had fuzzy bushy ginger hair and always wore old plimsole type footwear in all seasons. She wore thick knitted sort of stockings and she always pushed an old pram around with either gardening tools in it or sheep's heads which she would collect from the butcher's shop.

'On the following Monday some local men came to work at the camp. One of them, who I had worked with before, said, "Bad job about Miss Francis wasn't it?" I asked him what he meant and he replied, "They found her dead in her bungalow". I was very upset about this and I wished so much that I'd stopped work on the Friday for a few moments to bid her the time of day.

'On the way home from work that evening I called at the church parson's house as I knew that Miss Francis had no surviving relatives. I asked him when the funeral was to

107

take place, thinking that, just in case no one turned up, at least we could be there.

'He told me that she was to be cremated at Grimsby which was about 30 miles away but they would be holding a special service for her two days later, on the Wednesday. On that day our family went along to the service. I must admit that I was a bit surprised to find that the church was full.

'Before the service I managed to have a word with the parson to thank him for telling me about the service. Just as I was about to walk away from him, I remarked that I was still quite shocked as I had only seen her the previous Friday afternoon. He just looked at me in a funny sort of way and said, "Oh, did you?"

'The next day I was talking to the men at work about the service. I remember saying to the man who had told me the news about Miss Francis's death that the parson gave me such a funny look when I'd told him that I'd only just seen her on Friday afternoon.

'I got another funny look from my work mate, who answered, "I'm not surprised, it was Friday morning when they found her dead. The dogs had been barking so much and her milk had not been taken in so the police had broken in to her bungalow. They reckon that she had been dead for about two days."

'I went cold when he told me this but I did not elaborate on my seeing Miss Francis as he was one of those people who would have laughed at me. There was no mistake though. I definitely saw Miss Francis and we waved to each other and about five minutes later – the time it would take to walk from the camp to the junior school, my sister had seen her and the old woman had said "Hello, Elaine" to her.

'Something else came to light just as strange, a very long time afterwards. Quite by chance someone told me that when Miss Francis had been a young girl she had lived with her parents in one of the big posh houses on the road which ran up by the side of the junior school.

'I've often wondered what would have happened if I had taken the time to speak to her that Friday afternoon.'

∞

KERRY ANNE from Mansfield in Nottinghamshire was out with her friend Kelly during the school summer holidays. 'We heard a commotion and went to see what the trouble was. There were two black Doberman dogs fighting each other. Not wishing to be attacked we looked about for the owner of the dogs.

'A rough looking man came towards us and then went straight over to where the dogs were. He was quite a thin man, very tall and was dressed in shabby looking clothes. He collected the two dogs and walked off with them and we went on our way quite relieved to be out of danger.

'The following day we were walking through the same park and there were the same two dogs and again they were fighting and barking. We were quite shocked to see one of the dogs attack the other one's throat and the second dog seemed to die right there in front of our eyes. We saw the same thin owner run over to the dogs but we took to our heels and got out of the park fast. We were both shaken by what we had seen.

'The following Saturday we were walking through the park again as there are very few places to go near where we live. We could hardly believe our eyes when we again saw the same two Doberman dogs fighting with each other.'

∞

BETTY MASON of Dursley had worked in farming in the 1950s and 1960s. Her husband's mother and father had lived in the old farmhouse and Betty lived in a cottage with her husband and three children.

'The cottage dated back to the 1800s and had old stairs that curved round as they went up, like a lighthouse. We were all in bed one night and had been asleep for a while. I woke up with a start as I thought that I'd heard one of the children coming into our bedroom for something.

'To my surprise I saw a girl standing at the bottom of the bed. She was not our little girl. She had long plaited hair and was fully dressed. Our own daughter was much younger and had short curly hair.

'I sat up and looked at the child, too surprised to even speak. As I looked at her she gradually faded away. I never saw her again but I often wondered if she could have been connected with a Quaker graveyard which was just across the field.'

∞

A GLOUCESTER lady once lived in a bungalow which had at one time been a small private school. 'When we moved in we made quite a lot of improvements, which included the blocking off of the original doorway into the dining room so that we could make two smaller rooms out of this very large room.

'One day we were in the sitting room watching television. Our Alsatian, Sheba, was stretched out on the rug. We decided that it was time to make a cup of tea so I went into the kitchen followed by Sheba who knew that a trip to the kitchen usually meant biscuits for her.

'I made the tea and took the tray back into the sitting room where my husband was. I found him staring white-faced at the wall where the doorway had been blocked up.

'I asked him what on earth was the matter. He told me that he had just seen a woman walk through the wall where the door used to be. She had walked into the corner of the room then vanished through the wall. He described her as a small lady with grey hair wearing an old fashioned wrap-around pinny.

'I found it very difficult to believe him at first but he was so adamant about how she looked and it was totally unlike him to make up anything like that as he could never be thought of as any kind of practical joker. Also the shocked expression he had on his face convinced me that he must have seen something.'

∞

WHEN Mrs. June Harvey of Luton lived with her parents, in the Midlands, they took in a lodger named Jeff. 'I was 13 at the time and I shared a bedroom with my sister. Every night without fail Jeff used to pop his head round our bedroom door and say "good-night" to us.

'Sadly, some time after Jeff moved in with us he committed suicide. A couple of weeks afterwards, when my sister and I were in bed one night and our parents were downstairs watching television, we heard the sound of gargling coming from the bathroom. We thought it was a bit odd because the only person who ever used to do that was Jeff. We became alarmed when we heard footsteps going from the bathroom into what used to be Jeff's bedroom which was still unoccupied. Mum had left it exactly as it had been while Jeff had lived there. I think she hadn't the heart to go in there much.

'Every night for about six weeks both my sister and I heard the same thing. When we told our parents they of course put it down to childish imagination and we were told to put it out of our minds and to think no more about it.

'One night we were in bed and I thought that I had heard our bedroom door open. I opened my eyes and looked up to find Jeff standing there just inside the doorway. He was looking down at me. I did not feel one bit afraid at the time, he looked so sad. I got the feeling that he was trying to tell me something.

'Because of how our parents had reacted when we told them about hearing the gargling and the footsteps I decided not to say a word to anyone about seeing Jeff, not even to my sister. The following two nights the exact same thing happened. I heard the door open, looked up and there he was, just standing there, looking down at me, with a sad expression on his face.

'On the third night I looked him straight in the eye and said, "What do you want, Jeff?" He smiled and then he mouthed the words, "I'm sorry, June." I knew immediately what he meant. I had been the one who had found him dead in his bedroom.

'Because of the tragic atmosphere in the house my parents decided to sell up, so we moved to another house which was just around the corner. One day when I

112

happened to be passing our old house something made me look up at one of the front bedroom windows – the bedroom which used to be Jeff's.

'I saw the outline of a figure at the window. Suddenly it flashed and became very brilliant. It was Jeff, and he was dressed in his pyjamas. He lifted his hand and waved to me with a broad smile on his face. I never saw him again.'

∞

PETER of Warwickshire was riding his horse home one misty afternoon towards a village just outside Leamington Spa. 'The long straight road had houses on one side and a wide grass verge and open hills on the other.

'We were quite near to the entrance of my paddock when I saw, about 500 yards away, a figure standing on the grass verge. As I got nearer I saw that he was a soldier with a kit bag by his side. Nothing strange struck me until I got still nearer and I could see him more clearly. I saw that he was dressed in the uniform of the First World War with a peaked cap, jacket with brass buttons and khaki trousers.

'It was at that moment that "Bryn" my horse suddenly stopped. He started to shiver uncontrollably and began to move backwards. I talked to him and urged him forward but nothing I said or did would persuade him to advance.

'I turned him round and rode back up the way we had come for about 100 yards or so, turned round and started back down towards the paddock again. Thankfully he seemed quite happy to proceed this time. When I looked down the road the soldier had vanished. When we reached the spot where the man had been standing by the side of the road, I noticed that "Bryn" slowed down almost to a stop and kept looking all around him. He then seemed quite contented to carry on towards the paddock and was no longer acting as if he was afraid.'

∞

MR. PALING once lived in a house in Derby which has now been pulled down. 'I was born there and as soon as I was old enough to know about things, say about five or six, I became aware that there was a ghost in the house. It was taken as a matter of fact by all of the family. There was nothing scary about him, in fact he was almost accepted by all of us as part of the family and we had christened him "Harry".

'The stairs went up to the bedrooms between the front room and the middle room and countless times while the whole family sat in the front living room we would hear Harry walking up and down the stairs and along the corridor and through the upstairs bedrooms. He was such a part of our family life that often my mother would shout up to him, "Pop the kettle on, Harry, we could do with a cup of tea." We would all roar and laugh. Sometimes the living room door would just open by itself and we could all feel that Harry was in the room with us. My father would always make a joke on these occasions.

'Being brought up with the presence of Harry always about seemed completely natural to me and it just never occurred to me to be afraid. He was like a kindly uncle to me, always around, but never seen.

'My father told us, quite openly, that before he had moved into the house a man had committed suicide in the middle bedroom by cutting his throat with an open razor. He told us that the blood stains were on the floorboards and that they were still there under our lino because although he had scrubbed and scrubbed the floor before he moved in he just could not remove the stains so all he could do was to lay the lino over them. This was the bedroom I slept in.

'Sometimes at night I could hear old Harry breathing. His breath was always heavy. I could feel him get into the bed and I could feel his breathing down the back of my neck. I must admit that although I was not exactly afraid because I felt no menace from him whatsoever, sometimes it used to make me hot and uncomfortable. I used to call out, "Oh, for Pete's sake." My father would come into my bedroom and say, "Is it Harry again?"

'These things went on with Harry five or six times a week for all the years that we lived there. We left when I was 13. Sometimes I would go to sleep at night and he would not be there and then I would wake up two or three hours later and he would be breathing down the back of my neck. His breathing noise used to wake me up and his hot breath used to make my neck cover with sweat.

'My father always told me that there was no need to worry about Harry as he was a friendly enough old chap, and then he would say, "Poor old soul, he just can't settle down." My father used to get us all feeling quite sorry for Harry.

'I remember one night when my mother and father had gone to the pictures and my brother and sister were out with friends, I got home and of course there was no one in. It was in the summer time and it was still broad daylight so not having anything to do I thought that I would wander up to the top of our lane to watch for my mother and father

115

coming home. A friend of mine who lived across the road came out of his house. His mother had sent him to the off licence for something. I asked him if he would like to come to my house to play with my train set. He agreed so I went with him for the errand and after we had delivered the item back to his home we made our way down the lane to our house.

'We went round the back as the key to our back door was always hidden in the outside toilet. We went in and got the train set out on the living room floor. We had just clipped the railway lines together and put the engine and tender and carriage on the lines when my friend said, "I thought you said that no one was in." I told him that there was no one in. He said, "But someone's coming down the stairs." I just shook my head as if to dismiss it although I too could hear the footsteps. I just wanted to get on with sorting out the train set.

'The door of the living room then opened. My friend got up from the floor and went over to the door to see who was there. He let out a gasp followed by an ear-piercing scream, ran straight across the living room, through the kitchen and out the back door. I ran out after him. He had cleared our back garden and was racing along an alley which fed about a dozen houses. He went at the speed of light. I swear no Olympic runner could have kept up with him.

'I locked the back door and made my way back down the lane to the spot where I had been standing to watch for the return of my parents. When I told my father what had happened he said that Harry had probably only wanted to see who I had brought into the house.

'The next day at tea time I was in my friend's house when his father came in from work. I got quite a turn when the man said to me, "What do you think you are doing frightening our Tony like that? He came rushing in here last night scared stiff saying that he had seen a ghost." I was so upset I just got up and left their house.

'Later on my friend's father came across to our house to have words with my father because Tony was still in a state of fright. I am not sure what was said between the two men but all I know is that Tony was never again allowed to come to our house. We still remained good pals but he was always too frightened to come near our house. For years he used to wait for me at the end of our lane refusing to put a foot inside our door.'

∞

RACHAEL BUTLER from London was once on holiday in Northampton. 'It was a very hot summer's day and I was walking down a lovely peaceful country lane with my twin sister. Everything was still and quiet except for the sound of the birds chirping.

'There were only a few isolated cottages scattered here and there and when we passed one delightful little house we both remarked on how lovely and inviting it looked. It was whitewashed and almost dazzling in the bright sunlight. All the windows were wide open and the front door, which was painted a fresh bright blue, was ajar. The main front window was quite close to the roadway and was very large so we could see right into the room. The table was set with glasses of milk and a plate of cookies and there was a vase of beautiful flowers in the centre of the table.

'To the side of the house there was a small courtyard and

we noticed that there was a bright red bike lying on the ground. Everything was silent and motionless with not a living soul to be seen anywhere.

'We carried on with our walk as we had never been down that way before and we were eager to see what lay ahead of us. About two hours later when we were walking back along the same road we came to the same house. This time it did not appear so white. Then we saw that the windows were all boarded up with planks of old wood that looked as if they had been there for years and years. The front door was barricaded over with strips of rusting iron bars and the whole house was in a state of dilapidation. In the courtyard the bike was still there in exactly the same position but it was covered in rust.'

∞

MRS. ANDREWS of Eagle in Lincolnshire has never seen a ghost but she did have an experience when she was about 12 years of age which she will never forget. 'I was at school as usual one day and I was playing rounders in the playground during the dinner break. The ball was hit and it went up into the air. A boy and I both ran to catch it. Now I don't know if the ball hit me or the boy, all I can remember is looking upwards to catch it and as I did this the sun dazzled me.

'The next moment I found myself travelling through space at a lightning speed. I then turned and could see quite clearly the entire earth shimmering in vivid light. I could see all the continents as if I was looking at a globe. I then started to shoot towards the earth at a breathtaking speed. I could then clearly see the outline of Britain which closed down to just England. At this point I was travelling at an even faster rate rushing towards the land. Then I could see, far below me, a school playing ground and as I got nearer I could see a group of children playing rounders. There had been an accident and two children were carrying a third child towards the school building.

'I realized, with the greatest shock imaginable, that the third child who was being carried was me. I could clearly see my physical body and I could tell that I was unconscious – except that I was conscious up in the air where the real me was. I was travelling so fast that I sort of whizzed straight into my body and immediately opened my eyes and felt sick and very dizzy.'

∞

MAY from Warwick remembers when, during the last war, her mother was the house-keeper for the council of a hostel for bombed-out people.

'We called it a hostel but in fact it was a large Elizabethan house which had been given over for the purpose of housing the poor unfortunate people who had found themselves homeless. One room at the front of the house was used as a billeting office by a gentleman called Mr Saunders. We all just called him the billeting officer and it was his job to try to place the homeless people from the hostel in houses around the town.

'I was a teenage girl at the time. I remember that any time Mr Saunders had cause to come to the living quarters – usually the communal dining room – to talk to my mother about the evacuees I suppose, I noticed that he spent a lot of time staring at me although he never spoke directly to me.

'My mother had a private sitting room. Because of the

lack of available sleeping space in the house, I slept in the sitting room. I woke up in the middle of the night one time and was most surprised to see Mr Saunders standing at the bottom of my bed. Although it was quite dark I could see him clearly and recognized him instantly. He did not speak to me but just stood there staring at me in much the same way as he always had done.

'The strange thing was, I did not feel frightened or threatened in the least. I just couldn't figure out why he should be standing there. I was so sleepy that I just couldn't be bothered to think about it any more so I just lay back down on my bed and went back to sleep.

'The following evening when I had just come home from work, I nearly jumped out of my skin when my my mother told me that Mr Saunders had died at his home the night before from an asthma attack.'

∞

JOHN CRADDOCK of Northampton had a bad motor accident in 1974 when his car landed upside down on a banking by the side of the road. At the other side of the banking there was a very steep drop into a water-filled ditch.

'I was crushed under the vehicle and firemen had to come to cut me free. They gave me a mixture of gas and air to breath in – something like an oxygen mask – which I suppose was intended to ease the pain.

'I then realized that I was watching the firemen from up above them. I was dangling in the air. I could even look down on the parked ambulance and see the head and shoulders of one man sitting inside. Over by the bank I could see three men struggling with my car trying to hold on to it to stop it sliding down into the ditch. I became quite intrigued at seeing the underneath part of the car as I'd never seen this before.

'I watched them pull a man out of the smashed up car. He was on his back being dragged out arms first. I got the shock of my life when I realized that this man was me. Then, in mid air, I saw a very large clock, about the size of Big Ben, and I heard the loud strong sound of ticking. It was as if I was being shown the seconds ticking by. A rush of panic swept though me as I grasped the significance of this. I knew, beyond any shadow of a doubt, that I was being shown the last moments of my life on this earth.

'My attention was gripped by the hands of that clock as they slowly moved in accordance with the sound of the ticking, and all the time the clock was getting smaller and smaller. I was overwhelmed by the notion that the moment that clock got so small that it disappeared, I would be dead. I felt utterly helpless and I could feel my heart pounding as the clock got smaller and smaller until it was only about the size of a shirt button.

'A deafening scream jolted me back to my senses and I found myself being tied down onto a stretcher. I was rushed to hospital to be sorted out and although I was out of action for quite a while I managed to pull through.

'Before this happened I used to be quite a sceptic and just refused to believe in anything that I could not find a logical explanation for. This experience certainly has changed my views. I know that when I was hanging about in the air above that ambulance I had all of my senses with me and I was able to think calmly and reason things out. It was just the oddness of the situation that I found disorientating, but nevertheless there was no way that I could deny what was happening. If some other bloke had related this story to me I'm sure I would have just thought he was a bit loopy but since my accident I have had my eyes truly opened. The main thing that has changed is that I now know that the spirit goes on no matter what happens to the physical body. Once this fact has been grasped, then all other things are possible.'

∞

MARGARET, a young housewife from Derby, lost her father when she was only two-and-a-half.

'My mother was left to bring up a young family and she took the death of my father so badly that no one ever thought she would get over it. In fact I don't think she ever did. Even at that young age I was acutely aware of the misery she was going through. Although we were not what you would call in abject poverty, life was not easy by any means.

'As I grew up, always aware of the terrible struggle my mother was having, I used to sometimes sob myself to sleep, feeling so helpless to do anything to make life easier for the family.

'One night I was feeling very low and as I lay in bed whimpering to myself I felt the air suddenly become cold. It was a very marked change of temperature, not just like a draft, but a drastic biting chill which went right through me stinging me inside. I got an overpowering smell of pipe smoke and I felt somebody or something sit down on the edge of my bed.

'At first I felt afraid, but after a moment or two when I

122

had got over the initial shock of the cold, all trace of fear and anxiety left me as I felt a wave of peace and calm spread over me. It was as if I was being surrounded by a sort of protective barrier keeping everything that was sad away from me. I must have drifted off to sleep because I don't remember anything else that night.

'On and off over the next few years the same thing happened and I noticed that it was usually when I was very upset. I always felt the cold, followed by the smell of a pipe, then felt someone sitting down on the edge of the bed. This protective feeling always stayed until I dropped off to sleep.

'When I became a teenager I had all the usual problems what with school and boyfriends, etc, and then the visits started again. At first I was a bit afraid, but as soon as I felt the familiar comforting feeling as if someone was looking after me, I started to relax in the knowledge that no harm would befall me. I suppose I was too young to figure things out when I first experienced the visits, but later I knew that I was being watched over by my father. I had heard my mother remark about his pipe smoking once and when I started to think about it, I remember, as a tiny girl, seeing him smoke a pipe. Somehow I had never tied this up in my mind before, but then when he had first come to me I was very small, always sleepy and always upset, so I suppose I was beyond figuring things out at that stage.

'One night, just about a week or so before I was due to be married, my mother became desperately ill. I was worried out of my mind about her and very upset at the thought that she would not be able to attend my forthcoming wedding. I lay in my bed thinking about the difficulties when again the coldness permeated the room, then came the smell of pipe tobacco. I could sense the presence so vividly that I actually spoke to him out loud, saying, "I know you are my dad, and I know you have come to help."

'My mother died the following year, just before my first baby was born. I was so disappointed knowing that she would never see my baby. Anyway when my little Paul was only three months old I was at home alone with him. My husband was away and it was a cold January night. About 10 o'clock I lay in bed watching the portable television. Paul was fast asleep in his cot next to my bed. The gas fire was full on and the room was nice and warm and cosy.

'Suddenly it grew very cold and then came the familiar tobacco smell but even stronger than it had ever been before. I had patio doors leading to a small balcony and very heavy curtains were pulled closed across the doors. The curtains were made of heavy velvet and were fully lined with small lead weights inserted in the hem to keep them hanging properly. These curtains never moved as no draft whatsoever came in through them.

'There was a tremendous blast and these long heavy curtains suddenly blew apart and were waving up in the air. I could see the patio doors behind and they were closed tight as normal. I just lay there watching the curtains then I heard little Paul wake up. He did not cry but he was looking down towards the end of his cot. He then started to chuckle and wave his arms and legs in the air as if someone was playing with him. A few seconds later he just settled back down and went to sleep. I noticed then that the pipe smell had gone and the room felt warm and snug again and the curtains were back to normal.'

∞

KEVIN from Cambridge remembers the summer of 1969

with mixed feelings. 'My parents lived in the Cambridgeshire village of Harston, about six miles south of Cambridge itself, on the A10 London road. At the age of 12, the school holidays seemed wonderfully long, and one of my past-times was to cycle around the easy flat East Anglian countryside with my friend Graham. In those days it was nothing for us to cycle 20 or 30 miles in a day. Our mothers often made us packed lunches to take with us on these trips.

'I have sadly lost contact with Graham who was cycling with me on the day that I will never forget. He was the son of the headmaster of the school we both attended at the time. Anyway, one bright sunny morning we set off from my home, Seddlers Cottage, Harston. We cycled over the hill to Newton and then followed the road down to Fowlmere. At some point we took a left turn towards Duxford.

'At this point, I should mention that both Duxford and Fowlmere were wartime fighter bases. In fact the legendary Douglas Bader was part of a squadron there for some time.

'It was on this road between Duxford and Fowlmere that Graham and I noticed a radio-controlled model aeroplane flying in a field to our left. I had my own model flying aeroplanes and so I wanted to stop to watch it for a while. At the point where we stopped there was an old concrete structure with a flat roof. I believe it was probably originally part of the defences at Duxford airfield, as there were many such structures around the countryside at that time.

'To get a better view, we climbed on top of the flat roof of the structure. There was grass and the odd weed growing in the cracks on the roof, but there were certainly no bushes up

125

there or anything else of a bulky nature. As we watched the model plane flying around the field a man was suddenly standing there on the roof with us. He had not climbed up or walked from anywhere and he couldn't have come from behind a bush because there were none. He just appeared from nowhere in front of our eyes. It was the strangest thing I'd ever seen – one minute Graham and I were there alone standing on the roof in broad daylight and then suddenly there was this man standing only a few feet away from us.

'It was not a blurred image, misty or hazy or anything like that. In fact it was horribly and frighteningly clear. The man was dressed in what looked like a policeman's uniform, including the classic bobby's hat, except his uniform was grey and not dark blue. Even now after all these years I can describe his face clearly. It was chubby and very red. He wore a pair of round, wire-framed glasses like the type you could get on the National Health.

'I had never ever been so frightened. Graham and I looked at each other so I knew that he had also seen this man. We were too terrified to even speak so we both started to back away, still looking at him and as we did this, he reached into his breast pocket and took out a notebook and pen or pencil. At this point we both turned and scrambled down from the roof and ran as fast as we could towards the cycles which were just below us on the ground. I looked back in case he was following us, but there was no sign of him. I assumed that he was coming down from the roof around the other side of the building.

'We got on our bikes and as we started to move off we both looked back but the man was nowhere to be seen. I can remember being so frightened that I was shaking like a leaf.

We pedalled fast towards Fowlmere. From the slight rise in the land we were able to see back down to where the structure was and we could also see all of the surrounding countryside for miles and miles in every direction. There was not a trace of any other human being in sight.

'We were both so preoccupied with getting out of that area as soon as we could that our two bikes collided and we both fell off onto the road.'

∞

MARJORIE MARTYN of Stroud in Gloucestershire was once out walking with her sister Doreen when they had been sent to stay with her mother's cousins who lived near the little town of Nailsworth in the Cotswolds.

'It was during the month of August and at the time I was aged 14 and Doreen was 10. We had been thoroughly enjoying ourselves exploring the area known as St. Chloe Green, about a mile from our relatives' house. The weather was warm but on this particular day it was downcast, though people said that it would remain fine for the rest of the day. It had rained quite heavily during the early morning so the ground was soft and in places fairly muddy.

'Adjoining some common land at St. Chloe Green we saw a pleasant wood. A woman told us that it was part of the estate of a big mansion house called Rodborough Manor which was in the next parish and had been derelict for years and years since it had been burnt down. No one had been injured in the fire but the losses were so tremendous that the owners of the manor had been cast into financial ruin as seemingly the property had not been insured.

'The woman showed us where a carriage drive, so overgrown with brambles that it looked like a narrow footpath, led downhill towards Woodchester Valley. She told us that the drive turned north before it reached the bottom of the hill. She thought that if we followed the driveway all the way it might lead us to the ruins of the old manor house but nobody had ever bothered to go there since the fire. She intimated that she felt that there was some kind of restriction on the land which forbade trespassers.

'Naturally determined to defy the prohibition, we climbed over the wall into the wood, the gates of the drive being padlocked, and began to go down the narrow path which was all that remained of the driveway. There were no human footprints but we saw where foxes and badgers had been walking. We soon found a part of the woodland where blackberries were ripe so we began to pick and eat them. Doreen went to a patch a few yards further ahead of me where the undergrowth was fairly sparse.

'Suddenly she signalled to show that someone was approaching from below then she took cover behind a holly bush. I hid by crouching down among ferns behind a bush. From this position I got a view of a stretch of driveway more than 20 yards below me. I could clearly see two women walking up the slope. They moved slowly. One was old and frail, dressed in black with a grey shawl around her shoulders. Her hair was wispy and white. The other woman was middle-aged and wore on her head a very old-fashioned looking bonnet. Her dress, which was also old-fashioned looking, was a mixture of grey and black and it seemed to be made of a fine quality material like heavy brocade.

'I was worried that if they caught us trespassing on their

property they would be angry and I started to get scared. I was also afraid that when they reached the bend in the driveway they might catch a glimpse of Doreen for her hiding place was not really a good one.

'I waited, trembling, for several minutes trying to think up some explanation which would sound reasonable, but the women did not reappear so I thought that they must have passed into the woodland behind the trees and bushes, or perhaps another pathway had branched off from the one we had been following further up out of our view.

'I left my hiding place and went straight to Doreen and asked her if she had seen the women. She said that she had. She then asked me what they looked like. I described them as I had seen them. "Yes" she replied, "they were just like that – very queer looking ladies."

'Plucking up courage we went to look further on round the bend in the driveway but we both got quite a shock for there was no junction in the roadway and no path in any direction where they could have turned down. I could hardly imagine two such elegant people just wandering through the high grass within the woods, but we looked all around just the same, thinking that they could not have travelled far, especially as the oldest one was unsteady on her feet and moved very slowly. The natural terrace on the wooded hillside had become so narrow and so muddy that no one without wellies could have walked along there without a real struggle and without making deep foot-marks.

'It did not appear that anyone had walked around that area because we could see no footmark of any kind.

'At this point real panic seized us both. We ran back to

St. Chloe faster than I could have thought possible and never ever ventured near that place again.'

∞

A DERBYSHIRE woman, Eveline Walker, had only been married for about a year and was living in a farm cottage which could only be reached by a long lane. 'One night we were late going home as we had stayed longer than usual at my mother-in-law's house. I was walking beside my husband who was pushing the pram with our baby in it.

'The moon was out but there were a lot of clouds in the sky. As we made our way up the lane we came to the level-crossing where the railway ran straight across the lane. There was no bridge over the railway lines and we could hear a train approaching so we stopped to wait until it had passed.

'As soon as the train had passed I took over the job of pushing the pram and I had to walk slightly ahead of my husband because the footpath narrowed considerably at this point. There was a small cemetery which we had to pass and as the moon had gone behind the clouds it was very dark.

'I felt someone take a hold of the pram so I instantly turned around expecting to find that my husband had decided to push it up the rest of the lane. I then saw another man standing holding onto the pram. I was so surprised that I could not speak. My husband was also there just behind me as he had been. The man was dressed in working clothes and I could see that with his other hand he was holding on to a barrow. The hand on the pram was very forcibly guiding the pram off the pathway.

'I was so shocked that I pushed the pram out into the middle of the lane and then froze on the spot with fear. I again looked back at my husband, most surprised that he had not said anything as he was always so quick to come to my rescue for the least little thing, and here was a strange man pushing the pram about and he did not seem to be interested.

'I was even more bewildered when my husband asked me why I had stopped, then he asked if I was alright. I looked around me and there was no sign of the man. I was in such a state that I just burst into tears asking him why he didn't talk to the man. "What man?" came his reply. I was stunned and couldn't believe my ears. I said that I was talking about the man who had just that second pushed the pram off the pathway.

'I'm not quite sure what my husband really thought at that moment but he said nothing and just put his arm around me and took control of the pram. He turned to get the pram back on the pathway but then he too quickly swung the pram back out onto the lane. When we looked, we saw a massive deep hole in the centre of the path, just at the spot where I had been guided off, which I could not possibly have seen from my position behind the pram.

'The following day I mentioned the incident to the farmer's wife who told me that she had not wanted to tell me before for fear of frightening me but the cemetery gate was reported to be haunted by a gardener.'

∞

MICHAEL from Northampton was once engaged to a young lady called Virginia. They were very much in love and planned their wedding day for the following spring-time. Michael was devasted when Virginia suddenly took ill and within a few weeks she was dead.

'One night after I had been working late I had gone to bed in my bedsitter and had fallen asleep as usual. It was only about two month's after Virginia's death and I had taken to working late quite a lot, not being able to face going out socially. I had a strange dream about Virginia and I was aware, even though I knew somehow that I was having a dream, that I had never ever dreamt about her before, even when she had been alive.

'In the dream I saw Virginia's face looking very worried. She was holding out her two hands towards me as if she was beckoning me to follow her. I was well aware of the fact that she had died and I remember asking her what it was like being dead. She did not reply to this but kept trying to get me to follow her. I reckoned I had nothing to lose so I reached out to catch her hand but as I did this she kept moving backwards so that her fingers were always just out of my reach.

'I wondered if she was playing some kind of game with me but somehow the expression on her face told me that this was not the case. She looked really alarmed. I then asked her if she was feeling alright. I just could not figure out what was going on. I then heard her voice shouting out my name, only the sound seemed to come from a long way away. I kept trying to catch her hand and she kept moving backwards but the odd part was that her voice kept moving nearer to me and was getting louder and louder. At first she was only calling my name, "Michael, Michael" over and over again. Then in a scream I heard her yell out the words "Wake up".

'The impact of those words made me jump up in the bed. I had woken up. There was a strange smell in the room and then I heard a hissing sound. I then noticed, to my horror, that my gas fire had been on but not lit. I dashed across and switched it off at the mains and quickly opened the window as the room was filled with gas.'

∞

WHEN John of Kettering in Northamptonshire was courting he once missed his last bus home after leaving his girlfriend safely at her house.

'I started to walk back to my own house which was not all that far away but because it was just on the outskirts of the town I had to pass by a few fields to get home.

'As I walked along I saw a man standing over by one of the fields close to the fencing. He was in a dark suit and trilby hat. It was a bright moonlit night and I could see him quite distinctly but he was no one I knew. I just nodded over to him and he said, "Excuse me, have you got a light please?" I walked over and sparked up my lighter, holding it up to his face so that he could light his cigarette.

'At that moment a car came up the road and as its headlights beamed onto the man I notice that his face seemed to get pale. I nearly died as I watched his face slowly evaporate into thin air, then all of the rest of his body disappeared from the head downwards. I stood there in utter amazement, the lighter still burning, as I was hardly able to believe what I had just seen.'

∞

A LADY from Cambridge remembers an incident which

happened about 15 years ago. 'My husband and I came home from a friend's 21st birthday party in the early hours of the morning and went straight to bed. As soon as my husband's head hit the pillow he fell fast asleep but I could not sleep despite my tiredness.

'What seemed about two hours later, I heard the sound of a woman weeping right outside our bedroom window. I got up to investigate thinking that she must be in terrible trouble. I could not see any sign of anyone outside and I did not think that it could have been cats or a baby crying because it was distinctive sobs.

'Although I could not see anything, the sound of the sobbing continued and got so bad that I had to waken my husband to ask if he could hear it. He said that he could not hear anything and promptly went back to sleep. I could still hear it all the time, sometimes getting slightly louder, then going down to little more than a whisper, but always there.

'The following day, which was a Sunday, at exactly 1.20 p.m. I got an overwhelming feeling that I wanted to see my father. I was busy with the Sunday lunch so I told myself that as soon as we had eaten and I had washed up I would give him a ring.

'At 2.30 p.m. two of my father's friends called at the house unexpectedly. The moment I saw them I called out, "Something has happened to my father – he's dead, isn't he?" They told me that he had suffered a massive heart attack and he had been rushed to hospital but they were unwilling to elaborate further, suggesting that I go straight to the hospital.

'We immediately went to the hospital but I did not need to be told. I knew that he was dead. I was informed that he had died at 1.20 p.m. My father was Irish and I've always wondered if I had heard the banshee.'

∞

WHEN Mrs. Crane, a Cheshire lady, was on holiday with her mother in 1926 they stayed with friends in Buxton, Derbyshire. 'On the Friday morning, after doing some shopping in Spring Gardens, we sat on the slopes above the crescent where St. Anne's Well is situated. I was playing with a ball and my mother was reading a morning newspaper. I bounced the ball and missed catching it and it rolled away downwards along the path. I ran after it.

'I was almost at the bottom near the road, when to my surprise, I noticed a lady who was a friend of the family, sitting on the bench by the roadside. She reached out and grabbed hold of me as I ran past. In a quiet voice she told me, "No Grace, let it go." I obediently remained motionless, watching my ball roll onto the road. At that second a car sped round the corner and ran over the ball, bursting it.

'I turned round to say something to the woman but she was not there anymore. I slowly climbed up the path back to my mother who looked up at me and asked me where I had been running to. I went across, sat down beside her and told her that I had just seen Emily Charles at the bottom of the hill. I then asked if my mother had seen Emily come up the hill because I didn't know where she had gone to.

'My mother went white and told me that Emily had died in hospital two weeks earlier.

'There is a strange sequel to this story. The following month my grandmother visited Buxton for a few days, staying at the same place that my mother and I had stayed.

She had gone out for a walk and just as she was standing by the same bench on the side of the road, waiting to cross over, she dropped dead.'

∞

WHEN Rosanne of Shropshire was a child she had a very unusual dream. She was outside her house which was very old style with lots of firewood stacked carefully in bundles against the walls.

She was standing by a duck pond at the front of the building and she knew that she had several brothers and sisters and she was the oldest child. Her mother had died some time before and she was helping her father to look after the family.

'I remember being dressed in a long dark dress with a white apron over it. My hair was very short and I got the feeling that I was something to do with the Quakers. My father came towards me from the house, followed by a lady who was our tutor. My father told me that he was going to get married to our tutor and that she was to be our new mother.

'I always remembered that dream but never told anyone about it as although it was interesting enough there was nothing really extraordinary about it. To me it was just a dream.

'Years went by and I married my husband Terry in 1982 when I was 20. A few weeks after we were married he was made redundant so he decided to have a go at running his own business. In the August of 1982 we started the business but because people did not pay their accounts we started to struggle financially.

'We discussed the situation and we concluded that I should try to find a job to help ease the stress. I managed to find a job canvassing for a company but after three months they hit hard times and became insolvent.

'I had a friend staying with me at the time so we both put our thinking caps on and she came up with the idea that maybe I could become involved with party plan selling. She knew a company who operated in this way and they were always on the lookout for new people to join them.

'She made a telephone call to that company on my behalf and an interview was arranged for me. My friend very kindly agreed to go with me to the interview as she was vaguely interested in learning what it was all about in case she ever needed a job.

'We were shown into an interview room and introduced to the boss of the company and his wife who also worked for the company. I nearly fainted when I recognized him as my Quaker father from my dream. His wife was the tutor.'

∞

KATE FOSTER of Dudley in Worcester was brought up in a medium sized villa built at the turn of the century. The bedroom at the top of the stairs had been made into a bathroom and the other bedrooms opened on to a landing.

'When I married I moved about half an hour's drive away from my parent's home. After my little daughter was born I used to take her to my parent's home two days a week as I used to help my father with his paper work. He had a business which he ran from home and I looked after his books for him. So it was as if my daughter had virtually

137

two homes and was always a happy and well balanced child.

'At the age of five and a half she began not wanting to go to the bathroom on her own at my parent's house. She refused to even go upstairs without me going with her. I did not make too much of an issue out of it however, and as time went on it was all forgotten about.

'When she was 16, my husband died, but we coped as a family has to. One night we sat consoling each other and having a real heart to heart talk. Out of the blue she said to me "Mum do you remember when I was little and I refused to go upstairs alone in Nan's house?" I told her that I did remember it and she went on to relate the following:

'She had gone up to the bathroom with Mac (her constant childhood companion, a boxer dog). When she was washing her hands Mac started jumping up and scratching at the door trying to get out which was most unusual for him. She felt herself being pushed out of the bathroom and forced out onto the long landing towards the foot of the second flight of stairs. She then saw a little blond boy dressed in a blue velvet suit. He was standing on the first step with his right arm round the newel post and he was gently rocking back and forwards smiling at her all the time.

'The next time I went over to my parent's home I told my mother who reacted in a most alarming manner and accused my daughter of making it all up and telling lies. Mum was in a terrible state so I let the matter drop. However quite some time later she told me that my brother, who I knew had died in his second year, but who I was too young to remember, had received a blue velvet suit from my aunt for his first birthday. He had been buried in this suit.'

138

Chapter Three
THE NORTH OF ENGLAND

BUD FLANNIGAN, the well loved entertainer, ruled for years as the 'King' at the Victoria Palace where he had the audiences either screeching with laughter at his antics with the Crazy Gang or singing their hearts along to his tuneful melodies like "Underneath The Arches", "Hometown" and "Strolling" which he performed with Chesney Allen, the other half of the great Flannigan & Allen duo.

Years before Bud became a household name he used to work the old music hall circuit up and down the country. One such trek took him over the hills in the north of England to Lancaster where he always stayed in the same theatrical digs. Here, like all the other travelling entertainers of the day, he was welcomed by Sadie the landlady and her husband Bert as if he was a long lost son returned home. She adapted her catering arrangements to make sure that there was always a hot meal on the table at ll.30p.m. as Bud and his colleagues got home after the final performance of the night. Sadie enjoyed the chit-chat which would go on to the early hours as the entertainers told their funny stories. Every now and then they'd burst into song or play her a tune on the old upright piano she kept in the dining room.

When Bud Flannigan found stardom he never forgot the gracious lady who had opened up her home to him when he had been a struggling young comic. Every Christmas he sent her a lovely present and any time he was in the area he would pop in to say hello and have a cup of tea.

The fame of good theatrical landladies travels fast

around the show circuit so when Bud's sister and her husband were on tour around the north with a travelling company they remembered the address that Bud had given them. They were subsequently welcomed to Sadie's guest house with their small son John and the other members of the cast.

John was only seven years of age at the time but he remembers those days vividly. 'All the world was new to me, and being the only child in the company I remember everyone being really kind and nice to me. We met a lot of people as we travelled around the theatres staying in different theatrical boarding houses.

'We arrived at the digs in Lancaster and as usual we soon got acquainted with the other people who were booked into the house. That was when I first met old Teddy and his wife Martha; they were two watercress peddlars. Teddy had a limp and used to walk around the streets carrying a huge wicker basket on his back. He was a wonderful, kind old man and he used to sometimes take me out on his rounds with him – carrying me in the wicker basket. Martha, who smoked a clay pipe, would walk along beside us all the time telling me jokes. I only realize now, on looking back, what a peculiar sight we must have been as no one could have seen me in the basket but I expect they might have wondered at the yells of childish laughter that would come from the basket in response to Martha's brilliant sense of humour. I became very close to the two of them and looked upon them as uncle and aunty.

'I used to sleep in a tiny attic room at the top of the house. The electricity supply had not been extended to the attic so there were two small oil lamps to light my bedroom which had only a small skylight window and was therefore fairly dark even in the day time. When it was time for bed my mother used to walk up the narrow stairs with me, holding a lighted candle to take us up the last flight to the bedroom.

'One night we were going up to my room as usual when one of the other guests started speaking to my mother on the first landing. I was used to climbing the stairs so I took the candle and continued up on my own. As I got to the top landing on the third floor I was surprised to see the light of another candle. There right outside the door to my little room I saw an old lady. She was just standing there, but then she started to knock on my bedroom door. As she moved, the slight draft made the flame from her candle wave back and forth, lighting up her face. I could see that she was wearing a brown beret and had silvery hair. She looked as if she was worried about something. I ran up to her and asked if I could help her telling her that I knew how to open the door. (There was a trick in the way the handle had to be turned.) She looked down at me but said nothing. I put my hand out to grasp the door handle but she was in the way and she did not move. Again I asked if I could help her, and asked if she was trying to get into my room. She completely ignored me and continued to knock on the door. I then thought that maybe she was deaf and hadn't heard me telling her that I knew how to open the door so I yelled out quite loudly: "Let me show you." She did not even look down at me but again started to knock on my door. This just didn't make sense to me and her silence was really beginning to frighten me.

'While she was still knocking on the door she looked down at me so I knew that she had seen me. She still did not say anything but I noticed that her eyes were full of tears. She then turned her face away from me and started knocking on the door again. I suddenly became terrified and I turned and ran back down the stairs so fast that my own candle flame went out. I didn't stop running till I got to the door of the living room at the bottom of the stairs on the ground floor where I was met by old Teddy. He caught me up in his arms and whirled me around as was his usual manner of greeting.

'As much as I was full of fear I told Teddy that an old lady was trying to get into my room and that she had frightened me. He listened, and then asked me who she was. I told him I didn't know, that she wouldn't speak to me but she was wearing a brown beret. He put me down and rushed up the stairs as fast as his limp would allow. I just sat myself down on the bottom stair until he came back down. He was as white as a sheet. He took me up in his arms and carried me into the living room where my parents were talking to some of the others. He took my mother aside and handed me over to her.

'They questioned me about the lady with the candle and I told them exactly what I had seen, describing her to the best of my ability. It turned out that the only person who always wore a brown beret was Sadie the landlady. She had been dead for three days.'

∞

THE northern holiday resort of Whitby is situated on Cleveland's North Sea coast and has a lovely little harbour. Captain James Cook, the famous explorer, lived in the town as a young man. It was there that his ship "The Endeavour" was built, in which he set out in 1768 to voyage to Australia and New Zealand. His house in Grape Lane is marked by a plaque.

Whitby holds many memories for Eileen Smith who

visited the town for the first time a few years ago. She had arranged to go on holiday with her sister, but not having enough money to go abroad, they thought that it would be nice to see something of the north of England.

'We stayed in a big old house which had been converted into holiday flats, and from the start I had a strange feeling of having been there before, although I knew this was impossible as it was my very first visit to that part of the country. Somehow I seemed to know my way around the house, and on first entering the room I was to share with my sister, I had a most peculiar feeling which I could not understand.

'It was the usual sort of room you find in holiday flats – twin beds, a wash basin, a modern bedroom suite. But as I crossed the threshold I seemed to see, for a mere fraction of a second, a room which was entirely different! Not a bedroom at all, but a sitting room, dark and rather over-crowded, with heavy looking old fashioned furniture. On one wall there was a huge oval shaped mirror in an ornate gilt frame. The impression lasted no more than a moment, then I saw the room as it really was.

'Although I was shaken and bewildered I said nothing to anybody about the experience but during the first night in that room I awoke for some unknown reason. Moonlight was streaming in at the window and at first I thought that my sister was up and moving about the room. With a chilled feeling of pure terror I saw simultaneously that my sister was fast asleep in the other bed. Over by the wall where I had seen the gilt-framed mirror there was the figure of a young woman. She wore a long flowing skirt, a high-necked blouse and a silken shawl. She was half-turned, looking at me over her shoulder.

'The most horrifying thing about this woman was that she had my face! I was looking at another version of myself – or my absolute double. Feature by feature we were identical, even to the hairstyle - long hair drawn smoothly back behind the ears and tied with a ribbon. It was the briefest of encounters, yet so clear and vivid that I could note every detail of face and clothing before she simply disappeared. I lay, rigid with fear, afraid to move, afraid even to close my eyes for fear of opening them to again witness the return of the figure but nothing happened and I eventually fell asleep.

'Throughout our stay in Whitby I had a feeling of apprehension whenever I entered that room, wondering if I would see it again transformed to an old-fashioned sitting room. I was dreading the thought of seeing that girl again, however I saw nothing more and had no further disturbed nights. The weather was fine all week until the very last day of our holiday when it rained heavily. More for shelter than from any desire for culture, my sister and I went into the local museum and art gallery.

'There in the second room of the art gallery I saw it – just a small picture in a corner behind the door – a painting of the room I had glimpsed. There was the dark old-fashioned furniture, the gilt-framed mirror, and yes, the young woman. She was dressed in the same flowing skirt, high-necked blouse and silken shawl, half-turned and looking over her shoulder. She stood in front of the mirror and was therefore portrayed as a double image. She was exactly like me.

'With my flesh crawling I stood and stared at it for such a long time that my sister, who had moved off to another room, came back to see what was holding my interest. I asked her if the painting reminded her of anyone. After a brief scrutiny my sister said, "Goodness, I think she looks astonishingly like you."

'We sought information but as the pictures in the gallery were changed frequently, especially during the summer months, there was no catalogue nor any reference book which could be consulted, and the young part-time worker at the reception desk had no knowledge of the source or origin of any of the paintings.

'We could not decipher the artist's signature but the picture had a title. It was called, simply "ELIZABETH". Elizabeth is my middle name!'

∞

THE Lake District is a well known beauty spot which lies among the Cumbrian mountains in the north west of England. The longest lake is Windermere and the most popular touring centre is the town of Keswick. There are countless scenic walks across the highest mountain passes in England, some of which are over 2,000 ft.

At the southern end of the village of Grasmere can be found Dove Cottage which was the home of the poet William Wordsworth from 1799 to 1808. Near to the house there is a museum which contains the original manuscripts and other memorabilia of the poet. Wordsworth also resided at Rydal Mount by the picturesque Rydal Water in the shadow of Rydal Fell. He was buried in St Oswald's churchyard in Grasmere in 1850.

Nan lives in the shadow of Crossfell or "Fiends Fell" as the mountain is known by the locals. In olden days, before the pass road over to Alston was made, a "corpse track" led over the summit of the mountain to link the parishioners of the Eden Valley and the North & South Tyne Valleys. Near a place called Little Durfell, a large stone bothy was built to allow the mourners to rest the coffins. Sometimes in mid-winter the weary travellers were forced to spend the night in the building for fear of being smothered in snow drifts. One wild night during a violent thunderstorm the bothy was hit by lightning and an entire funeral procession sheltering there perished in the fire.

For years afterwards shepherds and hill walkers could sometimes hear the dying screams of the mourners echo across the still air, and so to rid the ill-fated mountain of its restless spirits it was blessed by a bishop and a wooden cross was erected on the summit. This has long since gone but the name remains – Crossfell.

Nan describes herself as 'a very down to earth kind of person, I am not given to believing all the old myths and stories, but all the same I had a peculiar thing happen to me when I was walking on the summit some years ago.

'There had been a heavy snowfall but it was a beautiful clear crisp day with a deep blue sky, so I thought I would take a wander up the track to the top of the mountain. There was no one in sight and I could see for miles and miles. The snow covered the track ahead of me for about a hundred yards or so, pristine and untrampled but then two lines of footprints appeared. These led all the way up to the summit then completely disappeared into thin air.

'I turned round to come back down by the same route and found only my own tracks and those of my two dogs. There was no wind or snowdrift that could have covered up the other footprints. When I reached the last plateau on the descent I paused once more to admire the wonderful view and I noticed that my dogs were both staring back up the mountain. They were growling and the hairs were standing up on their necks.

'As I looked back up to the left of the track I saw four tall figures dressed in black. I was too far away to see their faces but I could tell that they were watching me and the dogs. They all stood perfectly still. Then a slight mist drifted over the mountain-top and suddenly a fierce wind started to blow. The next moment the figures were gone, the mist had cleared, the wind had stopped and it was a bright sunny day again.'

∞

LONG before Leeds and Bradford became the centre of the clothing trade, Wakefield was the most important cloth manufacturing area in Yorkshire. Although the clatter of the mills can no longer be heard, Wakefield's splendid Georgian houses still stand proud and strong as a relic to the prosperity of the past.

Nesta from Wakefield was sitting before her fireplace in one such Georgian house in January of 1980. 'I was reading a very nice book about a ballerina's life. It was a happy book, nothing about ghosts or anything scary. My brother who had called in for a cup of tea had just left to go to his own home and there was no one in the house except myself.

'Suddenly I thought that I'd heard my bedroom door open then I heard a gentle swishing sound coming down the open staircase. The stairs came down to the right of the lounge where there was a small hallway. I was too frightened to look around behind me towards the open door so I just sat motionless staring into the fire.

'Then out of the corner of my eye I saw a lady come into the lounge and move into the centre of the room. I forced myself to turn round and there she was in full view just a few feet away from me. I can describe every detail of her dress – it was grey stiff silk, with a very tight bodice and a full skirt which reached down to her ankles. There was embroidery on the neck and cuffs.

'She stood behind my late husband's chair – the one that my brother had only just vacated a short time before. She put her hands on the back of the chair and then she slowly melted away. The next day she came again at about the same time but this time I was not so afraid. I watched her glide over to the same chair. Then I remember I so much wished that she could somehow or other bring my husband back to me. Suddenly he appeared but he was not looking my way. He did not look ghostly, in fact he looked quite young and I was surprised to see that he was dressed in a long white gown.

'I then realized that he was looking at the wall behind me. I turned to see what he was looking at and suddenly my daughter (who is very much alive) came through the wall. My husband held out his arms and she went into them and they both slowly disappeared. The woman in the long dress had also vanished.

'I was worried that something had happened to Kath, my daughter, so I immediately telephoned her to find out if she was alright. I was relieved when she answered the phone herself and assured me that she was fine. When I asked her not to drive too fast she wondered what had prompted me to say such a thing as she was not in the habit of driving fast. Although I did not wish to alarm her I felt that I had to tell her that I'd just seen her father. I did not mention anything about the woman.

'She told me, "Oh Mum, don't worry, he comes to the foot of my bed many a time and he holds out his arms to me. I always say that I am not ready to join him yet. He is always dressed in a long white gown."

'I wondered how my daughter could have known about the long white gown because I had not mentioned a word about this to her or to anyone else.

'One afternoon, shortly after that, my brother came to visit me. He was sitting in my late husband's chair and I was in the kitchen making a cup of tea but I could see through the wall-hatch into the lounge. I was just looking towards my brother when the grey outline of a woman's long dress seemed to loom out of the thin air. The figure gradually became clearer and I recognized her as the same lady I had seen in the room before. She bent over the chair and put her arms around my brother's neck. I was shocked as I couldn't imagine what on earth my brother was going to say finding such a strange creature bending over him.

'I'll never ever know what he thought because I never discussed it with him then and that was the last time I saw my brother alive.'

∞

THE Wirral peninsula juts out into the Irish sea north west of Chester, the old Roman city north of the Dee. In the year AD 79 the Romans established their camp to fortify themselves against the savage tribes of Wales. Many Roman remains can still be seen in the Grosvenor museum and all around the city; its ancient heritage is evident in the excellently preserved ramparts and the spectacular amphitheatre which lies near Newgate.

Mrs Browne, a Wirral lady, recalls the story told to her by her late mother Flo who had left school at the age of 13 to follow her sister Lucy into service as a housemaid.

'In the year 1917 when my mother was just 17, she worked in a large house on the Wirral with Lucy. One evening Lucy asked Flo if she would like to go to the pictures with her and a friend. Flo was not really keen on the idea as she had a great deal of ironing to get through so she declined the offer and decided to stay in to finish her chores.

'It never really worried her to be left on her own in the house. The owners were away and there were no other servants around so she was able to get on with her work without any interruptions. In those days the irons were heated on the kitchen stove and regular changes of irons were needed as they soon became cold in use. Flo was ironing in a room across the hall from the kitchen with its stove and so she was able to run back and forth across the hall fetching irons to and from the hot stove.

'On one such trip she could not put the light on in the hall because she had a hot iron in each hand. It was then, as she came out of the doorway into the hall that she came face to face with a man floating in mid-air. His arms and legs were outstretched and his eyes were staring straight ahead. His hair was combed back flat to his head. He was dressed in a night shirt which reached down to his feet. It was all very plain to see and very real.

'Flo felt as if she was frozen to the spot, still holding an iron in each hand. As she stood there, the figure floated past her, turned and went up the stairway and out of sight.

'She was so afraid that she dropped the iron and ran as fast as she could down to the lodge where the gardener and his wife lived. By the time her sister Lucy had returned from the pictures, Flo was in such a terrible state that the gardener's wife insisted she stay at the lodge with them until the following morning.

'The next day Lucy took Flo back home. When their mother saw the shocked condition Flo was in she immediately called for the doctor. The doctor said that the girl had suffered a severe shock and he advised that she be kept quiet with plenty of rest.

'Flo never went back to that place again. Her mother went to the house a few days later to explain to the owners what had happened. The lady of the house had only just returned from her holiday and upon hearing the story did not show the slightest surprise. She said that she knew the house was haunted and that she herself had seen things on occasions but she had never guessed that anyone else had seen anything.

'The lady explained that a man had been murdered in one of the bedrooms some time back. Flo had often told Lucy, long before that terrifying night, that whenever she was in the Blue Room, as they called it, she always felt uncomfortable and cold. She was always glad to finish her chores in that room and get out. She never felt this way in any other room in the house, only that bedroom. Could this have been the room where the murder had taken place?

'As a result of her experience Flo had a nervous breakdown and was away from work for quite some time. She could never forget that house and that terrible evening. The memory of that experience stayed with her until the day she died.'

∞

IN the year 1934 Florence lived with her parents in a remote stone house between Keighley and Bingley in the heart of the Yorkshire moors.

'My father kept pigs and their sty was about three quarters of a mile from our house. One night he went to feed the pigs as usual, taking with him a bucket of prepared food and his faithful springer spaniel. As we lived in such a lonely place it was my mother's custom to lock the door when alone in the house at night. My father was not long gone when my mother was terrified by the noise of the dog whining and scratching at the front door. She came upstairs and lifted me out of my warm bed and wrapped me in a blanket so that I could sit with her on the stairs listening to the whimpering dog. Although she was too afraid to open the door she kept trying to assure me that everything was fine and that daddy would be home soon.

'I was only five at the time but I remember every detail as if it was yesterday. After about half an hour we heard my father's footsteps and his knock on the door. My mother opened the door to let him into the house and the dog rushed into the kitchen and dashed straight under the sideboard to hide.

'My father explained that as he had turned from one lane to another he had heard footsteps. He felt that he was being followed so he sent the dog back to see who it was with the instruction "Get it Sam." Sam had obediently run towards the noise but then stopped in his tracks and started to whine loudly before taking off in the direction of our house.

'Unnerved, my father decided to go ahead and to feed the pigs, but again he heard the footsteps following him. He pushed open the large gate at the entrance to the sty area and waited. The footsteps continued and went past him down the lane. As the sound of the steps passed him he went stone cold. He saw nothing but he heard and felt a presence and he knew that something uncanny was going on to have frightened Sam off. My father was a big sturdy quarryman, very fit and strong, but he never again fed the pigs in the dark.

'In 1947 in a public house in Keighley my father met a man who had been walking his dogs one night from Bingley to Keighley and he told an almost identical story. That man had not heard of my father's experience and had never even met him before. It appears that Hainworth Shay Lane is still a haunted no-go area late at night.'

∞

ROBIN BALL used to teach at a boys school in Doncaster in 1962: 'There were 18 of the boys whose homes were outside the town and who used to board at the school from Mondays to Thursdays. I was required to have charge of them at night, together with a younger colleague and a matron.

'It was very noticeable that once it turned dark in the evenings the headmaster liked to get away to his own house. Only little by little did we come to learn why. While I was still fairly new, I was puzzled by boys in their dormitories calling out "Goodnight George". When I asked them what it was all about they told me that George was the school's ghost who walked up and down the stairs at night. All they could tell me about him was that he was middle-aged and wore a tweed suit.

'The boys were not frightened of him in the least. Eventually both my younger colleague, Stephen, and the matron had encounters with George. Stephen was a hardy

Cumbrian and the last sort of person to be afraid of ghosts, I would have thought, but he was visibly shaken after seeing George disappear through a wall. I only saw him once on a flight of stairs above me. I took him for an intruder and I rushed up the staircase only to find the place deserted. There was absolutely nowhere that he could have hidden himself.

'The headmaster was a little tyrant who used to cane the boys savagely on occasions. He seemed to live just for the power which he exerted over others. However, during the winter months when it turned dark early, if he came back for a snap inspection, expecting to catch a boy misbehaving, the boys always knew how to get rid of him: "Sir, George went upstairs five minutes ago," they would say; "He should be coming back down again fairly soon." Although the boys were not frightened of George, the headmaster was clearly scared out of his wits at the very thought of him.

'During the summer term the headmaster felt free to stay for the evening meal one night. He had taken more wine than I think he realized and he told us that when he had only just started in the school as a young man, one of the other teachers had hanged himself in the cellars where the boys hung up their coats and caps. From that moment on the ghost of that teacher had appeared on the staircase. As the school was in an old Georgian house, the boys had christened him "George".

'Apparently George had died with a serious grudge against our headmaster, who at the time of the suicide lived in the school with his wife. It appeared that the headmaster had made life unbearable for this teacher and had some sort of hold over him which made it difficult for the man to find

154

another job. He was eventually to take out his revenge, as night after night the headmaster and his wife would wake up to find the ghost of the dead teacher standing over them. On some nights the bedclothes had been thrown off them. This was the reason that he resided outside the school grounds.

'I was not surprised to find that the boys were not afraid of George for he obviously bore no child any ill will – he would not have been a normal teacher if he had.

'Our school, and other schools in the South Yorkshire area, were owned by the headmaster's very rich brother, an unscrupulous businessman. The headmaster had only limited powers when it came to the school's finances. His brother, who was totally unqualified as a teacher, found the headmaster a suitable man to govern that part of his kingdom in that the latter had a good university degree and proper teaching qualifications. So under the headmaster the school had gained a reputation for succeeding with boys aged seven to thirteen. The headmaster allowed for no failures.

'For a time the businessman brother had been the headmaster of a school in Sheffield which he owned. But, after knocking out the front teeth of a boy in his charge in a fit of rage, he had been taken to court by the boy's parents and dealt with appropriately by the law. After that his only interest in the schools he owned was in financial gain for himself. At least his brother, our headmaster, would ensure a good reputation for his school at Doncaster and his successor in Sheffield ran that school on much the same lines – scholastic success above all else.

'Eventually the headmaster and his wife found residence inside the boys' school in Doncaster no longer tolerable because of the hauntings by George. As salaried teachers they depended upon the rich brother as they had nobody else to turn to. The businessman reasoned that if he could make good profits out of boys' education in Doncaster, why should he not do the same with girls. The headmaster's wife was a qualified teacher and suitable as a headmistress. So the businessman brother bought a large house in the wealthiest suburb of Doncaster and converted it into classrooms with the necessary additions for a girls' non-residential school. He made the garden into playing facil-ities and allowed our headmaster and his wife to stay in a flat within the school buildings.

'From all that I saw, the headmaster's wife was perfectly competent and her school had a good name. It was only 1 ½ miles away from the boys' school where I worked, fairly near to the town centre, so the headmaster could get to us in his car in a matter of minutes. Of course his brother took all of the profits out of both schools for himself and he refused to release our headmaster from his contract with our school and made it clear that he would not be of assistance if any references were ever asked of him to enable the headmaster to leave his employment.

'When the cat's away the mice will play and so each night when the headmaster got into his car and drove off towards the girls' school, our boys heaved a huge sigh of relief. Not only the boys, I might add but Stephen, matron and I were also glad to see the back of him. It was only after he would leave the building that we could ever relax and be our normal selves. Under such a tyrant we became a very close knit family. The matron was the widow of a teacher and being the oldest amongst us she was our natural leader. Boys of that age need plenty of love, care and attention, even tough South Yorkshire ones, we all agreed, so when the headmaster was not there they were allowed to be themselves and were not punished for every minor infringement. We treated them as younger relatives rather than pupils under severe discipline as was the case when the headmaster was there.

'In the winter of 1962-63 it was so cold that a bathroom froze up and the temperature in the dormitories fell well below freezing. We allowed the boys to take hot water bottles to bed and gave them cups of hot cocoa before they went to bed. We paid for this ourselves but the headmaster accused us of stealing the cocoa from the kitchen. He stated that the boys should grow up tough and that we were spoiling them with such considerations. George must have agreed with us as every one of us got the distinct feeling that he was happy about how we were trying to help the boys.

'Although the headmaster used to drink, he opposed the drinking of any form of alcohol by members of the staff. Being in charge of boys at night time certainly made spending any time in a pub an impossibility. However, Stephen, the matron and I felt no sense of guilt in having the odd small bottle of lager or cider and in no way did it place any serious restraint on our abilities. We had a cupboard with a key (which the headmaster did not have) in which we kept our meagre supply. When one of us went out to dispose of the empty bottles and replenish our stocks (always after dark) we would call it disposal operations to keep the boys ignorant, but this proved to be totally in vain. If you live closely with boys of that age they soon discover or deduce the truth.

'They knew all too well that the headmaster considered our drinking beer or cider in much the same way as if they themselves had been doing anything naughty. We used to watch out of the staff room window in case the headmaster's car would appear. The boys in their dormitories did the same thing and we would all warn one another if the head was in sight.

'One evening Stephen, the matron and I were in the staff sitting room marking the boys' written work and preparing the next day's lessons, when the headmaster arrived unnoticed by us – but not by the boys. We were surprised when 12 year old Richard burst into our room saying, "Quick there's no time to lose. Get all of those bottles and glasses out of sight, open the window, and Mr Ball, smoke one of your smelly French cigarettes, the head is here."

'In less than a minute all that the child had suggested had been done. The head arrived and demanded to know what young Richard was doing in the staff sitting room. The matron answered, saying that Richard had come to her with a headache. The headmaster said that he would give Richard a tablet, but Richard knew how to get rid of him. He told the headmaster that George had been very active all night. He had been spotted on the stairs, in the dormitories and all over the place. The headmaster turned as white as a sheet then drove away within a minute.

'I couldn't help feeling that although George could not speak to the boys he had used his own means to communicate with them, and, to a lesser extent, with us. It seemed as if he wanted to unite all of us against that cruel headmaster and his ruthless brother. In that, he succeeded. The atmosphere inside that school was an unhappy one and one which I will never forget. The boys gave it the only brightness and relief from the depression which existed. Without them, we adults would have been suicidal ourselves.'

∞

THE small industrial town of St. Helens is situated north east of Liverpool, the main port on Merseyside. Norman has lived there all of his life and he can verify, 'Yes, there is some very nice countryside in the industrial north!

'About two-and-a-half miles from where I live lies a hamlet which is skirted by a stretch of lush woodlands. In a hollowed-out section of this area can be found mysterious caverns.

'Some of the old timers remember seeing the remains of an old chimney, an engine house and a well around the caverns. From time to time enterprising explorers would arm themselves with torches and boxes of sandwiches and delve down into the depths to try to uncover what lay beneath. Many visitors have ventured past the entrance but at the awesome sight of dozens and dozens of caves and twisting narrow passageways they quickly emerged with a sense of relief at once more seeing daylight. One journalist trudged for two miles underground and came across an intricate arrangement of walled-up passages. One of these had a gap just big enough to enter. He crawled along on his hands and knees for some yards until he found that this path opened out into a maze of smaller tracks and a labyrinth of caves so complex that he did not dare to venture further for fear of getting lost forever.

'However, one nearby opening, being the largest, caught his eye and he noticed that the entrance had been smoothed over for some reason, making this particular cave stand out from the rest even in the dim light of his torch. He braced himself and entered. His breath was almost taken away when he found himself in a kind of church complete with pillared arches and smooth walls. At one end of this church-like place a flight of steps led up to a gallery and an altar. There was an overwhelming sense of pending doom about the place, the silence was not peaceful but of a threatening nature. Although the cave looked exactly like the interior of a church there was something wrong – something he could not come to grips with. His immediate reaction was to run as fast as he could, out through the gap at the walled-up section and towards the long winding tunnel. By the time he had travelled the two miles to reach the exit he was in a state of near-collapse and counted himself lucky to be still alive.

'The last man to have officially worked in the caverns was a fellow called Bill Rigby. It is on record that he had explored the caverns in 1865 when he was a boy of nine. He had begun his working life there four years later when the caverns were owned by a Mr. Charles Howarth, nick-named "Yorkshire Charlie". Over 40 men were employed in the caverns, cutting out huge slabs of stone which were then transported by local farmers to the various building contractors.

'Bill remembered a deep shaft going down two layers of caverns beneath the ones which the journalist had encountered. This section had been filled in when the quarrying work had been completed there in 1870. Could the church have been built for the underground workers of that day or had it a more sinister sacrificial purpose? Judging by the atmosphere in that particular cave it would seem that the latter was nearer the truth. There was no sense of positive good vibrations which one would normally find in any bona fide church.

'Throughout the years there have been many dramatic incidents at the caverns. In 1960 and again in 1977 boys from the neighbouring localities of St. Helens and Billinge had gone on exploratory outings to the caverns and they had become hopelessly lost. After their non-appearance rescue parties were sent down to search for the youngsters and their guides. During the 1977 operation photographers went down much deeper than anyone had ever explored before. They emerged with impressive shots of stalagmite and stalactite formations.

'It is believed that the caverns are haunted by cavaliers who were chased down there by Oliver Cromwell and did not get out alive. In 1650 there were no such things as torches (other than live flames) and the cavaliers had no chance in the spider's web of passages. Several people have reported hearing moaning sounds in the caves from which they got the impression that men were dying.

'A few years ago a group of potholers from St. Helens Technical College spent nearly eight hours exploring the caves. Someone was posted outside the main entrance to keep a watch for them and to look after the gear and change of clothing. When the potholers eventually came staggering out of the caves the blood was drained from their faces and their hands were trembling uncontrollably. They were so petrified that not one of them would utter a single word about what had happened underground, and to this day, they have all kept their frightening secret.

'About ten years ago when I was at the caverns someone there told me about a weird and gruesome happening. Apparently a scout master and his pack went deep into the

161

caves but when they came out some time later, they discovered that two of the scouts were missing. They retraced their steps back into the complicated cave system. Eventually they found one of the boys hanging dead from a stalactite with a rope around his neck and with both his legs missing.

'They then heard a chewing sound and deep in a dark corner of the cave they found a kind of dwarf with a large head chewing the body of the other scout.'

∞

HELENE of Stretford, Manchester, became seriously ill with diphtheria when she was not quite five years of age. 'High fever raged and the nights were especially bad for me,' she recalls. 'It was during these nights that the old nurse used to come to see me.

'She would sit herself at the side of my bed and her lovely cool hands eased my congested chest and aching limbs with their soft stroking. Her voice was very low and had a curious and unfamiliar accent. Later, much later, she would tell me that she had to go and I would beg her to take me with her but she always replied that I could not follow her just then and I would have to bide where I was. She always promised me that she would be waiting for me at her home and that one day I would meet her there.

'Then she would rise from her chair and leave, moving very quietly, and I would follow her with my eyes, taking in every detail of her appearance: very straight-backed, small head with thick white hair, black blouse and skirt.

'She always came during the hours of the night, never in the day time and to my greatest vexation, nobody could

162

ever produce her for me however much I pleaded with the day and night staff to fetch her to my bedside.

'I recovered and my questions about the old nurse ceased after my mother had explained to me that one often imagined things during a high fever which might not necessarily be there. Trusting my mother implicitly I accepted this but the memory lingered and I was often grateful that the figment of my feverish imagination had been such a pleasant one.

'When my dear mother passed away it fell to me to take charge of her papers. She had always been a most methodical and tidy person so everything was carefully sorted and annotated in her neat handwriting.

'Amongst her treasured photographs I found something which startled me. It was a picture of my old mysterious nurse who had come to me all those years earlier. I picked it up and saw that on the back my my mother had written: "My Grandmother, aged about 65 years. Photo given me by my friend Lizbeth in 1957. So glad she found it, no other exists."

'I was stunned and sat motionless for a while. There was no possible doubt that this was the woman who had sat at my bedside and helped nurse me back to health. I had never ever seen this photograph before. I even telephoned my mother's old friend Lizbeth to check and she confirmed that she herself had only found it in 1957 amongst some old papers belonging to her own parents who were great friends with my late great-grandmother.

'Somehow the fear of death which I had always felt acutely suddenly left me as I remembered her words – that she would be waiting for me at her home and one day I would meet her there.'

IN the year 1950, Ben, a resident of Marton in Middlesbrough, Cleveland, was contemplating a big step. He was thinking of giving up his safe regular job to start up in business on his own selling tiled fireplace surrounds. He did not tell anyone about his tentative plans.

'We were living at that time in a terrace house, two up and two down. We had no children and I had only £10 in the bank. Starting any business would have been a dicey step but with virtually no capital it was almost an impossibility. But I reckoned that I would be able to arrange initial supplies on a monthly credit basis.

'One evening my wife had gone up to bed and I had checked all the downstairs doors and windows to make sure they were locked. I lit my last cigarette of the day and just stood in the middle of the living room with my back to the dying embers of the fire. I was thinking about a little corner shop which I had considered renting and I remember coming to the conclusion that the particular shop in question would hardly be spacious enough to display the various designs of fireplaces. I did not have the agent's details so I was trying to recall the exact address and street number, but for the life of me I could not remember what the proper postal address was.

'My cigarette was down to the last quarter inch when something drew my attention to the open door which led to the hallway and the stairs. A rough looking woman walked right into my living room and seated herself on the nearest dining chair with her hands resting on the table. I was so taken aback at the cool way she just came into the room I could not utter a word. I wondered if she could be a vagrant from the street, but then I remembered that I had definitely locked the doors. She was obviously harmless and I was in such a confused state I just stood there watching her. I was just as bemused by her attire as by her sudden appearance from nowhere. Her hair was dark and straggly and her features were gaunt. Some sort of woollen jumper was held together at her throat by an ordinary safety pin. Her skirt was hidden under an apron which seemed to be made from an old sack, fringed at the hemline.

'She turned her face to me but she did not raise her eyes as she spoke. In a low gravelly voice she told me: "Take one A." I had no idea what on earth she meant. I glanced down to flick my cigarette which had burnt my fingers. I only averted my gaze for a fraction of a second but when I looked back she had gone.

'Next day I found that the little shop which I had been thinking about was No. 1A. I took it and I am glad to say that from that moment on my fortunes changed for the better.

'I often wondered who that lady was, where she had come from, how she knew my thoughts, and where she went to. Nineteen years passed and in 1969, when my wife was a Commandant in a world-wide voluntary organization I was elected to become her dogsbody because she did not drive.

'My brief, each September, was to drive my wife and another lady to their annual conference at a Yorkshire seaside resort. Most other members went by bus, particularly a huge young woman with arms like tree trunks. She suffered because Marks & Spencers never had any clothes large enough for her and she had to wear men's shoes.

'On one occasion I had dutifully deposited my wife and her friend at the conference hotel when I noticed that the bus had managed to convey the extremely large lady safely to the venue. I had a snack, took a photograph and departed after promising to return two days later.

'Before I had left the outskirts of the town a terrible unaccountable feeling hit me. Although I was in perfect health at the time my whole body ached and a throbbing headache racked my senses. Thinking that maybe I was suffering from car fumes I wound down the window, but that made no difference. I still felt a melancholy wave engulf me.

'I don't know what happened next because I suddenly realized that I was driving through the market town of Helmsley. I was terrified – I had driven 30 miles in what seemed like just a few seconds. The body aches had gone but I still had the splitting headache, and a roaring sound almost deafened me. I drove for about two miles until I felt that my head was going to burst so I pulled into a lay-by and got out of the car.

'I stood looking over the wide span of scenery taking in gulps of fresh air in an attempt to clear my head. I could see for miles across a vast stretch of land with isolated farmhouses dotted along the valley. An arrow pointed to public conveniences which were hidden from view about a 100 yards inside the pine woods which covered the top of the moorland. I walked down the gritted roadway towards the conveniences which were clean and cool.

'I emerged and there, beneath the nearby trees, stood the old vagrant lady. She wore her tattered jumper and apron which advertised somebody's sugar. She had not aged and this time she looked directly at me – eye to eye contact. Her

166

gaze did nothing for my headache, except I momentarily forgot it. In that same low gravelly voice she said, "Go back." The next instant she had vanished. I stood there wondering what she meant exactly. Go back to where? To the toilets? To the car? Completely flummoxed I made my way back to the car and started to drive home. The headache started to ease as I drove.

'Two days later I was back at the conference hotel. When I drove my wife and her friend back home they seemed cautiously subdued. When we arrived home I got the full story. Moments after I had left them at the hotel they had drifted towards a room which had a bar. The extremely huge lady had landed a playful thump on my wife's shoulder blades, knocking her out cold. It seems that there is a junction of nerves at one point and a blow to that precise spot can almost kill. My wife had found herself seated on a chair at the hotel doorway, crying uncontrollably and had spent most of the following days in bed feeling unwell. The unexpected blow had triggered off an illness which eventually led to my wife's death.

'I was in deep grief trying to find some kind of explanation for what had happened. I remember discussing everything with an aged uncle and I found myself pouring my heart out to him. He told me about the time when my farmer grandfather had been killed in an accident.

'My uncle had been loading hay onto a farm cart and grandfather was working on top. An insect had stung the horse making the animal jerk forward in the shafts. Grandfather fell off and suffered a broken back. As a very small boy I remembered being present when my grandfather was brought into the house on a hurdle. My uncle then said that he had been struggling trying to lift my heavy grandfather onto the hurdle when he became quite annoyed at a woman who just stood close by staring at him. "She was no help to me at all, and even when I called over to her to go and fetch help she just stared right through me. I was so concerned at getting your grandfather moved without causing him extra pain that I just ignored her. She was raving on in a cracking old voice trying to tell me something but I was so confounded that I just snarled back at her telling her to mind her own business. She was wearing an old jumper that had seen better days and she had an old apron affair wrapped round her, made out of a sugar sack or something like that. The next thing there was nothing there. She had disappeared.'

∞

A BRISTOL man used to live in the north of England. 'I am a third generation railwayman,' he says. 'I use that word to distinguish between people who are real railwaymen and those who merely work on the railway. My grandfather was in the carriage works at Crewe after he left the army and all my uncles, except one who died early, were in the loco works along with my father. I followed him in 1939 and spent a long happy working life on the railway. I am currently interested in a couple of restoration projects.

'Once in 1951 I was riding an Austerity 2-8-0 freight engine over the Pennines finishing at Farnley Shed around 5.20 a.m. This was in February and it was therefore dark. I washed and walked along the track to Farnley Junction Station (which is no longer there) to wait for the 5.50 a.m. from Leeds due to arrive at Farnley at 6.00 a.m. to go on to Stalybridge, Stockport and then home.

'It was freezing with an east wind blowing that would cut you in half. The station gas lights were lit and I waited on the westbound platform. I was just standing looking over at the other platform where I saw a man standing under a lamp reading a newspaper. Although the lamp was fairly dim there was reflected light from the frozen snow on the platform so I could see him quite clearly. I was anxious to get home after a long night on the footplate. (I was not footplate staff but was on the engine observing the effect of new balance weights on the coupled wheels.)

'I did notice however that the man was wearing a top coat and trilby hat. Because he was the space of two running lines away and there was only the gas light, I can't say what paper he was reading but I assumed that it must have been the newspaper of that day. I say this because shops opened earlier then than they do now and in the latter stages of the trip from Mirfield I had seen shops with lights on.

'My train approached and just as it slowed down at the platform I saw the man across on the other platform turn and walk straight towards the track. I'll never forget the wave of panic that shot through me as I was certain that he would go over the edge of the platform in front of the engine. I roared over to him to stop. I did not take my eyes off him as I watched him move over the edge of the platform, then he was gone in a whirl of mist which drifted up and merged with the steam from the engine.'

∞

ROBERT CHAPMAN of Preston in Lancs used to be a church warden in 1972 at St Helen's Church, Garstang.

'I had a plan of the location of every grave in the

churchyard, also a list of them so I knew them all well. There were two which I always wondered about. One was a flat slab with a legend: "Leonard Foster, 1632" engraved on it. The other, a few yards away, was a shaped slab, upright, which bore the legend: "Elizabeth Foster died 17th October 1632". I knew that they had both died of the plague in 1632 for they were so entered in the register for that period and they were in fact father and daughter. I was well aware that having grave markers in 1632 meant that they must have been persons of some importance.

'One night, for no particular reason, the two tombstones came into my mind. Although it was 10.30 p.m. I took down the printed copy of the register for the years 1597 to 1686 and located the page on which the Foster entries had been made.

'At that precise moment the telephone rang and I answered it. A voice asked me, "Bob, do you believe in ghosts?" I instantly recognized the voice as belonging to a local farmer's wife. I answered, "Well, on Sundays I swear that I believe in the visible and the invisible...." She went on to tell me that her husband now believed in ghosts because he had just seen one that evening in the field. I remember reminding her that it was getting late but I asked if it would be convenient for me to visit them the following day at around 4.30 p.m. when I could hear the whole story.

'I arrived at the farmhouse on the dot of time as arranged. The farmer explained that the previous evening he had been spraying the young corn by tractor, moving up and down the field in sweeps the width of his boom. Moving parallel to a stream bordering the field he had noticed a figure walking in the same direction as he was travelling but on the far side of the stream. He of course assumed that it must be a local taking an evening walk. On his return sweep the figure had moved along and as the farmer was now travelling in the opposite direction he was able to take a closer look. He began to wonder who it could be, eliminating in his mind all of the locals who were well known to him.

'The large hat of the stranger made the farmer wonder as he had never seen such a hat on anyone before. Also the type of boots he was wearing seemed a bit unusual. As the farmer passed by, he watched the figure cross the stream where there was no means of crossing, and enter the field which was being sprayed. The figure had passed beyond the sweep he was making on the return, so the farmer turned the tractor in a circle to see better and to his horror he saw the spray boom pass right through the figure of the man. The next second the man was nowhere to be seen.

'I was shown the field, and I witnessed the tractor wheel marks in the young corn and the circular sweep which the farmer had taken to enable him to take a closer look at the figure. I asked the farmer to describe the clothes the stranger had been wearing. From what I was told they appeared to be of the type worn in the early 17th century. I requested that if the farmer ever saw the figure again that he would inform me.

'A week later he telephoned me to say that he had seen "it" again in mid-afternoon in a wood and he had been able to see the face. The clothing worn was exactly the same as he had seen previously. He told me that he had been talking to a lady in the village who knew nothing about what he had seen but who had reported that she had seen a figure similar in description on the site of a former coach path in the village.

'After a bit of searching through the old parish books

and a few visits to the local library I found out that the coach path runs directly across the land upon which the house of Leonard Foster once stood.'

∞

A WOMAN from Doncaster fondly remembers her late father as 'a very down-to-earth kind of man, certainly not given to fanciful notions.

'Some years ago he had been out on a shooting trip. Coming back in his van along a country lane which had hedges on either side and fields beyond, he glanced to the right to see a car coming straight across the field. It was not quite dusk and he had to pull up sharply, jolting to a stop just as the other car came straight through the hedge. It moved across the road in front of him and then evaporated into the opposite hedge and vanished into the field.

'For some reason my father always associated that experience with some kind of warning, or preparation. He'd had the strangest feeling when he saw the phantom car that it was meant to be taking him on some kind of journey. Although it did not make a lot of sense to him at the time, he seemed to feel that it was in some way significant.

'Shortly after this event I had the most weird dream. I'll always remember it because of its strange content, so unlike any other dream I have ever had. I was in a cemetery walking along with my mother trying desperately to find a way out. On one side of the path there was a larger than life white owl sitting on a tombstone. The moon was shining and as I looked at the owl, wondering if it could be alive, it blinked.

'We passed by the owl hoping that the path would lead to

172

the way out but I was horrified to find that the exit was blocked by several grey wolves who were snarling at us, their eyes gleaming with menace. On turning back round to retrace our footsteps there were more wolves blocking every pathway. I woke up the next morning with every detail of the dream vivid in my mind but I did not mention it to anyone as I did not feel that there was any reason to do so – after all it was only a dream.

'Very shortly after that my father was out on another shooting and fishing trip. This time it was at Howden near Goole. He stopped his van to speak to a farmer because he wanted to buy a sack of potatoes. The farmer's van was parked up ahead of him. They talked for a minute or two then a lorry approached up the narrow road. The farmer had been looking ahead and had seen the lorry coming. He called to my father to mind his back, but his warning came too late. My father was knocked into the farmer's driving mirror then he slumped down on the road unconscious. He died the following day never having regained consciousness.

'A few days later my sister, brother and I were looking at some of father's belongings; a lovely ivory chess set, a microscope and a three dimensional viewer which, it was unanimously agreed, I was to keep, together with a pack of little picture slides which went with the viewer. I had never seen these before and in fact I was not even aware that my father had owned such a thing.

'Eager to have a look through the viewer, I placed the first slide in position. I thought it rather odd when it turned out to be a picture of a graveyard. I quickly pulled the slide out and inserted the next one from the pack. I nearly died when I found myself looking at the very same large white

173

owl which I had seen in my dream. It was sitting on a tombstone.'

∞

HULL, on the north side of the Humber, is Britain's third largest sea port after London and Liverpool. It was originally known as Wuke-upon-Hull until King Edward 1 bought it and re-named it Kingston-upon-Hull. It was in the Humberside area that the Vikings invaded Britain in the l0th Century.

Some years ago Barbara Bayes was employed as a "Mrs. Mop" for a company in Albion Street, Hull. 'A large Victorian house had been converted into offices and I always thought what a lovely private house it must have been in its glory with sweeping oak stairways and high ornate ceilings and doors.

'There were a few private flats on the upper part of the building and I had to collect the key from the ground floor office to gain access to the second floor flat. This flat still retained a lot of its original beauty even with the mod cons installed. The cleaning of the flat was simple. The problem was with the door.

'For some reason it would close just when I was on the point of re-entering, armed with pails and brushes, or worse, when the latch was down and the key was on the inside. It wasn't as if it was swinging closed naturally, it was more of a slam as if someone was slamming the door in a bit of a temper. It had happened time after time, even once when I put a pail down to keep it open while I went to collect some cleaning materials from the little storeroom on the ground floor. I'd heard the slam from downstairs but even though I heard it I thought at the back of my mind that it must have been from some other door as it could not possibly be the first floor flat. But I was wrong. When I got back upstairs sure enough the door was shut fast. However, a pass key was kept in the office downstairs so although the closing of the door was an inconvenience it was nothing too drastic.

'One day I had arranged to meet a pal of mine to do some shopping in the town. She called into the downstairs office to wait until I had finished work as she had arrived a bit too early. I heard her voice drifting up the stairway but I just continued to vacuum the carpets with my back to the entrance door of the flat.

'I felt two hard taps on my left shoulder. Turning the machine off, I said, "Joan, you did give me a start. I won't be long, but don't sneak up again like that." I turned as I spoke and realized that I was speaking to an empty room. I walked over to the door and called out, "Have you just come up, Joan?" Joan answered me from the ground floor office saying that she had never left there. After handing in the key I again asked her if she had played a trick on me but she clearly did not know what I was on about, so I dropped the subject. But I thought that I'd better double check to find out if there was anyone on the third floor. I opened the top flat with the pass key but found it completely empty as it had been for months, awaiting new tenants.

'The following day I was polishing the stairway between the second and third floors. I distinctly heard footsteps going up the stairway just above me towards the third floor. I looked up but could see no one. I even called out but there was no reply. It was only then it dawned on me that no one had passed me on the stairway which was the only method

175

of reaching the top floor, and in any case the flat on the top floor was still vacant.

'Within a few minutes I heard the footsteps again. They were quite soft to start with and sounded as if they were walking across the floor of the top flat. To my horror they got louder and sounded as if they were at the top of the stairway. They were coming down the stairs towards me. I broke out in a cold sweat as I felt completely trapped. To make matters worse they were now running. I was peering up the stairs but could see nothing at all. The next moment an icy cold wave went through me as the sound of the footsteps went right past where I was standing. It was as if a freezing draft had just whizzed past. I heard the footsteps run straight into the flat on the second floor and I nearly fainted when I heard the violent slam of the flat door.

'I was so terrified that I was rooted to the spot, not daring to go back down the stairs in case I would meet anything as I passed the second floor flat. I'm not sure how long I stood there but I felt nauseated and I was trembling like a leaf. After what seemed like ages of silence I tried to muster up enough courage to make myself walk back down those stairs. Slowly I tip-toed down, keeping as far away from the second floor flat door as I could. As soon as I got past that door I galloped down the rest of the stairs two at a time until I got to the offices on the ground floor where I grabbed my coat and ran from the building.

'I rang up my employer later that day to tell him that I would not be returning to work. I must say that he did not sound too surprised then he admitted that no char had ever stayed to work in that building for more than a few weeks. I had been there longer than anyone and I'd only been employed for just over a month.

'This got me wondering, for although there was no way that I ever wanted to enter that building again, I was curious as to what was really going on there. I made some enquiries in the library and around the locals and I found out that many years ago a young girl had lived in the house and had fallen in love with a young man whom her parents disapproved of. Apparently there had been a violent row and the girl had been confined to her bedroom at the top of the house. Despite continuous running up and down to plead with her determined father she was forbidden to see her young man ever again. The parents found her dead in her room the following morning.'

∞

MR. HAITHWAITE from Ripon in North Yorkshire remembers: 'Some years ago I had caught a bus from town which stopped not far from where I live. It was about 9.30 in the evening and it was quite dark. As I walked along the road I heard a child crying over to the right.

'Thinking that the child must be in some difficulty I crossed over the road to see if I could help. I could still hear the crying, and moving along the other side of the road I saw what I thought was someone in a white coat.

'At that moment a car approached along the road so I thought that I would probably be able to see whoever it was in the car's headlights. To my surprise there was no one anywhere along the road or footpath and there was absolutely no place that anyone could have gone to. The crying had now stopped.

'I went home, mentioned what had happened to my mother and thought no more about it. A few days later a little boy who lived just down the road from our house was killed by a car on that very spot.'

∞

FROM Bradford in West Yorkshire a lady recalls when she was a young bride in 1942. 'I had only been married six months and was delighted about the fact that my new sister-in-law was very friendly towards me and used to call frequently for a chat and a cup of tea. One day she told me about a very vivid dream that she had had the night before.

'In her dream she had seen a young man, a soldier she thought, who had knocked on her door and she had invited him inside. She was surprised to see when he was next to her, that he wore a navy blue uniform with a white webbing belt and a white peaked hat. There was a red stripe running down the side of the trousers. It crossed her mind then that perhaps he wasn't a soldier but a sailor. She remembered being quite puzzled about this in the dream.

'He held out his hand, took her hand and said, "I've come to say goodbye because I must go now." He then turned away and waved goodbye to her.

'The very next day my mother and father received a telegram from the war office to say that my brother, a Royal Marine, had been killed in action by a direct hit along with six other men. They were on board Bradford's adopted cruiser, *The Aurora*.

'My brother had been on constant active service and was unable to attend my wedding and so my sister-in-law had never met him. His dress uniform was exactly as she had described in her dream.'

IN 1932, Mr. Anderson of Newton Heath, Manchester, used to live in a house in Bridgewater Street, Oldham, Lancs. The house has long since been demolished and the site is now part of the local school grounds. 'It was a single house, one up, one down, no back door and the front door opened directly onto the street.

'I was about eleven years of age and one lovely warm sunny day I was playing a game of football outside in the street with a gang of my pals. The ball burst, and as I had a football upstairs in the house I told the lads that I would run up to fetch it and I'd be down in a minute.

'On entering the house, the door to the stairs was facing the main door from the street. My mother and my sister were in the downstairs room sitting on rocking chairs at each side of the fireplace and they saw me come in through the living room door which was ajar.

'I opened the door to the staircase and went up, turning round the bend of the stairwell. I stopped in my tracks when I saw a woman at the top of the stairs. She was tall and straight and she wore a long dress that covered her legs. Her hair was done up in a bun. I thought my mother had sent this woman up the stairs for some reason although I couldn't really imagine why because my mother never let anyone other than the family up the stairs as our bedroom was not a pretty sight.

'The woman seemed a bit startled, then she smiled at me and I smiled back. She came down the stairs and I had to

179

press myself to the wall as she passed me as the stairs were very narrow. As she passed I turned to continue up the stairs but there was such a blast of coldness which seemed to smack into me that I lost my balance and fell down on my knees on the stairs. I couldn't get my breath and I'd never felt so cold in my life. I felt as if my blood was freezing up inside me. I remember thinking that I was going to die. I was fighting for breath for what seemed like a very long time but it must have been only a matter of seconds.

'Eventually I recovered and went up to the bedroom to collect the football. When I went back downstairs I was amazed to see only my mother and sister sitting in the living room. I said, "Where's that woman?" My mother asked me, "What woman?" I dashed out hoping to see her still in the street but there was no sign of her. I went all round the block followed by the lads who were only interested in getting the ball from me to continue the football match. The woman was nowhere to be seen. I even asked the gang if they'd seen a woman come out of our house as they were all waiting right outside our door. None of them had seen anyone.'

∞

MANY years ago, Doreen Bennett, a Leeds lass, was on a week's walking holiday in the Yorkshire Dales with a friend and a small brown poodle.

'We arrived very hungry at Barnard Castle. It was about 4.30 p.m. and on seeing a large notice advertising mixed grills on a cafe window, we needed no further encouragement. It was a very old building called Cromwell House Cafe.

'After a huge mixed grill with apple pie to follow, we enquired if the waitress knew of anywhere we could stay for bed and breakfast. Much to our surprise she told us that we could stay right there at Cromwell House.

'It looked such an ancient place we were not too sure but because it was getting late we thought that we'd better accept in case we couldn't find anywhere else. We were taken up the stairs to our room which had a thick heavy old- fashioned door with a large metal lock.

'During the night I awoke in horror. The hair was prickling on my head with sheer fright. The floor seemed to have opened up and there in the middle of the bedroom floor I could see about a dozen bone-thin people all stretching out stick-like arms. Their faces were so gaunt that they looked like skulls but they were alive and all the time reaching upwards as if they were trying to rise up out of the floor. I'll never forget the pleading expressions in their sunken eyes. One word came into my head – Belsen!

'I tried to sit up in the bed but I found that my body was rigid and I was unable to move. I had all my senses about me and I could see the mass of twisting limbs before me. I tried to call out to waken my friend who was fast asleep in the other bed but when I opened my mouth no sound came out. This made me go into an inner panic as I felt completely helpless.

'It was then I heard the most pathetic wailing sound. I kept looking from one tortured face to another to see who it was that was crying out. Although the sound continued I could not distinguish exactly where it was coming from. I still could not move anything except my eyes. I looked over to the far corner of the room and I saw my little dog cowering into the wall. The wailing was the sound of my poodle's terrified whimpering. I could see it virtually quivering with fright and looking at the figures.

'All I could do was just stare and stare at these tortured people for what seemed like ages but I expect that it was no more than a few seconds in reality. Very gradually the faces faded and eventually all of the bodies had disappeared and the room was back to normal. It was only then that I was able to move so I jumped up out of the bed and ran to pick up my dog which was still shaking with fright. I woke up my friend who had not heard or seen anything.

'The next morning after breakfast, the owner asked us if we would like to see the dungeons in the cellars where at one time men had been imprisoned, starved and tortured.'

∞

A LADY from Wakefield in West Yorkshire used to know a girl called Clara Gill who was a member of the same Methodist chapel and who attended Sunday school. 'She left the area and for years I never saw her. One day she came back to Wakefield to settle down. She was married and I noticed that her husband was a very smartly dressed young man although I never really got to know him very well.

'Clara died and her widower lived on his own in their little house. When I used to walk to chapel I used to pass the end of the road where he lived and on several occasions we walked part of the way together. I was always struck by how smart looking he had remained despite his lonely life.

'After a few years however he became unable to live on his own and went to stay in a local communal home. I never saw him after that.

'One day I was walking from my home into town and as I

passed a flower shop I suddenly began to wonder about this man. The only name I could think of was Mitchell but I knew perfectly well that this was not his name. I noticed, for some reason, that the time was 3.00 p.m.

'I thought no more about the matter until the next day when I again passed that same flower shop. As I passed the entrance, two of the members of our chapel came out of the shop. They were called Mr & Mrs Mitchell. We started to talk and they told me that they had just been into the flower shop to order a wreath on behalf of the chapel for Clara Gill's husband who had died the previous day at 3.00 p.m.'

∞

A LADY from Liverpool remembers when her daughter was born, 32 years ago. 'It was in the days before husbands were encouraged to stay with their wives during childbirth. The general attitude was that the men were just in the way and therefore after my husband had accompanied me safely to the hospital he was sent home with instructions to ring the ward the following morning.

'He went home and went to bed as usual but in the middle of the night he awoke with a start. There at the foot of the bed he saw his late mother who had died the previous year. She was nodding and smiling. He looked at the clock by the bedside and saw that the time was 4.45 a.m.

'At that precise moment I gave birth to our daughter. The first thing I noticed was that she had a mop of bright auburn hair exactly like my late mother-in-law.'

∞

MRS. E. Edgar, now a resident of Audenshaw, Manchester, at one time lived in Singapore. 'I had come home for a holiday just at the time of my nan's 89th birthday. My mother had arranged a party for her and of course all of her friends and relations were invited.

'On the day of the party my nan took me aside and quite calmly told me that she would not see me again. She said that she knew I would be going back to Singapore and that she was going to die very soon. I immediately got upset at her words but she told me that I was not to grieve because she was prepared to go and it would only make her unhappy if she thought that I would be miserable. She said it all in such a simple direct way that I believed her. She added that wherever she was she would be looking after me.

'I went back to Singapore and exactly three months after her party my beloved nan died. I was living in a large house with very wide stairs up from the living room. There were eight stairs up then a passage turned round and more stairs continued upwards to the next floor. One day I was just pottering about the house and I had to go up the stairs for some reason. Just above me at the top of the first eight steps I saw a flitter of light in the shape of a human figure. I watched it go up the remaining steps then turn and move along the winding passage.

'I was not sure what to make of it. I was alone in the house at the time as my husband travelled a lot and was away on business and both of my sons were out. I just got on with things and tried to put it out of my mind. A little later I had to go upstairs again but this time I was a little worried. Just as I started to walk up I saw it again – the same glimmering shape about the size of a person. It was in the exact same position and it was moving up towards the passage.

'It then hesitated, and started to glide back down the stairs coming towards me. By this time I was most alarmed. The only thing I could think of was that this light was my nan who had returned to look after me just as she had told me she would.

'I stood at the bottom of the stairs and shouted up towards the shape as loudly as I could: "Nan, I will always love you, but if it is you, you are frightening me. Please leave me alone." The light instantly disappeared and I never saw it again.

'Since that I have had only two dreams about my nan. In the first one she was crying but the second time she was laughing and looked serenely happy and contented.'

∞

GORDON, a Humberside man, remembers a story told to him by his mother: 'In January 1934, my mother was in the centre of Hull having just seen her mother onto a tramcar. She suddenly felt overwhelmed by a sense of her late father's presence. He had died four years previously. She felt that if she turned around she would most certainly see him.

'She was aware of his voice ringing in her head telling her, "Get a bus and go home." At the same time she felt as if someone was tugging at her coat to try to prevent her from going the way that she had intended to. She looked all around her but no one was touching her coat or was even near her.

'Having more errands to do before she could go home, she just pulled herself together and told herself that she was being foolish. She went on her way as per her original plan.

Within seconds, as she was crossing over the street, a mineral lorry came speeding round a corner and ran right into her knocking her unconscious. She was rushed to hospital with near fatal serious injuries and for a few days it was uncertain whether or not she would survive. She has always been convinced that her father had tried to save her from that catastrophe.'

∞

MANY people may have had an experience similar to that of Mrs Cantrill of Rotherham, South Yorkshire. 'At the time I was a young married woman with a baby and two other young children. Although my mother was dying of cancer I could only visit her rarely as my husband was at the office all day and we lived in a little village, well out of the city with hardly any bus service.

'One night I went to bed as usual and in the very early hours of the morning, for some reason, I woke up. I was very surprised to see my mother standing by the bed looking at me. Half in panic, I woke my husband who told me that I must have been dreaming and to go back to sleep. My mother had been dressed in a coat and hat which I knew well, but when I turned back round again she was gone.

'Whilst we were having breakfast the following morning, one of my sisters who lived with my mother and father opened the door and walked in. She looked at me and I said, "No need to tell me. Mummy's dead. She came to say 'goodbye' in the night." My mother's appearance in our bedroom had occurred at approximately the same time as her death.

'My older sister told me that for the last two days of my

mother's life, her eyes had been constantly looking round her bedroom searching for me. I couldn't get to her but she found a way to get to me.'

∞

ANOTHER short story comes from Mrs Grimmer of South Yorkshire: She reports, 'During the last war my husband was sent up to Fulford, an area of York, to a makeshift army hospital. He had tuberculosis. I had to go to Fulford with our two children and we were billeted at Park Grove.

'There was a great view of York Minster in all its glory from our room. One night we were sleeping on our bunks and I suddenly woke up. I felt completely paralysed and stone cold. I just couldn't understand what was happening to me for no matter how hard I tried to move I found it impossible. After a tremendous effort I managed to turn round on my other side. There, floating in mid air I saw the head and shoulders of an elderly lady. She had her hair piled up on top of her head and she was staring at me with her piercing blue eyes which I could see clearly. Although the room was in darkness she appeared in a luminous surrounding light and her face was brilliant as if it was somehow lit up from inside.

'My first thought was to lock the door but then I told myself that it wouldn't make any difference because being that she seemed to be just floating around without the rest of her body, she would probably be able to pass through doors. On thinking back I am amazed that I was able to think clearly about anything as I was so frightened at the time. The following day I happened to speak to a lady from downstairs. I just asked out of curiosity if she knew anything about the building. She told me that an old lady had once thrown herself off the little balcony outside my room window.'

∞

TINA of Manchester reports: 'Several years ago, when I was aged ten, my father died. A couple of months after this I used to see his face smiling in the centre of a halo of light up in the corner of my bedroom.

'At the time it frightened me even though I could hear his kindly voice saying to me, "Don't be afraid." Nevertheless I was afraid and used to run into my mother's bed.

'This carried on for about a year – not every night but about one or two times a week. By this time I had become used to seeing him and I was no longer afraid. The peculiar thing was that he no longer said anything but his face appeared smiling directly at me and very much alive.

'Ten years later, after I had married and moved away from home, my brother and his family (who had emigrated to Australia and then returned) were living at my mother's house. My niece who was aged seven at the time and had never met my father, occupied my old bedroom.

'One night she came running downstairs quite upset saying that she did not want to sleep in that room any more. When my mother asked her why, the child replied, "Daddy's daddy keeps smiling at me."

∞

PERHAPS one of the strangest stories of the north comes

from a lady from Kirkhamgate near Wakefield in West Yorkshire.

'We had six ponies in 1984 and since we had had a fair show season, we rented a field for a month from a farmer we were friends with in order to give the ponies some freedom. Show ponies are normally kept in the stables for most part of the time.

'One Friday evening my daughter and I went down to the field where five of them had been left to run around. They all came running towards us as usual. They were having such a great time that we decided we would leave them out overnight and check them again first thing in the morning.

'Early the following morning we were wakened up by someone thumping on the door of the house. My husband went down and was told that the ponies had got out onto the motorway and there had been a dreadful accident. Two of them had been killed outright and another two had been seriously injured and probably would have to be put down. Only one white pony, "Holly" had remained in the field and was safe. "Foxie", the sixth pony, was in the stable.

'We all got dressed quickly and went down to the scene of the accident. A huge opening had been made in the fence, possibly by vandals, but we might never know for sure. My youngest daughter's pony, "Cha-Cha" had lost one of her eyes and she had bad head wounds. The other injured animal was a pathetic sight to see. She was in foal and in a serious state of shock. She just stood still with her head dangling down towards the ground like a football. Our own vet arrived but informed us that both of the surviving ponies' injuries were so severe that they would have to be put down.

'We were all absolutely shattered and of course we

blamed ourselves for not bringing them up to the stables the previous night. After the animals had been put to sleep we went over to where they were lying on the ground to cover them with blankets until they could be taken away.

'My daughter Karen looked down at her pony "Cha-Cha". As she stood there, an icy feeling crept over her. At that very moment, my other daughter Elaine saw "Cha-Cha" rise up from the ground shrouded in swirling mist. The solid body of the animal still lay dead on the ground. She could only see the top half of "Cha-Cha" in the mist.

'On the following Tuesday afternoon my husband was driving me down to the stables to feed our two surviving ponies, "Foxie" and "Holly". Just as we were approaching the stables "Cha-Cha" ran right across the front of the car. My husband had to jam on the brakes making the car screech to a halt. The pony had just loomed out from the hedgerow and dashed right across the roadway and through the opposite hedge. We were both shaking with fright. He turned to me and said, "Cha-Cha".

'"Cha-Cha" was jet black all over except for a little white star on its forehead and it was the only black pony we had ever owned. We both got out of the car immediately and looked all over the place. There was no sign of "Cha-Cha" but up by the stables we were surprised to see "Holly" running about in a very excited state.

'We quickly got "Holly" back into the stable. We could not understand how she had got out as there were no signs of any break-in and her stable door was still shut.

'I couldn't help wondering if "Cha-Cha" had come back to collect her, or had she guided "Holly" back to the stable?'

Chapter Four
WALES

ONE afternoon Thelma was out for a stroll along the river near her home in Carmarthen on the western outskirts of the Brecon Beacons. In the distance she saw a figure standing by the bank facing the river. As she walked closer she recognized that it was a nun in a long black habit, but instead of the usual winged head-dress this one had a black hood over her head. She was quite tall and sturdily built.

'I could see that she was deep in thought' recalls Thelma. 'I found myself glancing over to see if she was perhaps praying on rosary beads but from the angle that I approached her I could not see the front of her at all.

'Being a friendly person and not wishing to appear rude by not speaking to her I just called over "good-afternoon" to her. I was a bit surprised to see that she totally ignored my words and continued to look into the water. I thought to myself that she didn't want to be bothered with anyone speaking to her so I went on my way.

'After only a few moments I looked up ahead of me and right there in front of me, standing on the bridge, was the same nun. She was facing in my direction this time, still staring into the water. Her black hood was pulled low down over the top of her head, almost covering her eyes.

'I looked back to see if maybe there could be two nuns – as to me they all look the same anyway – but there was no nun behind me where I had seen her on the bank. In fact there was only one man much further back walking in the opposite direction and a young woman walking with a pram.

'I kept watching the figure on the bridge as I walked along, not quite sure what to make of it. I passed the bridge, said nothing, and just kept walking. But curiosity got the better of me and I just had to look back at the bridge. This time I really did get a fright because the bridge was deserted, but far back along the bank I could see the nun in the very place where I had first spotted her. She was standing in the same position staring into the water but this time I got the impression that she was bending slightly more over the bank.

'I turned and continued my journey but in the matter of just a few moments a wave of icy fear ran through my body. I could hear footsteps very close behind me and the sound of heavy, laboured breathing.

'I knew that nobody could have caught up with me that fast. Only seconds before when I had looked around the nun was far back down on the side of the bank and no one else was in sight. There were no houses or other buildings by that particular spot from which anyone could have come. Even the man who had been walking in the opposite direction had gone.

'I quickened my pace, not daring to look round again. To my horror the footsteps behind me also quickened. They seemed to be making ground on me and the sound of breathing was getting louder.

'My mind was racing, trying to figure out what I should do. I turned slightly with the intention of crossing over to the other side of the road, but being a practical person I decided that the whole thing was getting out of hand and too ridiculous for words. I made myself turn around quickly. I screamed out in terror despite all my philosophizing because there, right behind me was the

192

black-clad nun still with her hood pulled down half covering her face.

'I took off at speed and ran down the road. After a few moments I glanced back to see if she was still following me. You can imagine my confusion when far away in the distance I could see the nun standing back on the bridge again. How she could possibly have got all the way back there in just a few seconds, I'll never know.

'By that time I'd had enough. I was a nervous wreck. I went straight to the first house I came to and asked if I could use the telephone as it was an emergency. I phoned my husband's work number and asked him to come and collect me, telling him that I would explain everything when I saw him.

'When my husband picked me up he could see that something had happened to upset me. Also he knew that I would never have interrupted him at the office if it had not been important. I told him to take me home by a different route and when we got inside I told him the whole story.

'My husband made some enquiries. He could find no one in the locality who had seen this nun on the day I had walked along by the river. He did find out something a bit later on however which I had never known about.

'Apparently in the year 1843 there were dreadful riots in Carmarthen when 400 men dressed up as women stormed the jail to protest against certain tolls which were being charged at the town gates. They called themselves "Rebecca and her daughters", taking the name from the biblical Rebekah. The men had been dressed in a great assortment of women's apparel.

'The more I thought about that nun – the height, strong build, and the way the hood was pulled down over half the face, I couldn't help wondering if "she" had really been one of the rioters.'

∞

ONE wild and windy night, William Davies was driving back from a football meeting in Abertillery. He saw two ladies at the roadside, obviously looking for a lift.

'One was elderly but the other was much younger and very pretty. I pulled into the side and offered to give them a lift which they seemed pleased to accept. It turned out that they were mother and daughter.

'They told me that they had been visiting relatives in Crumlin and somehow the time flew by making them late. Their house was in Glaswich Lane on the outskirts of Newport. On arriving at the big house they were most insistent that I went inside for a drink.

'The young one said, "You have been so kind, a small whisky will keep the cold air out and I will be pleased if you will accept." Her beguiling eyes were enough to persuade me and the thought of a Scotch was also tempting.

'On entering the hallway I was surprised by the old-fashioned furniture. The whole atmosphere didn't seem to be of this day and age. We went into the lounge and again this old world feeling was all around – the curtains, the log fire. I just thought that they must favour this type of decor and thought nothing more about it.

'They settled me into a comfortable chair near the fireplace and I asked would they object to me smoking. (I really should give it up, but there it is.) They both smiled their consent and as I lit my cigarette the girl said, "Oh what an exquisite lighter. May I look at it?" I handed it to her saying it was a family heirloom. Sipping the whisky, I felt a wave of tiredness wash over me so I felt it was time to go. I made my farewells and left.

'As I drove away, I thought, "Damn! I've forgotten my lighter." The girl had placed it on the mantelshelf. I could have kicked myself for not collecting it before I left. I turned around and made my way back to the house. The car headlights picked out an overgrown driveway and a derelict house. I immediately assumed that I had the wrong place but then I noticed the name displayed prominently: "Twm-Glas". I went to the door and even as I lifted the lion's head knocker I knew, I just knew, that I would get no answer.

'All the windows had a thick coating of grime and there was no sign of the heavy brocade curtains that only a short time ago the old lady had drawn. It was just then that I noticed a sign proclaiming that this property was for sale. I made a note of the agent's name and resolved that I would clear up this mystery in the light of the following morning.

'Bright and early the following morning I presented myself at the estate agent's office and informed him of the house I was interested in. He fell over himself in his haste to make me welcome, telling me that the basic structure was sound and there was lots of potential for improvements. I asked him who the previous owners were and he told me that the house belonged to the widow of Colonel Windrush – a fine family. He seemed to be edging a bit so I asked him if he was having trouble in selling it. He replied, "It's silly really. You see, years and years ago the widow and her young daughter were killed in a tragic accident near Oakdale and there has been some talk of ghosts."

'He told me that there was a reduction on the market value because of this, but who believes in haunted houses these days? I asked him if I could take the keys and view the place as I didn't believe in ghosts either.

'I must confess that in spite of that statement to the agent, I felt a strange tingling at the back of my neck as I entered that driveway. The key turned in the lock easily enough but I had to use some force to push open the heavy door.

'It was an eerie feeling, standing in that hall, now that it was empty. There was dust and decay everywhere. The door to the lounge was open and as I stepped inside I was horrified to see fresh footprints leading to the fireplace. Yes – my footprints, that I must have made the night before! I looked up towards the mantelshelf and I gasped with shock when I saw my lighter. I hurried forward, snatched it up and ran towards the hallway. It was then that I heard it – the voice of that young woman saying, "I knew you'd be back. It's such a lovely lighter."

∞

SIMONE remembers vividly the day she first took up residence at Alltyrodya Mansion near Llandyssal.

'We turned into the drive with its wrought iron gates and stone pillars on either side, our ancient 1925 Talbot car bumping along on the uneven surface. This was the entrance to the house that was to be our home for the next 18 years. Almost immediately on entering the drive one could see, on the right, the field belonging to our farm in which was a castle mound. This mound had been one of the earlier fortifications made of wood, before they were made of stone, and it had been the scene of a fierce battle in the 12th century with marauders from nearby Castell Hwyel.

'Continuing along the drive for perhaps 150 yards we

came to the cold bath. I do not know the age of it but I would surmise it had been built around the 16th or 17th centuries when some of the renovations to the property were carried out. Another 150 yards on and the large white house came into view. Here the drive widened and in the centre of it was an ornamental pond with a fountain. Steps led down into a field in front of the house. Years later, when we had occasion to call in plumbers to do some repairs, we discovered that from the field there was an entrance to a passage about four feet high. The two plumbers went in to explore and reported back that they had found a maze of passages under the main drive. They also came across a small padlocked door! How I wished I had told them to break it down to see what was beyond; it has bugged me ever since!

'Looking from the house towards the left we could see a field which had in it an unexcavated Roman Fort, the outline of which was quite clear. The then Curator of Carmarthen Museum was extremely interested in this and had certain documents in his possession relating to the fort. Briefly the history of the house is as follows: There has been a building on this site since the 13th century. In the 16th century a manor house was built for the first High Sheriff of Cardigan. During the 17th and 18th centuries additions were made to the house, with the last renovations carried out in 1820 and 1827 when the facade was altered and the stables, carriage house and granary were built.

'I was enthralled with my new home and not a little apprehensive. How on earth were we going to look after such a huge place? There was the running of the house, also the 475 acres of our farm which was on the opposite side of the valley, together with the 18 acres of gardens and woodlands. It frightened me – but not my husband David; who was confident that we could manage.

'Through the double doors of the entrance we came to the inner hall with its Georgian mirrors all round and Regency marble-topped table in black and gilt. The handsome staircase of polished oak with mahogany bannisters was magnificent. Leading off the inner hall was the most elegant room of the house. It had a polished oak floor, Regency alcoves and light sconces and two long Georgian windows overlooking the tennis lawn and Memorial Garden. A fine carved wooden fireplace graced this room and I learned later from a neighbour that it was a rare Adam taken from another mansion. The room was very large and had probably been used in the past as a ballroom.

'Here my imagination ran away with me and I could see a small orchestra playing with the ladies and gentlemen dressed in their satins and powdered wigs dancing to a gavotte or minuet. This room became our music room and David bought me a Broadwood grand piano. We did have a couple of Hunt Balls here and they were such great fun. I chose the Green Room for our bedroom with my son occupying the Green Dressing Room.

'Shortly after our arrival at the mansion my husband, myself and eight guests were sitting down to dinner when we all heard heavy footsteps approaching the dining room door. David supposed that it must be White, our estate manager, and that something must have gone wrong at the farm. I jumped up, opened the dining room door but there was nobody there. We thought it rather odd. Then, in the middle of that night, we were all disturbed by the son of one of our guests who had been put in the Brown Room to sleep. He was crying loudly saying that something had touched his face and wakened him up.

'My own small son slept in that same Brown Room for one night and woke up screaming: "Mummy, mummy!" I ran in to see what was wrong. He was so frightened that I got into bed with him and we went to sleep. After a while we were both wakened by heavy footsteps walking up the secondary staircase. They stopped right outside the other door of the Brown Room which opened onto a corridor.

'The footsteps were heard in other parts of the house by many of our guests. In fact one of the guests remarked to us the following morning that "someone was not wearing his bedroom slippers last night!"

'The following evening my sister-in-law, who was staying with us at the time, was walking down the main staircase when she saw a beautiful young lady dressed in an exquisite long blue satin gown. The lady was moving across the large main hall. My sister-in-law was taken by the formal period clothes the stranger wore and the way her fair hair was piled high on her head in an elaborate Regency style.

'She just assumed that the lady must be one of our newly acquired friends and that I hadn't mentioned that she had been invited for dinner, although she wondered about the style of the dress. Her musing was cut short when she watched the lady disappear through one of the large mirrors of the inner hall.

'White-faced and shaking she immediately reported the incident to us. It was agreed that we would keep quiet about it so as not to upset the other guests and particularly not to worry the children in any way.

'The following morning I was informed that one of the

servants had handed in her notice. The girl in question seemed to be a reliable sort and I was surprised to hear that she wished to leave our employment so soon after starting with us. I asked why she wanted to leave.

'It transpired that the servant had just finished her duties the previous night and was on her way to the secondary stairs which led to the staff bedrooms on the top floor. When passing the Brown Room something had caught her attention. There seemed to be a glow coming from the room and as the door was ajar the servant thought that she'd better check to see that all was in order. She entered the room, and there, sitting in front of a large blazing fire, she saw a beautiful young lady busy combing her long fair hair. She was wearing a magnificent blue satin ball gown. Thinking that the young lady was one of my guests the servant asked if she could fetch anything. The moment she spoke the young lady stopped combing her hair, turned round, looked the servant directly in the eyes then faded into the fireplace and completely vanished!'

∞

IN the summer of 1975 Kelly was working in Newport, Gwent, as a screen printer for Venture Carpets, an American company which had been established on the site of Stewarts & Lloyds, the manufacturers of steel tubing.

'It was quite a good summer in 1975 and even on night shift the air was still warm. I operated the print plant and although I say it myself I was very good at my job.

'The plant consisted of an eight screen print bed, a steaming chamber where the dyes would be set, a washing process and finally the drying area for the carpets. In the latter, the carpets were conveyed by huge rollers, gripped on either side by two belts with sharp steel pins. Throughout the process, smaller compensator rollers balanced the carpet tension. Should the carpet break, the entire plant mechanism would shut down automatically as there were electric eye sensors throughout the plant. Therefore the print plant could not be operated without the carpet running unless an "overide" key was used to bypass the electric eyes.

'On this particular warm summer night the printing plant had been shut down for maintenance so I had to operate the drying machine using the "overide" key. During the normal printing process I needed to work with several buttons and switches on the control panel but when the "overide" key was being used all I had to do was just sit there in case an emergency should arise as the machine was running itself.

'It was still warm, but suddenly I felt a chill and at that same moment the plant stopped. I was the only person near the panel as everyone else was working on the belt over 300 yards away. None of the emergency stop buttons had been pressed so there was no reason for the plant to come to a halt. Two electricians came and inspected it but they could not locate any fault. They were puzzled so they checked and re-checked but could not find the cause of the problem. The foreman came down to see what was going on so now there were the two electricians, the foreman and myself all trying to find a solution.

'It was then that the worried looking foreman told us that the previous week two men had left their jobs in the warehouse. They had been walking through the warehouse when an old man with a billycan came towards them.

Thinking that the old man had just newly been taken on, the two workers approached him as he seemed to be lost. As they moved closer and closer to him they both felt an overwhelming blast of cold surround them. The man, looking straight ahead, kept walking towards them and instead of stopping in front of them, he walked right through them and vanished.

'I immediately remembered the sudden coldness I'd felt at the exact moment the plant shut down. I had a deep down feeling that the man with the billy-can had something to do with it. From that night onwards I always felt apprehensive when I was on night duty and was on my own in that machine room. Although I never admitted it to any of the others, there were times when I thought the daylight would never come.'

∞

DURING the Second World War, a beautiful mansion house, Stout Hall in Pembrokeshire, was turned into a hospital for sick children. At that time, Jean was only 13 years of age but she remembers one experience as if it happened yesterday.

'I had been evacuated to North Wales with my eleven year old brother. We lived on a farm with eight other evacuees. Suddenly I felt desperately ill and it was confirmed that I had diphtheria. We were all sent to Stout Hall and I ended up staying there for 13 weeks.

'It was a beautiful building and I got to know all of the other children quickly. We always wondered why a certain part of the building was strictly out-of-bounds to us children.

202

'We had two maids who worked in the kitchens and slept in one of the attics. One night we were all awakened by the most hysterical high-pitched screaming. We were all terrified and some of the smaller children were crying with fright. The whole place broke into pandemonium but nobody seemed to know what was causing the uproar.

'It soon became apparent that the screams had originated in the attic bedroom which was occupied by the two maids. When the matron entered the small bedroom she found the two maids in hysterics. She tried to usher them out of the room but they were both so petrified that they would not move.

'They told the matron that an old lady had suddenly appeared to them by the door in the corner of their bedroom. She wore a long green dress and she had grey hair piled on top of her head. One of the maids had felt cold in the bed and had wakened to pull the bedcovers over her. She saw the woman just standing there looking at them in their beds.

'The first maid had let out a piercing scream which wakened up the other girl, and she also saw the woman. The vision stood its ground and the girls became more and more frenzied. One of them yelled "Go Away" and the woman moved backwards and just melted through the bedroom door.

'The girls were in such a state that they could not bring themselves to pass by the spot where the woman had stood. All they could do was to scream louder and louder.

'The news of the old lady went round the whole of the house. The maids were so excitable that it was impossible for them to keep quiet about what they had seen.

'When I was well enough I was allowed to go out into the

grounds which were at the back of the main hall. One day I was returning to enter the building. Something made me look up at the very large windows where I saw an old grey-haired woman in a green dress looking right down at me. I saw her quite clearly, then the next moment there was nothing at the window.

'Surprisingly enough I was not a bit afraid. I just remember thinking what a sad face she had. Years later, when I had grown up, I went back to that mansion for a nostalgic visit. I heard the story from some of the locals that years ago, in the last century, a gentleman and a lady lived at the manor and she met with a fateful end. Legend has it that the lady in green still wanders the hallways and attics – still with the same sad face – still searching for something.'

∞

WHEN Robin was courting Irene he was invited round to her parents' home one day to meet some of her relatives who were visiting them from Wrexham.

'Everyone was having a good old time chatting and having tea and some of the relatives' children were playing out in the enclosed garden. I got up from my chair and walked up the stairs to pay a visit to the toilet. On my way back down the stairs I tripped over a pair of child's shoes which were right in the middle of one of the steps, and I had to grasp hold of the bannister to steady myself. I didn't pay much attention to the shoes assuming that they must belong to one of the children of the relatives.

'I went back into the living room and sat on the couch beside Irene. I noticed that she had a strange look on her face. She seemed a bit frightened. I saw that she was staring hard over at her brother who was sitting in an armchair across the other side of the room looking quite serious. Just a few minutes beforehand he had been cracking jokes right left and centre.

'I asked Irene what was wrong. The first thing she said was to her brother Tony asking him if he'd seen it. He said that he had. I didn't know what they were talking about but I knew Irene well enough to know when something had upset her.

'She then told me in hushed tones so as not to alert any of her family, that she had just seen a small girl dressed in Victorian clothes run in from the hallway, across the living room and straight out through the wall. Tony verified the story, saying that he had also seen the girl and he added that she had bare feet.

'My mind rushed back to the stairs, so without saying a word I ran back up them but there were no shoes to be seen anywhere. None of the children had passed through the living room to go up the stairs and when we walked out into the garden where the children were playing all of them were wearing their shoes as normal.

'The three of us looked at each other completely baffled. We questioned the children – two boys and a girl – asking them if they had been playing with a little girl. They hadn't. The back garden was completely enclosed, and anyway, being strangers to the neighbourhood, they did not know any of the local children.

'Irene and I got married and went to live in Plymouth shortly after that. Her parents sold their house. My father-in-law told me that on the day they moved out, just as he locked the front door for the last time after all of the furniture had been taken out, something made him look up at the bedroom window upstairs. To his astonishment he saw a small girl looking out of the window from inside.

'He told me that he never told my mother-in-law about seeing the face at the window as he did not wish to frighten her. He is a very down-to-earth chap but he admitted to me that he could not get away from that old house fast enough.'

∞

MAUREEN from Mond in Clwyd was sitting by her fireside one night with her husband, two sons and a friend. 'In those days we had a coal fire and we always kept a large strong fireguard round the hearth in case any hot cinders spilled out onto the carpet. The guard was fastened to each side of the grate and was very heavy. Without any warning and for no reason at all it started to rattle and shake so much that the big clock on the mantelpiece fell down onto the floor.

'That night my husband went to work at the Sunblest bakery in Saltney. He was on regular night shift and usually left at around nine o'clock. Because of what had happened with the fireguard I was a bit scared, so as soon as he left I locked the outside door with the two bolts (top and bottom) plus the key which I took upstairs to the bedroom with me, knowing that my husband would not be home until the following morning. I put all the lights off and went to bed at 10.30 p.m.

'I had only just dropped off when I was wakened by a dreadful scream. I got up and ran into the children's bedroom only to find them all asleep. The room was perfectly quiet and normal. I ran downstairs and still found nothing. I then thought that I must have been dreaming and went back to bed. The next thing I knew, my husband was shaking me awake. I was flabbergasted to see him leaning over me, knowing that I had the only key to the door in the bedroom with me. I asked him how he got in. He told me to come down stairs with him so that he could show me.

'I slipped on my dressing gown and went downstairs with him. The door was wide open and the lock was hanging off. The two heavy bolts were lying on the floor just inside in the hall.

'We were so concerned that we got in touch with our local vicar that day to tell him what had happened. He came to the house and had a look around and then asked us if we had found anything in the house which did not belong to us or had we been given anything recently. The only thing we could think of was a photograph which an old pensioner had given my husband in return for doing some work in the old man's garden. It was a very old framed photograph of a woman dressed in a long white cotton dress with lots of frills and flounces on it. My husband did not really want to take the photograph as he felt that it was quite special to the old man but the pensioner insisted, saying that it was a photograph of his grandmother. We put the photograph on the wall above the fireplace.

'After the conversation with the vicar my husband took down the photograph and placed it outside on the road for the bin men to collect the following morning. I still felt very frightened inside even though the photograph had been removed. I was so perturbed that my husband stayed off work that night, not wishing to leave me alone with the children.

'We put the children to bed and settled down to watch

television. After a while we heard someone knocking on the door which that day had had new locks fitted. We both went to the door but nobody was there. We put on all the lights in the house and then we went to bed ourselves. The next day we decided to visit my husband's mother so we got the children ready and got into the car to set off on the journey. It was raining heavily and as we started off we saw a woman standing by the edge of the road. She was wrapped in a long shawl and was soaking wet.

'I mentioned to my husband that the poor soul must be wet through and I suggested that we give her a lift. He stopped the car and I opened the door for her to get in, shouting over to her, "Come on you'd better have a lift, we've room in the back." I realized instantly that I couldn't see her anymore. Only seconds before, she had been standing there and now there was not a person in sight. I even got out of the car to have a good look up and down the road to see where she could have gone to but the road was deserted. I got back in the car and we carried on down the road but after just a few seconds we suddenly felt a bump. I said to my husband, "Oh my God, you must have hit her!" We stopped straight away and both of us got out. Again there was nobody in sight. I got really worried at that point. I remember saying to my husband that the woman must be under the car. We looked underneath but could not see anything on the road, but just to make sure my husband moved the car forward a few yards. There was nothing there at all and by this time we were both soaked through.

'We got back into the car and had just moved off when I happened to look out of my window. I nearly died when I saw the same woman with the shawl staring in through the glass at me. I let out such a scream that my husband nearly crashed the car he got such a fright. Instead of going to my mother-in-law's we went straight back to see the vicar, Mr Davies and asked him to come back to the house with us as we were terrified to go back there. He came and blessed the house and said some prayers asking God to grant the woman eternal rest. He told us that there should be no further trouble and he was right. We never saw the woman again and all the strange noises have ceased.

'I have my own theory that the old pensioner's grandmother was trying to let us know that she objected to having her photograph put up in some strangers' house. She certainly convinced me in no uncertain terms.'

∞

ONE day Hannah, who was at that time living on the outskirts of Cardiff, took to bed with a bad attack of influenza. She felt very ill and restless and could not sleep.

'Suddenly I found myself struggling in a huge ball of cloudy gauze-like material. I fought hard for what seemed like ages, then eventually I managed to get my hand through this gauze. The moment I felt my hand break through the material which could be described as very thick heavy white cloud, I was entranced by what I saw before me.

'I was completely free of the gauze and found myself standing at the edge of the most beautiful stream you could ever imagine. The waters seem to dance by and each ripple was of a glorious vivid colour unlike anything I'd ever seen. The colours were dazzling in their beauty and surpassed the earthly spectrum by far.

'After a few moments I became aware of forms standing

on the opposite bank of the stream. I looked across and there was my mother, father and my brother-in-law, Walter. They had all died within the previous few years.

'Overjoyed to see them, I called out excitedly and started to wave across to them. They did not appear to hear me so I shouted even louder, asking them what they were all doing standing over there. I beckoned for them to come over to me but not one of them moved. I then called out to them saying that I would paddle through the stream to join them. At that moment I spotted my brother in the distant background still in his First World War uniform. Although he had died in 1918 I didn't seem to realize at that point that he was also one of the dead. I got the impression that he was trying to stop me from wading across the stream. He did not say anything, it's just the feeling that I got at the time, probably by the funny look that he had on his face.

'I had always thought the world of my brother but like a lot of brother/sister relationships I used to feel that he teased me quite a bit. He was several years older than me and I suppose I had been over sensitive as I'm sure, on looking back, that it was just his way of being affectionate towards me. When he used to come home on leave he was always playing little jokes on me, but I loved him just the same.

'Anyway I became slightly irritated by his attitude and I remember clearly calling across the water to him: "Go away. You are always teasing me." The instant I said those words he just moved away out of my sight. I was a bit sorry that I had yelled at him. I repeated my question to my mother, again asking what she was doing just standing there. At that point it dawned on me that none of them were looking directly at me at all but all of them seemed to be watching something high above my head. I was beginning to feel very frustrated and again I started waving my arms about trying to draw their attention to me.

'Finally my mother spoke. Still without looking at me she said, "We were not expecting you yet." Then my brother-in-law added, "We are waiting for Cecil." Cecil was my other brother who was very much alive. With those words ringing in my ears I found myself back in my bed.

'I remember feeling confused as I knew that I had not been dreaming – I had not been asleep – yet I could not understand exactly what had happened. To get my bearings again I looked at the clock by the side of my bed. It was 3.00 p.m. I told my husband immediately as I was so bewildered by what had just happened to me; I also told a friend who was in the house at the time. They both humoured me saying that it must have been the effects of the flu, and that I'd just had a strange dream. No matter what they said I KNEW THAT I HAD NOT BEEN DREAMING. My husband brought a hot drink up to me and then I did fall asleep.

'Shortly afterwards I was awakened by the telephone ringing. I heard my husband answer it and by the tone of his voice I knew that something was very wrong. I heard his footsteps on the stairs and as he entered the bedroom I could see that he was shocked. He told me that Cecil had been rushed to hospital with a haemorrhage and had died at exactly 3.00 p.m.

'When I think back now I can understand why my brother did not want me to enter that colourful stream. Despite all his teasing I feel that he saved my life that day for I'm sure that if I had waded across to the other side to join my relatives I would have been dead.'

211

CATHY had just finished shopping in Abergavenny one day and was making her way home with her shopping trolley. She had almost reached her home in a quiet part of the town in a road which was usually deserted.

'Being that I live in such a back street area I rarely see anyone passing through. I was just about to open the front gate when suddenly a young woman was standing immediately in front of me – so close to me that her face almost touched mine. She seemed to have appeared out of mid-air.

'She stood there smiling at me. She had the most beautiful face and wore a pink dress. She was in modern dress and was wearing make-up, and I could smell her lovely perfume. I got a powerful feeling that she was a good sweet person.

'I was so stunned at seeing this woman I could not move or speak. After a short space of time she turned to go then she looked back at me and said in a very cultured voice, "Isn't it a lovely day." I nodded and managed to mumble, "Yes." The word was no sooner out of my mouth when she faded into thin air right there in front of me.

'I looked up and down the street but there was no sign of a soul and all was quiet and still as usual. I was so bewildered because the scent of her perfume seemed to linger in the air. To this day I still remember the sweet expression she had on her face but for the life of me I don't know where she came from or where she went.'

∞

LIKE many people, Harry Everett, a Yorkshire man, spent many a happy holiday in Wales. One particular year he spent a couple of weeks in North Wales, making his base in one of the villages on the outskirts of Bangor. He got friendly with one of the locals – a chap called Alun who lived on his own in a small cottage in the village. Alun, who was in his early sixties, had been a widower for a number of years and had worked out his own little routine of going out on his bicycle each morning to his job as an assembly worker in a small factory then coming home each night to his little house where he prepared his own evening meal.

Harry relates that: 'One night Alun cycled home along the dark country lane which led to his cottage. He went into his kitchen as usual and prepared his simple evening meal and carried it through to the table in his living room. The table stood against the wall which was directly opposite the window.

'Alun started to eat his bread and cheese and enjoy his mug of tea when he became aware of a reflection in the window. He looked over and saw the reflection of himself but also of two other people on the other chairs round his table – a young man and a girl. He kept looking back and forward between the table and the window. Around the table were the two other vacant chairs but in the reflection in the window he could see two figures sitting in the chairs enjoying their meal. The man was some years younger than himself and was no one that he recognised. He was wearing a light coloured shirt which was open at the neck and a brown tweed waistcoat. He had no jacket on but wore a type of kerchief around his neck. All the details were vivid in the window which had no curtains across the centre, only side drapes which Alun always left open. The darkness outside heightened the sharpness of the reflection caused by the bright living room light. The girl looked as if she was in her late teens and was dressed in old-fashioned style clothes with lots of frills down the front. Alun could only see the figures from the waist upwards so he could not tell for sure if the girl wore a blouse or a dress.

'He thought that his eyes must be playing a trick on him so he got up to go over to the window. He watched his own reflection rise from his chair and move across the room towards the window while the other reflections were still sitting there eating supper. The reflections were so life-like that he found himself swinging round quickly, sure that he would see the couple sitting on the other chairs – but no, the chairs were still empty.

'Alun opened the window and instantly the reflected image of the other people disappeared. He had a good look through the open window but there was no sign of anyone outside. He even went to the door to have a better look, then he walked right round his cottage but all was silent and deserted.

'He returned to his living room and stared hard at the vacant chairs round his table. He looked across at the window and much to his relief he could only see his own reflection. By this time he was not feeling much like finishing his supper, so he made sure that all the windows were locked and he double-bolted the door and went to bed.

'A few days later, on the following Saturday morning, he happened to be doing a bit of gardening for one of the local council officials. His married daughter worked in the council offices as a secretary and when her boss mentioned that he could do with help in putting his garden in order she had suggested that her father who was an excellent gardener would be happy to help him out.

'After working in the garden for several hours, Alun was invited in to have a cup of tea by the official's wife. They got chatting in the kitchen and the conversation drifted to the subject of books. The woman mentioned that she was reading an interesting book but it was a bit creepy. This led to him telling her about the strange reflection he had seen in his window.

'The woman asked him if he had any idea who the people in the reflection could have been. Alun shook his head, explaining that he had never seen them before in his life. The woman thought for a moment then asked him what his exact address was. She made a note of this and said that if she found out anything she would let him know.

'Alun did not want to make too much of an issue of his experience and was beginning to feel slightly sorry that he had mentioned the incident in the first place. He told the woman that he was not really bothered about finding out anything and that he did not particularly wish to be thought of as some kind of crank. Nothing more was said about the matter and he went back outside to get on with his work in the garden.

'The following Saturday Alun returned to the council official's house to do some more gardening. The woman of the house told him what she had uncovered. She had asked her husband to look up some of the old electoral lists for Alun's address and it came to light that over a hundred years earlier the cottage had been owned by a young man called Phillip Mercer who was a shepherd for one of the local farmers. The cottage had originally belonged to the farm and had been used to house various farm workers but at one point the existing tenant had been offered the freehold of the property in return for some great personal favour bestowed upon the farm owner.

'The reason Phillip Mercer's name stood out among the various previous owners was that there had been a mystery surrounding this man. It appeared that he had fallen in love with the only daughter of a slate quarry boss. The girl's father felt that his daughter would be marrying below herself and he refused to give his consent to the marriage. The girl's mother had died when she was a toddler and she was very much subjected to her father and was caught up in an emotional conflict, not wishing to go against him but at the same time pledging her love to the shepherd.

'In an attempt to solve the situation the quarry boss banished his daughter down to Sussex to stay with his sister and refused to let the girl return.

'Every night for two long years Phillip Mercer trundled back to that lonely cottage and ate his evening meal in solitude waiting for the day that his girl would somehow return to him. He had tried to find out the address the girl had been taken to but without success.

'One day the news broke around the village that the girl had committed suicide. Her aunt had missed her from the house and when a search was carried out the girl's body was found washed up on the shore. Later a note was found in her room. It was a letter to be sent to Phillip – her last request. In that note she explained to him that she could no longer face the futile life which had been thrust upon her. She promised him that she would find a way for them to be together. The letter was brought to the village by the girl's aunt and much against the quarry boss's wishes it was eventually given to Phillip Mercer. The aunt was apparently full of remorse and felt that it was the least she could do to make up for the terrible tragedy which she had allowed herself to become involved in.

'From the moment he received that letter Phillip just gave up on life. He only ate one small meal a day – in the evening when he returned from the fields – and slowly his health began to suffer and eventually gave way completely. Those who knew him swore that he died of a broken heart.

'Alun is certain that death has not parted the shepherd and his love. He feels that their ghosts still meet in his little cottage.'

∞

A YOUNG Welshman, who had been brought up in Malaya and educated in Florida, met a beautiful Irish-American girl called Carmel, fell in love, married her and set up home in Jacksonville on her wealthy father's estate. Being the only daughter of a well-to-do family, Carmel had been spoilt as a child and given everything she had wanted. Tom got on well with her parents and it was obvious that they looked upon him as a suitable husband for their daughter.

Tom had fallen for her dynamic personality and striking beauty. Her shining black hair had never ever been cut in her life and so it almost reached her feet. She was full of beguilment but had a fiery temper which she was quite unable to control. Like a lot of infatuated young men, Tom thought that he would be able to make her change. In fact after they were married she became possessive and unreasonably jealous. Tom was totally devoted to his wife and found it difficult to understand her attitude, particularly as he never so much as looked at another woman.

When Carmel became pregnant Tom hoped that things would change. He so much looked forward to the new baby, but even this natural emotion did not please his wife. She accused him of loving the unborn child more than he loved her. Despite all his attempts to convince her that he truly did love her she continued to act with hostility towards him.

One night they had a blazing row. He had had enough of her scornful suspicions and he threatened to leave her unless she changed. At these words she immediately assumed that he must be seeing another woman. It was the last straw to Tom who stormed out of the bedroom and went downstairs. On his way downstairs he heard a thud on the bedroom door and he realized that she had thrown something in her frenzy. This was something he had grown used to and usually he managed to get out of the way of flying objects just in time but once she threw an alarm clock which hit him on the back of his shoulder.

As he reached the front door to leave the house he heard Carmel at the top of the stairs screaming abuse at him. The next moment she lost her footing and fell headlong down the stairs. As she lay silent at the foot of the stairs Tom knew that she had screamed at him for the last time. Her neck was broken. He had lost both his wife and his unborn baby.

Although Carmel had once told Tom that when she died she would like to be cremated rather than buried in the ground, when it came to making the decision her parents felt that she looked so beautiful in her coffin that they insisted that her body be buried on the family estate.

Completely devastated, Tom returned to Malaya in an attempt to push his painful memories to the back of his mind. Time went on and he gradually got over the trauma, all the time keeping in touch with his young sister in Carmarthen. He returned to visit his family and a pact was made between them that they would let his past life rest as whenever the subject was mentioned he became very upset and depressed.

Life went on and about two years later when he heard the news that his sister was to be married, he again returned to Wales for the wedding. He visited Carmarthen the following year for the christening of his first niece.

Perhaps his sister's new baby brought back memories of the unborn child that he had so much looked forward to seeing, but whatever the reason, Tom became very attached to baby Helen. He sent expensive gifts from Malaya and kept in constant touch with the family.

As Helen grew up she began to write regularly to her uncle Tom. He never re-married, having become absorbed in his career, and was a high executive for the company he worked for. Helen loved receiving his letters with the enclosed photographs and literature about Malaya.

The day after Helen's 17th birthday she was happily walking along the street watching her own shadow as it moved ahead of her. She suddenly became aware that another shadow seemed to hover around her own. After a few seconds when no one passed her as she had expected, she looked around to find that she was the only person walking on that part of the street. Certainly there were no other people near enough to cast a shadow beside hers. Still the other shadow was there. As she moved slightly to the right, then slightly to the left, she saw her own shadow move with her, and also the other shadow. She was most confused, but the confusion turned to fear when she realized that the other shadow did not move in unison with her physical movements. It could not be a double of her own shadow.

Helen recalls: 'After a short time the sun went behind some clouds and of course both shadows disappeared. When the sun came out again, only my own shadow was visible. However when I reached the house, as I walked down our garden path towards the main door, I saw it again, gliding along next to my own shadow. I turned around quickly to see if anyone could have entered the garden although I knew in my heart that no one could have. There was only me in the garden, yet there were two shadows.

'I became very frightened and ran into the house and went straight uptairs to my own room. I did not say anything to my parents as I was afraid that they would just tell me that I was imagining things. After all it does sound a bit soppy to say that I was followed by a shadow.

'That night I went to bed as usual, but around 3.00 a.m. something woke me up; I'm not sure what. The bedroom was filled with a beautiful perfume. I had never smelt anything so lovely. Then I noticed that there was a small orange coloured light in the corner of the room. As I watched the light it grew larger to about the size of a football. It continued to grow but as it did I was overcome by a fear that something evil was in the room. I remember trying to call out to my parents but to my horror no sound came from my mouth. I seemed to be struck dumb with terror.

'I was perfectly wide awake because I distinctly remember wondering to myself if I could possibly be dreaming. I glanced at the clock and it was four minutes past three in the morning. I had my normal presence of mind except that I was so frightened I was unable to make a sound. By this time the orange light had formed itself into a tall oblong shape and it floated across the bottom of my bed.

'There was some sort of mist which seemed to swirl around the tall light. I could not take my eyes off this thing which hovered in the bedroom. Very slowly the mist settled and gradually the shape of a person appeared. It was a woman with a beautiful face. The most striking thing about her was her long flowing hair which seemed to reach right down past the end of my bed. She was scowling at me with angry flashing eyes. It was at this point that I found my voice and let out a terrific scream. As soon as I did this the woman vanished through the bedroom wall.

'Both of my parents came rushing into the bedroom. I was in hysterics and could hardly talk to them. They brought me downstairs to the lounge and Dad made me a cup of tea while my mother tried to calm me down. When I regained my composure I blurted out the whole story to them about the shadow and then the light which turned into a woman. They did not make any comment that night but told me not to worry about it and that they were sure that nothing would harm me. I remember thinking at the time, however, that my mother had a very concerned look on her face especially when I told her about the woman's extremely long hair.

'The following day I had to return some books to our local library. Although I was still a bit shaken over what had happened the night before, I had tried to put the whole incident out of my mind. I was never so pleased to see the rain in all my life as I was understandably most apprehensive about seeing any shadows.

'After I left the library I was walking along when I came to some scaffolding. I stopped in my tracks when I got a hint of that same lovely smell that had been in my bedroom. Almost instantly I saw her. That strange woman with the long black hair was standing some way ahead of me inside the area where the scaffolding was. I was rooted to the spot with fear and could only stand staring, hardly able to breathe, unable to take my eyes off her. She smiled at me and then beckoned to me to follow her. As if in a trance I found myself walking towards her. It was as if she had some power over me and I was unable to help myself although I was fully aware of what was happening. I was dreadfully afraid as I moved towards her but I think I was even more afraid of what might happen if I disobeyed her.

'The next moment there seemed to be a loud uproar and I felt myself being grabbed from behind and pulled backwards. As this happened a section of the huge wall behind the scaffolding tumbled down in an explosion of rubble and dust at exactly the spot where the woman had been standing. I looked hard through the rising dust but I could see no trace of her.

'It turned out that some of the workmen on the site had noticed me walking past the 'No Entry' sign and one of them had just managed to drag me back to safety before the wall came down. I was in such a state that I could hardly talk to explain to them what had made me do such a stupid thing.

'When I told my mother about seeing the woman again and my near-miss, she told me the story about my uncle Tom's dead wife. It came as an awful shock to me as I had always believed that he was a confirmed bachelor. It transpired that unbeknown to me, my mother had tele-

222

phoned my uncle Tom and had told him about the vision I had seen the previous night. He had informed her that the estate of his late wife's family had been sold shortly after he had left the States. Before the family had finally moved to Texas they had decided to dig up Carmel's remains, cremate them and scatter her ashes at sea just as she had wished. When she had been buried her long hair had been heavily scented with incense.

'My uncle Tom had told my mother that he felt that Carmel was up to her old tricks again. She had always been insanely jealous of anyone whom she imagined her husband to be fond of – even her own unborn baby. Tom felt that because he had shown me such kindness over the years, Carmel – even in death – still felt threatened.

'I have no doubt that she was trying to lure me to my death. In a way I felt sorry for her because it seemed she was just as restless in the beyond as she had been when she was alive. I said a secret little prayer that her spirit would find peace. I really meant it as I was upset for my uncle having such sad memories. I know my prayer has been answered because I have never seen Carmel since and I have the feeling that she is finally at rest.'

∞

PWLLHELI is situated on the Lleyn Peninsula, North Wales, and is steeped in ancient traditions. The peninsula is believed to be the resting ground of King Arthur's magician, the famous Merlin, who is said to be lying in an enchanted sleep beside the golden throne of Ancient Britain.

Melvyn Thomas was most definitely not asleep when an

odd thing happened to him in his home town of Pwllheli. 'I was sitting up in bed one night reading a book. Apart from my bedside lamp there was a lot of light coming into the bedroom from the street lamp just outside my window. Something attracted my attention just above my head where I could see a dark revolving oval shape which appeared to come down from the ceiling; it was like a spiral of dark wires.

'This thing was moving round and round fairly quickly but it was also slowly moving the other way – down towards me. Thinking that I was going to be smashed on the head my natural impulse was to stretch out my hand to keep the thing away. I hadn't time to think about what was happening, I was so keen to keep whatever it was away from my head. When I reached out towards the spiral it quickly changed direction and started to move upwards and to go through the ceiling.

'By this time I had started to grow a bit alarmed because I couldn't figure out what was going on. The end part of the spiral could still be seen just underneath the ceiling rotating at a very fast rate. I thought it was going to disappear through the ceiling when it started to tilt over. As it did this more of the spinning form reappeared until the entire shape was now floating lengthways in the air, still rotating at great speed.

'The dark colour changed and became gradually lighter until it reached a light greyish colour. I sat there in bed hardly able to believe my eyes as I saw the figure of a man become formed in the centre of this spinning cocoon-like object. He was floating at an angle in the air. I could clearly see the facial features which I recognized as a Negro. As he grew more vivid I could see that he was wearing a suit of pure white material, like linen or cotton. He had curly hair and seemed to be quite a big man. He did not look at me, in fact I don't think he knew that I was even there. He stayed like that in mid-air.

'I started to feel panic setting in because I just did not know what I could do. Because he did not vanish straight away I got the feeling that he was going to stay with me in the bedroom. I jerked at the bedclothes to jump out of bed. As I as did so the man vanished up through the ceiling. I was sitting on the edge of the bed as he disappeared. I remained there for a time collecting my thoughts together.

'No one of that description has ever lived in my house as it is fairly new and has only had two previous owners. There is absolutely nothing to account for what I saw that I can fathom, and I have never seen the vision since. I always used to think that when people reported seeing such things that they were either imagining it or if not, there must be some understandable purpose for the visitation. This is where my story runs short because I am afraid I cannot supply any reasons or explanations. I just know that I saw that man. Maybe some day I will find out what he wanted from me, or could I simply have observed at random life in another dimension?'

∞

WHEN old John Evans was a younger man he had an experience which has remained as clear in his mind as though it happened yesterday.

'I was working on my daily rounds delivering sacks of coal around the doors. Most of the deliveries were for coal which had been previously ordered but I was authorized to sell individual bags of coal if anyone approached me so long as they were able to pay me in cash. At the end of each evening I used to report to the depot where the amount of coal on my lorry was checked against the amount of cash I paid in.

'One day I had just about finished my round in Pontypridd in the Rhondda Valley. I was walking back to the lorry after delivering the last order. I caught a glimpse of an oldish fellow who was sitting in a rocking chair outside the front door of his little terraced house. He waved over to me as if he was trying to attract my attention so I walked over towards him. I remember thinking at the time that it was a bit chilly to be sitting outside.

'I asked him if I could help. He told me that he had noticed that I had been delivering coal to a house across the road and did I have a couple of bags to spare. I told him that I would be pleased to help him out but there was only one bag left on the lorry. In those days the bags were loaded in amounts of one hundredweight. He asked if he could have the last sack of coal and would I mind bringing it through to his coal cellar which was at the back of the house.

'I placed the coal in the cellar and then went to be paid. The old man dug deep into his pockets, fumbled for a few seconds and then counted out the correct coins into my hand. I told him that I would be back round his way the following day and that I could deliver the second bag of coal then if he still wanted it. He nodded, then waved me goodbye.

'That night I checked into the depot as usual and counted out my money to my boss. It was easy to reckon up the day's takings because I had cleared the lorry completely and it was always loaded with the exact same number of sacks every morning. The cash tallied up OK so I went home as usual.

'The following day I returned to deliver the second bag of coal to the old man. I found the house and went up and knocked on the door. A youngish woman answered. When I told her why I was there she looked most puzzled and said she didn't know what I was talking about. I asked if I could please speak to the old man who lived there. She called her husband who came to the door immediately to find out what was going on. He was a young man, I would say in his late twenties. Again I asked if the old man was there but I was told that they were the only people who lived in the house and they had been living there since they bought the house two years previously.

'I thought they were pulling my leg so I told them that a sack of coal had been ordered the day before and I was just doing my job in delivering it. If they didn't want it that was up to them but all they had to do was tell me.

'At these words the couple burst out laughing. When I asked what was so funny they told me that there would be no point in them buying a sack of coal as their house was all electric and the fireplace had been blocked in when they bought the house. I was really getting cheesed off with them and by the look on my face they must have guessed as much. The man asked me into the house to see for myself. He showed me into the living room and sure enough there was a smart built-in electric fire where the old fireplace was. I asked if I could have a look at the back of the house where I had been the day before. With much hilarity they led me down the narrow passageway towards the back of the house.

'I was completely dumbfounded. There in the exact spot

where I had delivered the coal just the day before was a smart modern shower-room. I asked them where their coal cellar was. They told me that I was looking at it. They had converted it to a shower-room shortly after they had moved in as they knew that they would have no use for the cellar as it then stood.

'Feeling a proper Charlie I apologized for the inconvenience and quickly left. I had left my lorry just outside their house but before I got back in the driving seat something made me hesitate. I knew the people in the house across the road slightly as they were regular customers so I decided to go over and have a chat. I think I just wanted to convince myself that I was not going crazy.

'I told my story to Mrs. Hart across the road and she listened without saying a word. She could see that I was somewhat disturbed and she told me not to worry, that it was only old Percy.

'Who on earth is old Percy?" I asked. Mrs Hart told me that Percy was the old man who used to live in the house that I'd just left. She described him down to the last detail, even adding that he used to always sit outside his front door dozing away in his rocking chair. He had lived alone in the house and had not bothered to carry out any renovations and still used his coal fire with its back boiler to heat the water. The old man was a pensioner and had found it increasingly hard to cope, having no family to help him out. During the harsh winter his frozen body was found huddled up in the corner of his living room. He had died from hypothermia.'

∞

ROGER and Brian had been friends since childhood. They

started infant school together in Aberystwyth on Cardigan Bay. All through school they had been best friends and faced the joys of the Boy Scouts and Boy's Brigade as inseparables. They left school and both found jobs. Roger's joy was music and despite Brian's noticably tuneless voice, Roger lured him into his band – as drummer.

The little combo played around the local pubs and clubs and thoroughly enjoyed themselves, dreaming of the day that they would become rich and famous. They started to get noticed and gradually the diary filled up. Roger was the vocalist and front man of the four-piece outfit.

He recalls his early days with the band. 'When I look back I realize that we were not all that hot but at the time, like all youngsters, we thought we were great. We wrote our own songs and we were desperate to land a recording contract.

'As the gigs started to come in on a regular basis we had extra cash to play around with as the four of us still had our day jobs. I suppose we were quite sensible as far as that goes for although we were all longing for the day when we could go full-time professional we knew that it would be fool-hardy to chuck in our jobs before anything concrete came along.

'With our extra money Brian and I bought ourselves motorbikes. Our parents were not that thrilled about this but we wore down their resistance. One night we had been at a party and I admit that we had had a bit too much to drink. Anyway we left in the early hours of the morning to ride towards our part of town as we lived fairly close to each other.

'I'll never forget that night. I was in front and I took a

sharp bend. I was barely on the straight again when I heard the most horrendous crash. I looked back and couldn't see anything so I stopped immediately. I ran back a few yards and then I saw the twisted heap of metal lying in a ditch with Brian underneath it. He was unconscious.

'At first I was so shocked I didn't know what to do. We were out in a lonely road in the middle of the night with not a soul in sight. I was shaking when I lifted the bike – or what was left of it – off Brian. He was lying on his back. I thought I'd see if I could help him up, but as I took hold of him I felt something wet and I realized that he was bleeding badly, so I left him where he was.

'I ran to my own bike and rode like fury until I reached a telephone box by the side of the road. I phoned for an ambulance then went back to where Brian was still lying out cold to the world. Within a short time I heard the siren of the approaching ambulance with its blue light flashing in the darkness.

'Brian was rushed straight to the operating theatre. I sat outside in the waiting area for what seemed like an eternity. My mind was in a turmoil trying to think of what I would say to Brian's folks. The following few hours were a complete nightmare which I will never forget. I was taken to one side and calmly told that Brian had died on the operating table. Apparently he never stood a chance as he was suffering from massive brain damage. From then on I can't honestly remember anything clearly until the next morning. The hospital and police had been in touch with Brian's family and had broken the news to them. I felt that I was dying myself. I just lay in my bed and refused to see or talk to anyone. I just couldn't take in what had happened.

'Shortly after that I left home to go and work in London

as the band had packed up and I could see no future where I was. I was very despondent and I found every day a problem. I had taken to drink and was slowly going downhill. When I told my family that I had decided to move to London they were naturally sorry but at the same time they felt that a move might help me straighten out my life. I remember my father telling me that if I was really serious about getting my life in order he would encourage me and send me off with his blessing and that if things did not work out there would always be a welcome for me back home. My bedroom would always be there. I was very touched at this and made some grunts and groans to that effect. Then he delivered his punchline: on condition that I gave up the booze.

'When I got to London I quickly found a job and a flat and made new friends. My father's words rang in my brain and when I thought of Brian it all made sense to me. I remember distinctly that it was just after Christmas and before the New Year of 1983. I had had a lot of time to think and I decided that I could go either way – I could make an all-out effort to improve myself or it would be downhill all the way. The more I thought about it my fighting spirit suddenly returned to me. I became determined to prove myself to my father but even more to convince myself that I still had some character left in me.

'I met a nice girl at work called Julie and she started to build up my self-respect. I was getting used to going out for an evening and asking for a coke without feeling embarrassed. She was a marvellous help to me and I can honestly say that without her I am not sure if I could have pulled myself out of the rut.

'One day I was standing outside a cinema in Leicester

Square waiting for Julie. I noticed that the lace of one of my trainers had become loosened. I bent down to tie the lace and saw another pair of shoes right in front of me. A voice seemed to echo in my head telling me not to look up. I became petrified with fear and for some unknown reason I knew – I just knew – that it was Brian who was standing in front of me. I knew that if I raised my head I would see his face and I would be dead.

'I'm not sure how long I stayed in that awkward position, bent down as if I was tying my lace. I felt the hair on the top of my scalp rise up. My throat was dry and I could hardly breathe. Being very careful to keep my eyes tightly shut I slowly turned myself round until I was facing the other way. I could actually hear my heart beating inside me like a drum as I opened my eyes but I kept my gaze riveted on the pavement, not daring to look up.

'I was thankful when the other pair of shoes was no longer in front of me. It was then that I heard Julie's voice behind me saying that she hoped she hadn't kept me waiting too long. I was so relieved to hear her voice that I jumped up and hugged her as hard as I could without saying a word. I was so shaken I had lost the inclination to see the film that was showing. She must have guessed that something was wrong because she kept asking me if I was feeling okay.

'When I got myself together I asked her if she would mind not going to the cinema that night. We ended up walking along by the Thames Embankment and found an empty bench where we sat down and I told her what had happened. I thought at first that she might laugh me but I was really pleased when she didn't. She was very under-standing. We did not talk much more that night but just walked down by the river towards the City. Then we caught the bus back to her place. That was the night I asked her to marry me. I think the biggest shock of the night came when she actually said "Yes!"'

∞

MANY people believe that life and death continue on an ever turning wheel. This turning is often described as the wheel of fortune, life's recurring cycle, reincarnation, the spiral of destiny, etc. After being very ill in hospital, Terry Rogers of Newport now believes that life proceeds through cycles.

'I have heard of people who have reported having strange experiences whereby they (or their spirits) left their physical bodies and some of them assumed that they were, at the time, dead, or all but dead. In some cases the experience occurred while their hearts had stopped beating and they were clinically dead. Most of these people were somehow aware of the fact that efforts were being made to revive them. I am sure however that I was very much alive that night in the hospital in 1970.

'Although I had been suffering from a long illness eventually diagnosed as Hodgkin's Disease, I can say with all honesty that the thought of dying never entered my head. In my innocence I got quite a shock when the consultant told me at a later date that no one had expected me to survive. That was certainly news to me. All I had ever thought about was why they were taking so long to find out what was wrong with me and why could they not provide a cure?

'The doctors came to me one day and asked if I would let them try out a new treatment. Apparently everything else had failed, but of course they did not tell me that at the time. I agreed, thinking that anything was worth a try if it would help me to get better.

'I had an almost continuoùs high temperature and this, combined with the various injections and drugs, gave me such hallucinations that I was living a life totally different from the real one, but I was not aware of this. Everything that happened in my head was very real to me and I can recall a great part of it, if not all, to this day. The real and the imagined fused into one, and it was only after the event that I was able to separate them.

'The doctor and a nurse or two would come to my bed with a trolley full of apparatus – needles, drip tubes and various phials of drugs which the doctor would mix on the spot, like some witches brew. Then he would inject the fluid into the tubes which constantly seemed to be attached to my arms. I would watch all of this with a great deal of interest and some apprehension.

'All the side effects which I was experiencing gave me peculiar sensations. The medical staff's voices would be heard by me as booming loudly in my head or fading to a whisper. Sometimes I used to see their lips move but heard nothing. Figures around the bed would advance towards me or retreat into the distance yet with no sense of movement, in and out of focus, fading and reappearing. My own voice seemed to come from deep inside my body, and I had no real control over it. I never knew whether I was whispering or shouting. It was impossible to hold a conversation, yet everything else appeared to be quite normal to me.

'One evening they came to my bed as usual. At least it seemed as if it was the evening as the lights were on around my bed and the background was dark and shadowy. The doctor and a nurse stood at the foot of my bed. The trays of apparatus were between them on a trolley. I watched the doctor mix his potions and fill a syringe. I remember that there was some conversation and the nurse was laughing at something which had been said. I jokingly asked the doctor if he was capable of putting the needle in the right place – the usual banter – and he answered me saying that he'd never missed yet.

'I was lying back on the bed with my pillows bunched around me feeling strangely contented with my lot. I was wide awake, relaxed and pleased that everyone was in a good humour. Although I was apprehensive about what was happening to me, nevertheless I was always pleased to see a team of medical staff around my bed. It made me feel that something was being done and at least I was getting some attention. This was better than the long endless periods of isolation when I lay there alone, watching everyone pass me by, ignoring me, or so it seemed.

'This night was one of my happier times, I thought, as I waited for the doctor to go through his usual routine of injections. It all somehow felt so cosy as they gently drifted in and out of my vision.

'I began to realize that something odd was going on in the background, some ten feet or so above the foot of my bed, apparently floating in space. I watched, fascinated, as the scene slowly materialized out of the darkness. A life-sized figure appeared to be strapped to the side of a large revolving wheel. I then realized, to my astonishment, that the figure was me! Yet I knew that I was still lying safely in my bed watching myself on that wheel going round and round.

'On one side stood the nurse, not by my bed but next to the me on the revolving wheel. On the other side of the wheel was the doctor with a syringe in his hand. As I revolved past him on the wheel, on each occasion he made a lightening stab at me with the syringe and squeezed some of the contents into my arm, all the while saying something which I could not hear but which I supposed must have been funny judging by the nurse's laughter.

'I was amazed at the doctor's accurate lunges with the syringe thrusting it into my arm each time I swung around abreast of him. I felt nothing and it all seemed perfectly natural as I lay back on my bed and watched the proceedings until the syringe was eventually empty. When they had finished they walked away from my bed as usual pushing the trolley.

'As the vision of the wheel started to fade I got the overwhelming feeling that something of importance was being conveyed to me. I watched my own body gently fade with the wheel but the funny part was that I did not just fade as a complete entity but started to disappear from the feet upwards until there was only my own face which seemed to stare back at me.

'When I think about it now I don't know how I was not petrified with fear, yet I was perfectly calm and collected in the knowledge that everything was going to be all right. It was almost as if my face had been purposely left till the end to instil upon my brain the fact that things were about to happen in a revolutionary way. I did not grasp the entire meaning of what was happening but I knew that matters would be resolved by my living out a cycle. Or to put it simply, by going round in a circle.

'Unbeknown to myself I started to act in a most

unorthodox manner in the hospital, although at the time, of course, I lived through it all as if everything was completely normal. My reactions and my attitude were beginning to cause some consternation among the staff who did not seem to fully appreciate what was happening. In fact it took my wife to point out to them that some of the treatment that they were giving me was responsible for my weird behaviour and that I was not brain damaged by my illness as they all believed. She, very fortunately for me, eventually managed to persuade the consultant to give me a brain scan which proved that she was right in her assessment. She told me this later.

'In the year 1968, just before the onset of my illness, I weighed eleven and a half stones. At my lowest point when they all thought that I was on my way out, my weight had gone down to five stones. I could never understand at that point why I could see all my bones. I was in fact at that time nothing more than a living skeleton, too weak even to turn over in the bed. Now as I sit here in the full bloom of good health I weigh exactly eleven-and-a-half stones again. I've come round the full circle as I knew I would. While I was at my lowest ebb, somehow, someone or something gave me the inner conviction that I would surely pull through. For that I shall be eternally grateful.'

∞

FLINT Castle, now in ruins, was the first in a chain of medieval castles which graced the land of Wales to the north of Snowdonia from Clwyd across to Caernarfon which is the ancient ceremonial capital of Wales. In the magnificently preserved Caernarfon castle, Prince Charles was invested as Prince of Wales in 1969, following the tradition set by King Edward I whose wife Queen Eleanor bore a son in the castle in April 1284. That child was known as Edward of Carnarfon and he was formally created the first English Prince of Wales in 1301.

Just a stone's throw from the ruins of Flint Castle lives a lady named Gwen Evans. One winter evening Gwen walked across to close the heavy curtains of her lounge windows when something outside caught her attention.

'Our front garden is large with tall conifers bordering it and is completely private and cut off from the road. There is no reason for anyone, other than members of the family, to be there. At first it just looked like a whitish misty light, but then I noticed that it was moving slowly across the lawn. I put my hands up to shade my eyes from the light in the room and peered out with my face close to the window to get a better look. I had no sense of fear, more of curiosity. As I focused on the moving column of mist I saw the faint outline of a human body. At this point I did feel quite shivery and cold and I knew something was going on in my garden which was certainly not normal.

'There was no one else in the house with me at the time and I was not sure what to do. Although I was feeling a bit afraid there was something about this figure which kept my attention. It was as if I dared not look away, even for a second. I seemed to know inside that if I did look away the figure would be gone forever and for some unknown reason this saddened me. Apart from my natural apprehension at observing the unknown, I was calm inside, certain that whatever was out there was in no way going to harm me. I got the impression that I was meant to see it.

'I stood riveted to the spot as I watched the mist slowly

but steadily clear and there stood a young girl. Because of her strange dress it was difficult to say exactly how old she was but at a guess I would say about ten or eleven or perhaps slightly older. She did not look at me but just moved in a circle on the lawn. She kept looking up at different angles as if she was looking or talking to other people who were much higher up or taller than she was. I know that seems a strange way to describe her but that is how she struck me.

'The girl was surrounded by a light which seemed to grow brighter and brighter all the time while her form became more vivid. I could now see every detail of her appearance in shimmering vibrant colour. The thing that stunned me most was the fact that she was wearing a deep purple cloak over her shoulders which was trimmed with what looked like ermine. She had long dark hair decorated with strings of pearls or beads wound round her head. Her elaborate gown reached right down to the grass. I stood entranced as she moved around the lawn watching her jewels sparkle in the rays of the mysterious light which surrounded her. For someone so young she was most extravagantly laden with all sorts of precious looking stones. I then saw her expression change. She had a look of alarm on her face as she gazed upwards. I could see no one else there but it was as if she was looking up at someone, then she raised both of her arms as if to protect herself and the next second she had vanished and the garden was in blackness.

'I closed the curtains in a dazed state, ran and poured myself a brandy to steady my nerves and just sat there, unable to get the vision of that young girl out of my mind. Trying desperately to find some kind of explanation, I started to ask myself questions just to check things over in my head: Was it Halloween? Were there any fancy dress parties going on in the neighbourhood? Were there any plays or entertainments being presented in the locality? I had to answer all of these questions in the negative. For the life of me I could not fathom it but even as I carried out this self-interrogation I knew in my inner self that I would never find the answer because what I had seen was not of this world.

'When Robin, my husband, came home from work that night I told him what I'd seen through the lounge window. He looked at me with a grin on his face then he jokingly asked me if I had been at the brandy. I told him I had been, but only after I'd seen the girl. Because he knew perfectly well that I was deadly serious he immediately admitted that he should not have said that to me. He then began to take in what I was saying to him. I watched his expression grow strained as I went over and over the story.

'He then walked across to the windows and I have to say that he did hesitate slightly before pulling open the curtains. He looked out through the window but of course there was nothing there. He then went outside and had a good look around the garden, the driveway, the front of the house and the path and road in front. I just couldn't bring myself to follow him out. Nothing was amiss and there was no one near the house so we had dinner, but all the time the girl was on my mind. At that time two of our three sons were living at home with us so we decided that it would be wise to say nothing of what I'd seen to either of them, not wishing to upset them.

'That night we went to bed as usual and when I suggested that we should keep one of the bedside lights on my husband readily agreed. I think he was more concerned than I was because, having not seen the girl, he imagined the situation to be more frightening than it actually had been. I was perplexed yes, but not what you would call terrified as I felt that the young girl, whoever she was, seemed to be in a kind of vulnerable state herself and she appeared to be in need of some kind of help, for all her apparent riches. I got the impression that she was too involved in trying to protect herself to bother about harming others.

'That night I had a weird dream that someone was talking to me in a strange language. It felt like there was a lot of murmuring voices and although I could not hear exactly what they were saying I somehow knew that they were not speaking in English. Above the background voices I could hear a single frail voice speaking in the foreign language. I opened my eyes, and to my amazement I could still hear the voices. It had not been a dream after all. I could still hear the muffled sounds as if a group of people were talking in hushed tones together and then again I heard the other voice saying something like "ejappy" or "ijappy."

'I immediately shook my husband to waken him. He opened his eyes and I asked him if he could hear anything. He didn't say anything so I ran over to our bedroom window which overlooked the front lawn as the voices seemed to be coming from that direction. I looked out but could see nothing and the voices had faded to almost nothing. Then, as if away in the distance, but still merged with the voices, I heard the distinct neighing of a horse. The next instant all was silent. My husband had not heard a thing. I got back into bed and tried to get to sleep.

'A few nights later I was sitting in the lounge watching television with my husband and two sons. I was enjoying the programme and certainly not thinking about the recent goings on when I saw a swish of light move right across the room. As I looked and recognized the vague outline of a young girl within the oblong shape of light, my body went cold. She walked right through the lounge windows and out towards the lawn. This time I really was afraid and I just burst into tears unable to say a word.

'My husband Robin decided that he would try to get to the bottom of the strange happenings. He felt that the first clue were the words "ejappy" or "ijappy". After some deliberation he wondered if what I had heard could have been the French word échapper which means to break away or to escape from. Although my husband knew some French I knew none at all – just a bit of Welsh. He explained to me that phonetically this word would sound something like ejappy. He then had to consider whether the apparition was linked to me myself or the family, or to the property, or location. Considering that we had no connections with France whatsoever, in fact neither of us have ever even been there, he dropped that line of enquiry.

'Robin then thought about the muffled voices and the neighing sound of the horse. That indicated to him that the link could possibly be with the house or the immediate location. After a bit of investigation he found out that an old medieval roadway once ran through the site on which our house had been built. The roadway (more like a track) had led past Flint Castle.

'In the year 1399 while King Richard II (son of the Black Prince) was in Ireland trying to restore order amongst the rebellious chiefs, he received the news that there were also problems on his home ground. Immediately he set sail across the Irish Sea and landed on the northern coast of

242

Wales. The king's entourage marched down the old road-way and just as they were passing Flint Castle they were set upon by a band of noblemen. King Richard was taken prisoner on that very spot – now the land upon which our house stands. With him on that fateful journey was his wife who was greatly distressed by the sudden attack. Her name was Isabella of Valois – *a ten year old French girl, daughter of Charles VI, King of France.*

∞

BILL lived in Cardiff with his parents and his little brother and sister, and although they were not particularly well off, they managed. When Bill was about eight years of age his normal routine would be to come home from school, quickly clear any homework he had been given and then spend about half an hour reading to little Elizabeth from her story books. His parents felt that this exercise would be good for him in as much as it would hopefully improve his own reading technique and it was good for Elizabeth to have the exclusive attention of her older brother which of course she loved. Something happened in the May of that year which he will remember forever.

'I was always very close to little Elizabeth probably because we all looked upon her as the baby of the family although at the time I recall she was about three years old. My brother Richard – we called him Ricky for short – was two years younger than I was so he would have been six. I was reading to Elizabeth as usual when I heard a lot of noise downstairs. Ricky had been off school for a day or two because he had not been feeling too well. When I'd come in about an hour earlier I noticed that Mum had moved him from his own bed to the couch in the living room which was made up like a bed with a quilt over him. He was asleep when I peeped round the door so I thought that I'd better not wake him up or Mum might be mad at me.

'I went down to find out what was going on and I found the next door neighbour in the room and Mum was crying. She did not often cry in front of us, in fact I think that was the very first time I'd ever seen her in tears. I was soon to find out that Ricky had taken a turn for the worse and the ambulance was on the way to our house to take him to hospital. The neighbour had offered to look after Elizabeth and myself while Mum went to hospital with Ricky. I remember the panic trying to locate my father who was out at work on a building site and was therefore not near any telephone.

'I was told to go back upstairs and keep Elizabeth happy while the grown-ups organized things. I remember the job I had trying to explain to Elizabeth that Ricky was poorly but that the doctors and nurses would soon make him better and he would be back with us again. No matter what I said to her she would not be consoled and just kept screaming and screaming until the neighbour had to come up to try to pacify her. Elizabeth was not a spoilt child, my parents saw to that, and it was most unlike her to behave like that. It was not the selfish cries that you sometimes hear from children but there seemed to be genuine fear in her voice. We were a very close-knit little family and she was devastated at not having Ricky to play with.

'Two days later Ricky died from diphtheria. We were all terrified to break the news to Elizabeth, remembering how upset she had been when Ricky had been taken to hospital. My Mum came in to us both and she took Elizabeth on her knee and gently told her that Ricky would not be able to come home as he had gone to Jesus.

'I remember holding my breath and waiting for the awful reaction that I was convinced Elizabeth would give when the truth of the situation dawned on her. To my amazement she looked straight up at Mum and said simply, "I know."

'Mum was slightly surprised but more relieved at the philosophical way Elizabeth seemed to take the news. Mind you, I was not a hundred per cent sure that she really did understand at that point but with hindsight I now think that she probably did. In fact I believe now that she understood far far more than any of the rest of us.

'It took a long time for our family to get back to normal after losing Ricky. Everywhere, all over the house, there were memories of him that were sometimes just too painful to deal with.

'About a year later I was reading to Elizabeth as usual. My parents had made an enormous effort to try to bring things to as near normal as was possible in the circumstances so I had been encouraged to continue my reading sessions with Elizabeth. This particular evening I noticed that she was not really paying attention to me at all. Two or three times I had to stop and ask her if she wanted to hear the story or not. I then noticed that she was drawing something. Not the usual babyish scribbles but very distinctive little men and women and dogs and rabbits but all in the style of matchstick drawings.

'I had never seen her do anything like that before and of course I told her that I thought the drawings were very good. She looked up at me in a most matter of fact way and told me Ricky had just shown her how to draw them. Not wishing to upset her I merely mentioned that she must have watched him when he used to draw. I must just mention here that matchstick drawings were Ricky's speciality. He was always drawing little figures in a very distinctive way. I know most kids start drawing by making match-like people but he used to put special little hats and shoes on his drawings which were totally individualistic. Elizabeth's drawings had the same hats and shoes. I just assumed that she had seen some of his drawing books around the house, and I continued with the story I was trying to read to her.

'Again I noticed that her attention had wandered and she was back at her drawings. I asked her if she just wanted to get on with what she was doing herself and I would read my own book. She told me that Ricky wanted her to finish them so he could see them when he came back.

'I did not say anything to her and let her get on with her drawing, but later that evening I told Mum what she had said about Ricky coming back. Mum told me to ignore her as she was just imagining things as little children do. For several evenings the same thing happened but I noticed that the drawings were becoming more and more perfect and I couldn't help telling her that they were getting better, just to encourage her.

'She told me again that Ricky had shown her how to do them, then she added that the next day he was going to show her how to draw a horse. As gently as I could, I told her that Ricky could not come back, then I reminded her of what Mum had told her when Ricky died, about him going to Jesus. She nodded her head as if she understood completely but then she added, 'He does come back to see me. He came here today. He told me that when he comes tomorrow he will show me how to make a horse.'

'Her words really upset me as I had missed Ricky so

much and I would have loved to see him. I was a bit cross with her and I said that she was just making it up. How could Ricky come back if he was dead? She then said something I will never forget – and bear in mind she was only four years old at the time. She looked right in my eyes and said, "People are not dead when they're with Jesus. Ricky's not dead, he lives with Jesus." There was such conviction in her little voice that it left me speechless.

'After that I didn't bother saying any more to her about the matter. She continued to do her drawings – and yes, a few days later she drew a matchstick horse saying that Ricky had shown her how to do it. I just let her ramble on and on. One day she did upset me when she said that Ricky had told her that she could come with him soon. I remember thinking to myself that this game had gone far enough so I made a point of asking Mum to explain to her again that Ricky was dead and that she couldn't go anywhere with him.

'Elizabeth started school the following September. She too caught diphtheria and was dead within weeks.'

Chapter Five
SCOTLAND

WHEN Richard and his wife visited Edinburgh for the first time they stayed at the 16th century hotel, The Lady Nairn, in Willow Brae Road. He recalls being delighted with the hotel: 'I was particularly charmed with the old world furniture in our bedroom which graced a magnificent four-poster bed complete with drapes and canopy.

'As I lay in bed beside my wife who was fast asleep, I was reflecting upon the day and thinking how peaceful and serene everything was. Suddenly the bed started to move, slowly at first then it rattled and shook in a rocking motion starting at the bottom and working its way up towards the top. I was rigid with fear and kept looking at my wife who slept right through the commotion as if nothing was happening.

'I was certain that any minute there would be a knock on the door to complain about the noise. My attention was caught by a yellowish light which appeared in the centre of the canopy. I just could not take my eyes off it and as I gazed in terror I watched the light grow in intensity and gradually form itself into an oval shape which was hovering above me.

'By this time I had broken out in a cold sweat and my heart was thumping. The motion of the bed gradually calmed down and as this happened the light started to fade then eventually vanished and all was silent.

'I got up and went around the room switching all the lights on and checking the walls, doors and windows to see if there were any cracks. I looked out of the window to see if any heavy lorries were on the road then I started to pace the floor checking if the floorboards were sound. I knew in my heart that I was only acting on an impulse to take rational steps in an effort to find an explanation and in truth I would find none. I even looked under the bed for a clue which might explain what had just taken place, but all to no avail.

'I lay in that bed until dawn, unable to sleep, trying to work things out in my mind. The following morning I was expecting the manager to approach me but to my surprise he just smiled a polite good morning. I did not wish to alarm my wife so I merely asked her if she had slept well and she assured me that she had.

'Several years later I happened to be speaking to someone who knew one of the subsequent managers of the Lady Nairn. We were talking about hotels in general and the following story came to light: About two years after I had experienced the rattling and had seen the yellow light, a young chambermaid was working there. At that time the bedroom I had slept in – the only one with the four-poster – was under repair and three workmen had told the chambermaid that when they had stopped work to make some tea, all the dishes started to rattle furiously, so much so, that the three men ran in terror from the bedroom. The girl did not pay much heed to them thinking that they were just teasing her. The work on the room was eventually completed and it was once more in use. That same chambermaid was in the bedroom one day and she suddenly got the feeling that somone else was in the room with her.

'The girl turned round quickly and sure enough there was a man standing in the middle of the floor. She could not understand how he could have entered the room without her seeing or hearing him. He was staring at her with vivid blue icy eyes which sent a wave of fear through her. She was certain that he was going to attack her.

'The man started to move towards the girl. In an attempt to save herself, the chambermaid stretched out her arm to stop the man. Her hand went right through him. She screamed at the top of her voice as she watched him fade into the wall.'

∞

LESLEY had only just moved to the North of Scotland with her husband to take up residence near Aberdeen. She loved the fresh air and the scenery but she was deeply unhappy. The strife between her and her husband had not eased by the move north of the border as they had hoped. She was past knowing whose fault it was and past caring. The arguments were becoming more frequent, more bitter, and she was growing more and more depressed. One evening after a raging row, she ran sobbing, from their cottage, towards the cliffs which were not far away.

'I breathed in the fresh air amidst my sobs, thankful that no-one else was walking on the cliffs to see my mascara-run face. I climbed one of the hills facing the sea-front, climbed higher and higher to the top, and then sat down on the grass ledge over from the roadway which skirted the top of the hill. I looked out at the sea. The rosy glow of the sunset over the water was so beautiful and peaceful – why couldn't my marriage be like this? I have no idea how long I sat there staring out at the sea and feeling sorry for myself. I tried to analyse the situation, asking myself if things could ever improve, trying to think of anything I could do to redeem my doomed marriage. I could not think of a single thing. I'd tried everything to no avail.

'I could not face the thought of returning yet again to my husband the silent rebukes, the pain. There seemed no way out. I had nothing left on this earth to live for; I had come to the end. As the sun sank beneath the horizon I felt a sickening chill spread through me. I gazed down at the turbulent water far beneath and told myself it would only take a few seconds then it would be all over. No more heartaches!

'I felt myself break out in a cold sweat as I got up. My legs trembled so much I could hardly stand. In a thundering flash of realization I came to my senses. No, I wasn't ready to die after all – but I was too late! To my horror I felt the loose earth of the cliff move under my feet – I had started to fall – I screamed in terror!

'Suddenly I felt two strong arms grab me from behind and gently pull me back up on to the solid ground of the cliff-top. I'd had no idea that anyone was there and had been watching me.

'I turned round and found myself looking up into the eyes of a young man I'd never seen before. He was tall and strongly built, rather scruffily dressed, but it was his radiant smile that made me melt into his arms. I sobbed with relief and told him that I could never thank him enough for saving me.

'He held me for a long time, never once speaking as I blurted out my problems. He just stroked my hair and listened in silence. We walked together and he kept smiling kindly at me, touching my heart with his soft gentle eyes.

'I said that I'd have to be getting back. He kissed me

tenderly on the forehead and waved as I reluctantly walked off.

'For days I could not get him out of my mind, and I found myself taking the same route along the top of the cliffs secretly hoping that I would meet him again.

'About a week later I was strolling along the sea-front where I saw an old fisherman pulling in his net. He looked over at me and said, "Shouldn't be walking by yourself in these parts – not with Brian Symes around."

'My startled expression made him lay his net down and say, "Didn't mean to frighten you, Miss. I just assumed that you knew about Brian."

'I asked him who Brian was. He went on to tell me that Brian Symes was one of the local labourers who had helped to build the road along the top of the cliffs. A friendly lad he was, very popular with everybody, always a smile, no matter what. The fisherman's voice grew solemn as he told me: "This month ten years ago when the new road was almost finished, Brian had sat down on the edge of the cliff to eat his lunch. He stood up to go back to the others but the soft earth crumbled beneath his weight. God only knows how long he clung to the edge before falling to his death."

'I asked the fisherman, "But surely someone nearby must have heard his calls?"

"No one could," said the fisherman, "Brian was dumb. He hadn't spoken a word since birth."

'A shiver ran down my spine. I looked up at the cliff-top and wiped away my tears for the man who saved me but could not save himself.'

∞

'WHEN David Webb was 16 years old he was an ardent

member of the Christian Guild of St Mary in the Parish of Bernard Castle in Co. Durham. He was chosen to attend the Christian Summer Camp on the island of Iona off the west coast of Scotland. The object of the exercise was two-fold: to give him Christian leadership training; and for him to assist the monks in the rebuilding of the abbey.

'Iona, part of the Inner Hebrides, covers an area of about 2,200 acres, and has long been looked upon as the place of origin of Scottish Christianity, having previously been an important Druid centre. St Columba travelled from Ireland and settled in Iona where he founded a monastery in the year A.D.563. He sent his monks out to convert the savage Picts and Scots.

'In the 13th century the abbey church of St. Mary was made into the cathedral, which was destroyed at the time of the Reformation, the site becoming the property of the Dukes of Argyll. The 8th Duke of Argyll presented the ruins of the old abbey to the Church of Scotland and the work of restoration was instigated. In 1905 the abbey was re-opened.

'Iona is scattered with celtic crosses, tombs of ancient kings of Scotland, Ireland and Norway, and a wealth of memorials from the past.

'The abbey on Iona used to be a ruin but it was decided to rebuild it just before the second World War. The rebuilding was started by the resident monks and was carried out in excellent taste. They had tried very hard to retain as much of the ancient building as possible. The main interior pillars which had long been exposed to the elements were left with the ferns and lichen still growing from them. This gave the inside of the abbey a most atmospheric and mysterious effect, without, I must add, being eerie or frightening. Large

253

double doors led into the Abbey and the altar was at the far end opposite these doors. There was one other small door in one of the side walls.

'The following story was told to me by one of the monks in the presence of the then Moderator of the Church of Scotland who was living on the island at the time of our tutorial:

'One evening back in the early 1940's I was lighting the candles around the altar when I heard someone knocking on the main doors. I looked to the back of the abbey and saw the doors open. A young man entered wearing what I instantly recognized as a German Luftwaffe officer's uniform. He walked towards the altar and paused. I wanted to ask him if I could help as he seemed to be looking for something, but somehow or another I could not bring myself to speak to him. Perhaps I was daunted by his uniform, but it was more than that. There was just something about him that made me feel apprehensive. He did not look at me, in fact I got the impression that he didn't seem to know I was there. I admit that I was relieved to see him walk away towards the side door and leave the abbey.

'I reported what I had seen to my superior who in turn alerted the relevant authorities. The following day a search was made of the island but no trace of a German officer was found.

'On that second evening I was again lighting the altar candles at the same time and naturally my thoughts were on the man I'd seen the evening before. I was just a little uneasy but I cannot say that I was altogether frightened as I was confident that no real danger would come to me on the altar. Even so, when I heard the solitary footsteps making their way up the aisle I confess my heart skipped a beat. I turned around quickly and there he was, the same serious face, the same uniform; and I had the same feeling of foreboding.

'I stopped lighting the candles and stood silently watching him. I wanted to run to tell someone but my feet were rooted to the spot. He looked straight ahead, ignoring me completely. After a few moments he turned and walked towards the side door and left, exactly as he had done the previous evening.

'I gathered myself together and made myself follow him. I got to the side door and went out, expecting to see him walking away from the abbey, but to my surprise there was no one in sight. I guessed that he must have walked round behind the building so I ran round to the exterior of the altar section of the abbey. There was no one to be seen. By this time I was growing agitated at having lost sight of the man as I knew that I would be questioned as to which direction he had taken. I made a complete circle of the building twice, but the man was gone. I looked in every direction, but there was not a soul in sight.

'I reported the incident again exactly as it had happened. The following morning the matter was reported to the authorities on the mainland of Scotland. A thorough search was made of the whole island of Iona but no trace of the Luftwaffe officer could be found, and there was no record of any boatman having taken a man in a German uniform to the mainland.

'Several days later one of the residents of the island was out walking with his dog. He was strolling along on the sandy beach on the north side of the island when his dog, which had been running ahead of him, began barking excitedly. The man went to investigate. There, half buried

255

in the sand was the body of a young German Luftwaffe officer. It was later confirmed that the man had been dead for several weeks, although the sand had, to some degree, preserved the face. I was able to identify the corpse as the same Luftwaffe officer I had seen in the abbey.

'The final sequence to this old monk's story is that the body of that young German officer was buried in the small graveyard that lies next to the abbey. It was felt that the officer's appearance at the altar was his way of trying to communicate a plea for help. Whatever he was searching for will never truly be known, but the monks felt that the least they could do would be to ensure that he was given a decent burial.

'If you walk through that graveyard you will see the German officer's final resting place. A headstone marks the spot where lies the mysterious soldier. If you then walk past his headstone and go round to the other side of the small graveyard you will see another grave. The headstone on this grave reads MACBETH – KING OF SCOTLAND. Take care however not to tread in the graveyard around the midnight hour, lest you also hear the ghostly voice which warned Macbeth: "Sleep no more!"'

∞

WHEN Sandra was 14 years of age, like most youngsters she loved dancing. As she was the only daughter her parents were fairly strict, so when she asked their permission to go to a disco in the neighbouring village of Mauchline they were reluctant to agree. She used every means she could think of to persuade them, eventually enlisting the assistance of the parents of her friend Grace. It was agreed that the two girls would be allowed to go to the disco in Mauchline on one condition: they had to promise that whatever happened, and however much they were enjoying themselves, they had to be out of the disco in time to catch the last bus home. As in most rural areas of Scotland public transport had its limitations. The last bus that would take the girls home left Mauchline at 9.20 p.m. which would mean that they would have to leave the disco well before it finished. The girls promised faithfully that they would definitely leave in time to catch the last bus, and on this understanding Sandra's parents gave their permission.

The two girls danced their way through the evening, and, true to their word, they left in time to catch the bus. They were so brimming over with exuberance when they arrived home that their parents agreed that the girls could go to the disco on a regular basis. So it came about that every Monday night Sandra and Grace attended the Mauchline disco.

One night they become so absorbed in the fun they were having with their friends that they completely forgot about the time. Upon realizing that the last bus was about to leave, they dashed out of the hall and ran as fast as they could down the road to the bus stop. They were just in time to see the back of the bus as it sped off without them.

Sandra remembers: 'We were so upset that neither of us had the courage to telephone our parents to tell them what had happened. We decided that the only thing that we could do was to start walking.

'It was a lonely country road and it was very dark with no light whatsoever. Hardly any cars used that road, especially at night. We walked quickly at first, and chatted to each other about the disco and what we would be up against when we had to explain to our parents what had happened. Grace's parents were also strict and we both knew what we would be in for. After a while we stopped talking. We just linked arms and kept walking, hearing only the sound of our own footsteps which became gradually slower as we grew weary. The trees were casting odd shadows across our path. Although we did not admit it to each other at that point we were both beginning to feel a little bit scared.

'We must have walked about three miles, and after the evening's dancing, our feet were aching. Just then it started to rain, and in just a few mintues we were both soaked through to the skin. Then to make matters worse a streak of lightning shot across the fields and the thunder started. The noise was almost deafening, coming so suddenly in total contrast to the awful silence which we had experienced up to that point.

'Out of sheer panic we started to run, but we both quickly realized that running would not solve anything as there were still miles and miles to go and no houses or phone boxes along the way. Running would only make us more exhausted than we were already.

"What can we do?" asked Grace nervously. I tried to reassure her that there was nothing to worry about but inside I was just as frightened as she was.

'By now we were both very tired and thinking about the long journey still ahead of us we began to lose heart. After a few more minutes I had to admit to Grace that I was too weary to walk another step. My feet were killing me and I was growing more and more afraid.

'Grace suddenly suggested that maybe we should pray. We were not in the habit of praying and neither of us was particularly religious. However, we both felt at such a low

258

ebb that any suggestion was better than nothing, so we huddled down together in the horrible watery ditch by the side of the road and started to pray. We really begged God for help as we felt completely forlorn.

'We were still praying in the rain when a white car stopped right beside us on the road. We were taken aback because neither of us had heard it approaching.

'A man opened the car door and called over to us. He was dressed all in black with snowy white hair. He told us that he knew we were in trouble but he would be glad to take us home. We were both terrified but then I noticed that he was wearing a vicar's white collar. I whispered to Grace that he must be a minister. He beckoned to us to get into his car. We reckoned we had nothing to lose, so gingerly we got into his car. He leaned across and opened the back door so that we could both sit together in the back seat, which made us feel a bit better about accepting the lift home.

'There was an odd atmosphere in the car but I just put it down to the fact that we had been so afraid, also the rain was still pouring out of the heavens. Even with the car's strong headlights on we could hardly see more than a few feet in front.

'He did not say a word to us and we were both past talking. We just wanted to get home as quickly as possible. We were on the road that led to Grace's house. We were just about to tell him where her house was when we realized that he had slowed down of his own accord. He stopped the car right outside her house. She got out, waved at me and ran up the path to her front door. Not waiting to see if she got inside, the minister drove off in the direction of my parent's house. I wondered how he had known where Grace lived, but I just assumed that he probably knew her parents.

'Being alone with him in the car made me feel uneasy. After all I had never seen him before in my life and I'd no idea where he came from. He did not speak to me. By this time I was very frightened, especially when I could see he was taking all the correct turns to where I lived. I stiffened with fear. I seemed to be struck dumb. I was wet through and shaking with the cold. He started to slow down just as he approached my home, then he brought the car to a halt outside the door of our house. The man turned off the engine. I dashed out of the car as quickly as I could and ran up to the front door. I turned to see why he had not re-started the engine and I nearly died. There was nothing there! No car, no minister, nothing at all. Nor was there any sign of a car up or down the deserted road.

'I was trembling with shock as I stumbled into our hallway. My parents could see how distraught I was. My mother comforted me and explained that Grace's father had just telephoned to say that I was being driven home by the minister. "Shouldn't we invite him in?" she asked my father. I was too numb to tell them that the car and the vicar had just disappeared. My father went outside but of course he couldn't see anyone.

'The next morning, after the full story came out, my parents were most concerned. Even though they knew that I was not given to exaggeration they found it difficult to accept my story about the disappearance of the car and driver. They felt compelled to take the matter further. An extensive investigation was set up after first having established from all the churches in the area that no minister fitting that description was in our locality on the night in question. My parents' initial investigations sparked off a search throughout the whole of Ayrshire to try and find out who this person was who had come to our aid.

'I can't help thinking that the reason my mother and father were adamant that they should talk to this man was to put the "nonsense" about the vanishing car out of my mind once and for all.

'After a lot of letter writing and telephoning, it came to light that on the exact spot in that ditch where Grace and I had prayed for our lives, a minister had murdered two 14 year old girls in 1897 and buried them right there by the side of the road. Was our driver that same minister trying to make up for his dreadful deed?'

∞

IN the year 1939, John Ireland was sent to Grieff in Perthshire to take part in concentrated training along with other units of the 9th Highland Divisional Signals from Stirling and Aberdeen, all having been with territorial forces. They were billeted in the Crieff Hydropathic along with a company of Royal Engineers.

'We, that is the Royal Signals, also occupied Fern Tower,' explains John. 'It was a listed building which stood some three quarters of a mile away from the Hydro and which could only be reached by a path which was sand-wiched between two fields. It is well known that Charles Edward Stuart – Bonny Prince Charlie – spent a night in the Fern Tower during his retreat in 1745. General Johnnie Cope is said to have encamped in the same year in the grounds surrounding the house.

'It is interesting to recall that reveille at the Hydro during the war was announced every morning at 6.30 a.m. by the strains of the 9th Highland Division Pipe band playing "Hi! Johnnie Cope are ye wauking (awake) yet?" I can hear it still! The Hydro itself dates back to 1868 and in 1912 the Strathearn Hydropathic Establishment Co. Ltd purchased part of the Fern Tower Estate from Lord Abercromby who was the owner at that time. The tower was some 60 feet high.

'Fern tower had been unoccupied just prior to the war, and when it was taken over by the War Department it was discovered that a billiard table had been left in one of the longer rooms although no balls or cues were to be found. No one was really into billiards so the door to the long room was locked and the billiard table was forgotten about.

'In the early hours of one winter's morning, a soldier on guard duty distinctly heard a clicking sound. It was clearly audible in the still quiet morning just before dawn. He walked around, then his attention was drawn to a dim light coming from one of the windows of the tower. It was the window of the billiard room and the light was the light above the billiard table. The clicking was like the sound of billiard balls hitting against each other. He went straight to the room feeling sure that he would catch a game being played. On trying the door he found that it was locked. He hammered on the door calling in to the players that their game was up and would they open the door. There was stony silence. The soldier listened, puzzled, for a few moments, then went back outside to have another look up at the windows of the long room. Everything was in darkness – no light was showing and the clicking sound had stopped.

'He did not mention the incident to anyone, fearing that they would only say that it had been his imagination.

However, a few nights later, he was again on guard duty and again he heard the same clicking sound. He looked up at the window and there was the dim light glowing above the area in the long room where the billiard table was. This time he was determined to catch the culprits in action so he hurried straight to the room, all the time listening to the clicking sound of the billiard balls. He reached out to open the door and suddenly the clicking stopped. The door was locked and all was silent.

'This time the soldier did make a report and on checking it was found that the only key to the long room had never been removed from where it had been placed several weeks previously. There was no question of anyone entering or leaving by the one window to the room as there was a sheer drop down the side of the tower. The soldier knew that he had not passed anyone on the way to the room. He was at a complete loss to understand what had happened. However, the matter was forgotten and life went on as normal.

'Some time later, again in the early hours of the morning, another soldier was on guard at the door of the Fern Tower. He felt the cold intensify and he got the unnerving feeling that he was not alone. All of the soldiers should have been asleep but he wondered if someone had come outside for any reason. He felt the hair rise up on his scalp as he saw the misted outline of a kilted figure drift out of the darkness and glide about directly in front of him.

'The terror stricken guard took fright and ran into the tower. Although he had suffered no harm, it was several days before he regained his composure. From that moment on there was always a double guard at the door of the Fern Tower.

'A short time after the apparition was seen, two soldiers

on guard duty heard the sound of voices. They could not make out exactly what was being said, but got the impression that there were many men talking and that there was some degree of urgency in their conversation.

'The two guards became alarmed and quickly made a check of the tower and the grounds but everything was normal. The sounds had faded and everywhere was silent again. Suddenly there was an almighty blast of firearms, and the muffled voices returned. By this time the two guards were petrified, not knowing what was going on. Again they heard the sound of gunfire and the muffled voices grew louder. The soldiers almost froze with fright, as out of the darkness a misty figure moved towards them. They both saw him but were too afraid to move. The vision was shrouded in white vapour which seemed to be luminous. Amidst the vapour the two soldiers saw a tall kilted man with a young face. What struck them most about the man was the sadness of his expression. After a time – it was difficult to say exactly how long – the two soldiers started to walk towards the door of the tower. The moment they moved, the kilted man disappeared and the sounds of firearms ceased. It is important to understand that at the time both weapons and ammunition were in very short supply, especially to a training unit. All arms were kept locked up in the armoury and only withdrawn when training took place, and returned immediately afterwards so that all was accounted for.

'Sadly, Fern Tower was demolished in 1962 by arrangement with a territorial Army detachment of Royal Engineers from Sheffield and Nottingham as an army exercise.

'I've often wondered who the sad man in the kilt was and if the sound of the firearms was an echo from a battle of the

264

past. Some mornings I can still hear in the back of my mind the wail of the pipes sounding reveille to welcome in another Highland dawn and perhaps herald yet another appearance of the kilted, mist-shrouded stranger.'

∞

IN the year 1915 when Edith was fifteen years of age, she moved with her family from the south of England to a house in Barony Street, Edinburgh. This is her story.

'There was a large main door on the ground floor level and a kitchen with a passage leading to a two room flat in the basement. I chose to sleep in the basement bedroom thinking it such a cozy little room, while my brothers and sister were taken to sleep in my parents room. I used to wonder about this, but later I was to discover that mother was frightened for them to sleep anywhere else. They used to hear odd unexplained rattlings, bumps and clanking sounds and they saw unaccountable shadows.

'Firstly, cats would appear everywhere, mainly black ones, and they would be running through doorways, leaping off worktops and chairs. The strange thing was, I never ever saw their faces. Their heads were always averted or the cats would just turn away before I could see them properly. Mind you I was terrified that one day I would get a good look at a cat's face.

'Once, while baking, I felt a cat brush against my legs. I looked down expecting to see our own cat there and I nearly passed out when I saw this strange cat which turned and fled out through the door. Now our own cat was never allowed into my bedroom at nights, but one night I distinctly felt a weight on my feet. Presuming it was our cat,

265

I threw my legs up to get it off. I expected to hear the thump of it landing on the floor, but there was no sound whatsoever.

'When sitting on my own one day, my parents being in the front room, my own cat, which had been lying on my lap, suddenly jumped up. Her fur stood on end. She stared all around and then took to her heels and charged out the door in terror. I heard a noise on the stairs (one of the stairs used to bump when stood upon) and a sound like taffeta rustling. I ran to tell my mother.

'Until then I had never said a word to her but now I was well and truly shaking with fright. She was relieved that I had spoken out because she had been seeing things, hearing sounds and she had wondered if it was only her imagination. She went on to tell me about the ghost she had seen.

'She had been going down to the kitchen one day and she was walking towards the stairs. On looking down she saw a man standing there, gazing at the flagstones on the floor, his hand at the side of his face as if in thought. What he was looking at was a stone with the initials E.M.M. carved on it. These are my present initials. They had been there from the day we moved in but no one had taken any notice of them. The man was dressed in black breeches, red hose and shoes and a red tassled smoking-type hat. Mother let out a gasp and the man disappeared.

'Many's the time I attempted to lift that stone with the initials on it to discover what was underneath it but I never managed to.

'At other times I would knock downstairs because of the noise my little brother was making. Meantime he'd thought it was me who was rattling around, but we discovered that it was neither of us but another unexplained incident.

'One day my mother and I were drying some damp bedding when we heard what we thought was the sound of a ball bouncing and then we both felt the most terrible thump on our heads although we could see nothing. My wee brother started cowering and screaming "A man, a man." We saw no man in the room.

'My mother became so frightened in that house that she used to rush through the housework so that she could get out as quickly as possible. She was not to leave that terrible place for ten years although she tried desperately to get somewhere else.

'When I married at the age of 20, my husband and I lived in that same house with my parents. Things carried on happening and although my husband "didn't believe in all that rubbish" as he put it, he had to cut the wires to all the kitchen bells because they used to ring and ring for no reason. Even after he had cut the wires *they still rang!*

'Ten years after moving into that house my parents eventually found somewhere else to live and two weeks later, to my great relief my husband and I found ourselves a small house nearby.

'Some years later my brother sent me a newspaper clipping telling of men digging outside our old home in Barony Street. They were to install a generator and they unearthed a small barred cell.

∞

MANY people visit Scotland and come back home full of wonder at the breath-taking scenery, the grandeur of the mountains, the lush Galloway country, the awesome sights of the Valley of Glencoe and Culloden Moor. When Richard left his home in Cambridge to holiday north of the border he too was left quite breathless – but for a different reason.

'My wife and I were travelling around Scotland and arrived in Moffat. It was the first time in our lives that we'd ever been to Moffat and we were just looking around, enjoying the sights when I suddenly remembered that I needed to draw some cash out of the bank. I left my wife happily buying some souvenirs and made my way down the street.

'I saw a bank and was pleased to note that it was the T.S.B. – my own bank. Directly opposite I saw a gents' hairdresser which reminded me that I badly needed a haircut. I looked at my watch and saw that I would have plenty of time to visit the hairdresser then go to the bank before lunchtime.

'I remember looking at the outside wall of the bank to see if there was a cash dispenser as I was still toying with the idea of getting my money first. Where the usual cash dispenser would be set into the wall of the bank, I noticed that a metal plate had been placed across it. I then decided to go straight to have my hair cut.

'I was lucky to be served fairly quickly and got chatting to one or two of the locals. My haircut was soon finished, I paid and left. I made my way back to the shops where my wife had been browsing and soon we were back in the car on our way out of Moffat. It wasn't until my wife asked me where we should go for lunch that I suddenly remembered about the bank. What with chatting to the locals in the hairdresser and then worrying about getting back to my wife I had completely forgotten about the money.

'Since we did not have any hard and fast schedule mapped out for our holiday we decided that we would go back to Moffat the following day. I told her that it wouldn't take long because I'd seen the bank opposite the hairdressing salon and I knew exactly where to go. We decided that we would drive through Moffat, take out some cash, then continue driving northwards out of Dumfriesshire.

'The next morning we set out as planned back on the road to Moffat. We made our way down the street, saw the hairdressing salon, but to my utter amazement there was no bank opposite it. No T.S.B., with no metal plate over the cash dispenser. I just stood there staring in disbelief for on that very spot where I had seen the bank there was a photographer's shop with large blown-up photographs displayed in the window.

'My wife was tugging at my sleeve. She was wondering why I had stopped in my tracks. I reminded her of what I had told her the day before about how I'd seen the T.S.B. with the money dispenser on the wall covered over with a metal plate. I had even remarked to her that I'd wondered if the cash dispenser was going to be replaced or perhaps it had been sealed over because of vandals.

'I looked all around to see if I could possibly have mistaken the location of the bank but there was no T.S.B. in sight and no other building which even slightly resembled the bank which I had so clearly seen just 24 hours previously.

'Very puzzled indeed, I decided to make a few enquiries and I found out from a nearby shopkeeper that a T.S.B. bank did indeed stand on that very spot where I had seen it but it had been closed down for two years. When the photographer took over the building he changed the entire front facade to accommodate his line of business.

'The experience left me feeling most perplexed as I had distinctly seen the bank looking just like any other High Street Trustee Savings Bank building – apart from the metal plate over the money dispenser.

'Had I gone into some kind of timeslip? I often wonder what would have happened if I had not needed a haircut that day and had gone straight through the doors of the phantom bank!'

∞

JOAN tucked in her small daughter in the back bedroom, kissed her goodnight then went downstairs to rejoin her friend Dianne in the living room. Dianne had come round to spend the evening with her as both of their husbands were on back shift, being workmates, and the two women had become firm friends.

'I like Dianne to come round as it is company for the two of us. She hasn't any children and once my little girl is asleep the evenings can get very long, especially in the winter. I get fed up with watching television so when Dianne comes round it helps to pass the time.

'Anyway, one night just last winter Dianne was sitting in the living room. I'd just settled little Katie in her bed. She was tired and I remember thinking to myself that she'd soon be fast asleep. She's such an active little thing that she wears herself out now she has started day nursery.

'Dianne and I had just settled down to watch a video together when we both heard footsteps coming from upstairs. They were quite clear and sounded as if someone

270

was walking down our landing. We looked at each other. She asked me if Katie was up out of her bed although the footsteps seemed too heavy to be a child's. I rushed straight upstairs to the back bedroom but Katie was sleeping peacefully in exactly the same position as I'd left her. Just to make sure, I quickly looked in our own bedroom but there was nobody there.

'I went back downstairs shaking my head. Dianne looked a bit puzzled, then she said, "Maybe it's Mrs. Ross from next door." I looked at the clock and reminded Dianne that it was too early for Mrs. Ross to be back from bingo. We'd both waved to her as she was leaving just as Dianne came in earlier that evening.

'There is no other house adjoining ours so we just couldn't make out where the footsteps had come from. About 20 minutes later, during a quiet part of the video I thought that I heard the footsteps again. I did not say anything but glanced across at Dianne. Her anxious expression told me that she had also heard something. We both went upstairs straight to my little girl's room but again she was sleeping soundly. By her heavy regular breathing I could tell that she could not have just been awake. Nothing in the room had been disturbed. We then both inspected all of the upstairs area including the bathroom but nothing was out of place.

'We started to walk back downstairs. Dianne was in front of me. Something made me turn back and go into my own bedroom which was situated to the front of the house. I'll never know exactly what made me do it, but I found myself walking over to the bedroom window.

'When I looked outside I got the shock of my life to see a nun walking very slowly down our garden path from the

271

house towards the gate. I just stared at her huge white elaborate head-dress and long black robe. I did not know any nuns and wondered what on earth she was looking for. It crossed my mind that maybe she was going round the doors collecting for charity, but then I thought that it was a bit late for that, and anyway I'd always thought that they went out in twos.

'I wanted Dianne to see her, but I did not want to call out for fear of wakening Katie so I ran out onto the upstairs landing and went down three or four steps then called on Dianne to come up. I then went straight back to my own bedroom window.

'The nun was still there. She had reached the front gate. She turned around and looked straight up at me with eyes that made my blood run cold. I'll never forget that chilling gaze as our eyes met. It was dark outside yet there was something about her face – it was sort of luminous – especially those eyes.

'I absolutely froze with fright when I saw her raise up one of her arms, her eyes never blinking or looking away from mine, and slowly, with one finger, she beckoned me to join her.

'At that moment Dianne came into the room. I was in such a state of shock that I could not utter a word. The instant Dianne reached the window where I was standing the nun vanished into thin air, but the sickening thing was that she started to disappear from her feet upwards. It all happened in one swoosh but to the day I die I will still see those icy eyes staring at me – even when the rest of her body had vanished!'

∞

SOMETHING happened to Milly Martin when she visited

the Isle of Bute which she will never forget as long as she lives.

'We went to stay on the Isle of Bute just off the coast of Scotland – "Doon the Water" – as they say in Glasgow. We stayed in a small grey stone cottage just inside the grounds of what is now a British Rail convalescent home. There was only one bedroom with two beds so I shared one bed with my ten year old daughter, and my son, who was 14 at the time, had the other bed.

'Everything went well until the Wednesday. It was late afternoon, we had just finished tea and were planning to go round the island. I was hanging out a tea towel on the clothes line when I noticed just through the trees that a ship was leaving the island. It was a beautiful sight – the blue sea, white ship and so many shades of green from the grass and trees. I pulled the line down and was thinking what a lovely sight it was. I was feeling happy and relaxed when suddenly I bent double, overcome with grief and despair. I experienced utter mysery with a deep, deep down depression which was almost too much to bear.

'My son had seen me and came out. He put his hand on my shoulder and said, "What's up mum?" I opened my eyes and found that I had been not just crying but sobbing and sobbing. My face was wet with tears and I just cried and cried. My son waited until I recovered as I could not speak for several seconds. I told him that I was all right and said how stupid I felt. I had no idea why I had been sobbing.

'The next night about 3.00 a.m. I woke up suddenly. There was something in the room. Some *thing* – not someone – but a powerful feeling of something big and strong, just at the side of the bed. I went to sleep again thinking it was just another strange feeling I had had.

'The next morning at breakfast my son said that he had woken up in the middle of the night because he had felt something thick like a wall – a strong barrier – between the two beds. I was very shocked and told him that I had had the very same feeling. We thought it most odd.

'Friday night came, our last night on the island. The next day we were going to see an old ruined church half way up the mountain, the only place we had not seen on the island, then we were going home. We went to bed excited at the thought of seeing these old ruins in the morning. Then about 4.00 a.m. my daughter sat up, still asleep, and said in a loud voice, "Oh mum, look at those beautiful red roses."

'Thinking to myself that she was having a lovely dream I gently laid her down and went to sleep saying, "Yes they are nice aren't they," and said no more about it.

'The next day we went to the old ruin. It was very interesting. I was standing looking at a hole in the rock where the old monks used to wash. Suddenly I heard my son's voice behind me saying, "Oh mum, look at those beautiful red roses."

'I couldn't turn around for a moment as I remembered that I had already heard those exact same words in the middle of the night from my daughter. When I did look, my son was standing looking at an old half-sunken grave stone. I couldn't make out the words on it, but as I was standing there, that same terrible feeling of despair and hopelessness swept over me again.

'It made me wonder just what it was that was trying to get at us. Was something or someone trying to reach us across the years? Had someone been killed there in one of the many battles? Did someone leave the island to seek his fortune never to return? I can never, to this day, look at a red rose without remembering Bute. I have never felt anything like it before or since and I hope I never will.'

∞

FOR many years Jim worked in a large mental hospital in the Lothian area, the name of which he has asked to be withheld for fear that any of the present patients might become alarmed.

'The main reception office where I worked was normally staffed only by myself and my secretary Nancy. It was typical of hospital administration areas, being encased by a semi-circular partition, the top half being of glass panels that gave me a view of the large reception area and a corridor that led into the main office and ward complex. It had one communicating door to this area. To the right of the reception office were the waiting rooms and a large room that was used for medical meetings. Anyone entering either area had to pass alongside the reception office and would be plainly visible to whoever was in the office.

'On the afternoon in question it was quiet. A hospital shop in the main area had closed and the few people who were about passed up or down the corridor.

'With one eye on some paperwork and the other on the enquiry hatch I suddenly saw someone pass along by the glass-panelled front of the office. It was a woman and I had a fleeting impression of grey coat, hair, and some form of head-wear. She passed out of view and the only direction possible was that of the waiting room or the large main area. Nancy, who was also in the office with me saw her. Being a mental hospital we took particular note of everyone's comings and goings with a view to security and patient welfare. I said to Nancy that I would see what our visitor wanted and find out who she was. I went into the waiting room which was empty, as were the adjoining rooms. The rear exit door was, as always, locked, and I had the key.

'I went back into the reception office and told Nancy that I could not see the lady anywhere. She thought that I was joking so she went to find the woman herself, but came back shortly afterwards saying that she could find no trace of her. For some reason I noted the time. It had just turned 4.00 p.m.

'During the next couple of days Nancy and I mentioned to a few people what had happened. As is usual in hospitals the word spread and some thought that it was a joke until a night-duty nursing officer of many years service came to see me one evening. She asked me to describe what I had seen and at what time I saw it. When I went over the story with her she told me that I had seen Sister Alice – then she told me the story of Sister Alice.

'The large room next to my reception office had at one time been used by the Medical Superintendent and at 4.00 p.m. each afternoon it was Sister Alice's job to go to report to him on the day's happenings. Sister Alice was of medium height, wore a grey uniform and always passed alongside the glass panels on her nightly journey. She was found dead one morning in her room and a small metal plaque to her memory was placed in the grounds.

'This story was confirmed by several long service staff who worked with her. They feel she walks on her rounds to this day.'

∞

ANOTHER hospital story comes from Bob, a worker who

for some years lived in the grounds of the hospital with his wife and family.

'The house dated from 1898 and was one of a row of eight or nine. There were two rooms downstairs plus a kitchen and three bedrooms (one large and two small). All rooms were served by electric lights as was the hall and stairway. I mention this as it may be of importance. The bulbs used were all 100 Watt pearl for maximum light.

'Our daughter Jayne had been put to bed in her own room at about 8.00 p.m. Her bedroom contained toys, books and the pram used when she had been a baby. She was three years old at this time. My wife and I were downstairs when we heard Jayne screaming at the top of her voice. I jumped up and ran towards the door of the living room which led directly to the stairway. I switched on the stairs light then, looking up as I took my first step, I saw a figure some two or three steps from the top. I can describe it as every detail is still vividly clear to me after all those years.

'Using the stair wall as a reference point, it was about five feet tall, clad in a long white Edwardian style dress nipped in at the waist and with small red and white daisy-type flowers on it. I even noticed that the flowers were raised slightly above the dress material as if they had been sewn on. I did not see the woman's face, only a blur. As I started up the stairs the figure turned and went out of sight into the top of the stairway which was at right angles to the stairs themselves. I still remember clearly how the ankle length dress draped itself as the woman turned.

'Going into our daughter's room I saw her standing in her cot bed still screaming, "Don't let that lady take my pram." I took her downstairs, still very upset. She spent the rest of that night in our bed.

'Some days later our eldest daughter and little Jayne were in the front room. My wife was out. I was making coffee in the kitchen when my eldest daughter came in with Jayne in her arms. Jayne was crying and white faced. There was, she had told my eldest daughter, someone in the room – a lady who had frightened her, the same lady who had tried to take her pram away.

'Because the pram seemed to be the attraction we sold it a few days later and we never had any trouble since. I wondered if we had got ourselves caught up in some kind of time warp whereby moments from the past were somehow relived by the woman in the white dress. I wonder if she could have been a baby's nanny.'

∞

MORAG of Argyllshire wonders if anyone can throw some light on a mystery which has kept her guessing for years. She appeals to anyone who knows the Lochgilphead area, in particular the hamlet of Slockavullin which is situated about 8 miles north west of Lochgilphead.

'Slockavullin was built for the workers of the nearby Poltalloch Estate and there is only one road into it. It was around mid-day and I had taken my baby son who was in his pram and my dog Ziggy, a golden labrador, out for a walk. I was returning home when I noticed a young girl aged about six or seven standing at the entrance to Poltalloch Estate. I had never seen this girl before and the thing that struck me was that she was dressed in old fashioned clothes. Also I felt that she was standing in a most strange place. If she had been waiting for a lift in a car, the other side of the road would have been more appropriate.

'I walked on towards her feeling a little apprehensive and then I looked around for Ziggy. I was alarmed to see the dog standing right in the middle of the road stock still, the stick still in her mouth, staring at the girl. I walked on calling on Ziggy all the time but still she stood there not moving a muscle – just staring at the girl.

'I walked past the young girl, said hello to her then called on Ziggy again. My dog came slowly up the road with the stick still in her mouth, never taking her eyes off the young girl. Suddenly when Ziggy was about ten yards from the girl, she dropped the stick, started running and shot round the corner past the girl, barking furiously with her hackles up.

'This made the hairs on the back of my neck rise as Ziggy loves children and usually runs up to them to be patted. I began to push the pram faster and faster all the time looking back over my shoulder to see what the girl was doing. To my amazement she vanished completely.

'A few years after this I was talking to a friend who used to visit Slockavullin. We began recalling old times and I started to tell him the story about when I was passing the entrance to the estate. He immediately cut me off saying, "Stop. Don't tell me." It transpired that once he had been driving home to Slockavullin at three o'clock in the morning and he saw a young girl aged six or seven wearing old fashioned clothes standing at the side of the road about 50 yards from the spot where I had seen her.

'Naturally he was very interested to hear my story. Despite asking local people about this I was unable to find out anything that might explain what I had seen. Today I still admit to a shiver going up my spine when I recall this incident.'

∞

WHEN James Robertson, a resident of Morris Plains, New Jersey, USA, was on holiday in Scotland a few years ago, he found an old document in the archives of the Robertson Clan Museum at Bruar, Perthshire. The museum is located along the old road between Blair Atholl and Calvine near the point where the Bruar water empties into the Garry River.

It transpires that in the 1920s another James Roberston, who was a resident of the Loch Rannoch area in Perthshire, was confined to bed with a heart ailment. To while away the lonesome hours he decided to write down his recollections of his youth for the benefit of his children. He called it "Memories of Rannoch".

The work was divided into chapters, each on a different aspect of life in the Highlands during the 1860s and 1870s. The second chapter was entitled "Old Auchtarsin Ghosts". Auchtarsin was a small village east of Kinloch Rannoch where James Robertson had lived as a boy and which has now disappeared from the map.

The link between James Robertson of Loch Rannoch and James Robertson of New Jersey is that the latter's grandfather had been the gamekeeper for the Dunalastair Estate near the now disappeared village of Auchtarsin. He had emigrated to the States in 1875 bringing his wife, two daughters and a son. That son was the father of the present day American James Robertson.

James Robertson of Auchtersin tells his story as follows: 'On 16 April 1925 I had a recurrence of the cardiac trouble which brought my working life to a close in the middle of

June 1920. I had hoped at first that a few days rest in bed would restore me to that measure of health which I enjoyed for the four previous years when I was able to crawl about and do some useful turns in the little shop. But the days lengthened into weeks, the weeks into months and the months into years and here I am, still in bed. My friends and comrades of the busy world have passed out of my life, one by one, as the creatures of the wild drop away from their maimed or diseased fellows. Even my 40 years of activity with their seemingly purposeless striving have grown dim in retrospect and have now almost faded from my memory.

'The more dim those strenuous years become, the more clearly and lovingly I find my mind reverting to my early days and to the old familiar, kindly people. Alas! they have now passed away and

> Year by year the landscape grows
> Familiar to the stranger's child.

'My memories remain fresh and green within me and it is to pass them on thus to my children, as much as to beguile the tedium of the weary wait, that I have written down these rambling recollections in this book. I told some of these stories many times over to my motherless wee lassies at bedtime, but they soon forgot them – even as I forgot many old-world tales my father told me.

'If the writing of them down does nothing more, it will give them a glimpse of the world in which their father and grandfather lived. That is all I can hope for.

'With that, I will leave the manuscript, shaky and blotted as it is to the care of my children, and if they sometimes read it in their moments of leisure, I hope it will awaken in them kindly memories of their father.

'The greatest bane of my childhood and youth was the almost universal belief in ghosts. No road or path leading anywhere from Auchtarsin was without its ghosts and according to all accounts, few people who walked home at night from Kinloch, Bridge of Kynachan, or Trinafour, escaped their attention.

'My father's house at Easter Ballintuim, being an old farmhouse, had an exceptionally large kitchen. It also had a very wide fireplace round which a circle of neighbours sat, night after night during the winter, and told their awful tales. The children played about in the semi-darkness behind and listened with bated breath when some particularly weird experience was being related.

'The most frightful ghost on the Auchtarsin circuit was the one that haunted the road at Eas a' Chliabhain. Its *modus operandi* was to leap on the traveller's back from behind the milestone and try to throttle him. That is perhaps why its victims were unable to describe its appearance – if it had any – or to supply any definite particulars.

'Once a respectable kirk-going crofter affirmed that, on his way home, the ghost sprang on his back at the milestone and made a determined attempt to get at his throat. He managed, with immense difficulty, to keep it from getting a grip, running all the while at a great pace towards the curling pond, about a quarter of a mile further west. Where the overflow from the pond crossed the road, the ghost – being unable to cross running water – had perforce to drop off. The victim was found early next morning lying unconscious by the roadside.

'On another occasion a worthy young farmer was passing on his way home, whistling just to keep his courage cheery, when he heard, above the roar of the east wind, a rustle behind the milestone. With the greatest presence of mind, he quickly drew a sacred circle round about himself with his stick and stood in the centre waiting. No ghost came so he thought he would sit down. Time passed and still no ghost came. Feeling tired, he thought he would stretch himself. Still no ghost appeared. At daybreak he got up and went home. There was dust and gravel all over his clothes and it was fortunate for him there was no motor traffic in those days, as the circle that had protected him so effectively was in the very centre of the road.

'Another man, like a certain king of Spain, got his beard singed. He was very cautiously passing the milestone when he suddenly felt the grip of fiery fingers at his throat. There could be no doubt of the personality of his assailant for there was an overpowering smell of brimstone. After a desperate struggle, he succeeded in freeing himself, and so got home.

'All these incidents occurred before my time, but although I frequently heard the names of the persons mentioned, they have completely escaped memory.

'I can speak from my own recollection, however, of the Rev. Murdoch Corbett, the Free Church Minister of Bridge of Kynachan, who would on no account pass Eas a' Chliabhain alone after nightfall. Whether he had ever seen the ghost is not known, but when his pastoral duties detained him late about Auchtarsin, he invariably recruited a bodyguard of young men who saw him and his terrier safely across the Bridge of Tomain Buidhe.

'Prior to the 40s of the last century the road did not pass Eas a' Chliabhain at all. It struck off a few yards west of Dalreoch, passed up behind the Coille Beithe, and down through Baiul'Ur.

'The ghost at Eas a' Chliabhain must therefore have been a comparatively recent institution – a mere parvenu among ghosts. Indeed, there was no word or sign of a ghost at that place until after the death of young Tailor MacFarland of Auchtarsin who lost his life there on the night of Feill na Drochaid about 80 years ago. There was a mystery connected with the tragic occurrence that was never cleared up. His body was found the following morning in a pool among the rocks above the Eas. The discovery was made by his father and some other men who seemed to know fairly well where to look. It was conveyed, very carefully covered up, to his home at Auchtarsin where his parents, contrary to the usual custom, declined to allow the neighbours to view it.

'This unusual proceeding came to the ears of old Dr. Menzies, the local medical man, who resided a little distance below Auchtarsin, at the Home Farm (now "The Gardens") which he then leased. The doctor soon made a point of calling but when the parents demurred to let him view the remains, he peremptorily insisted and had his way. After a brief examination he informed the father that he was sure that his son had not met his death by drowning. But whatever the nature of the report, if any, that the doctor made to the authorities, no action was taken.

'The two persons last seen in the deceased's company, Ann Robertson – "Ann Mhor" – a young woman reported to be his sweetheart, and John Forbes, a middle-aged married man, both of Auchtarsin, incurred, perhaps unjustly, a good deal of obloquy from the neighbours and the people of the countryside. In partial justification of this hostile attitude, it was noted in particular, that neither of them ever again passed by Eas a' Chliabhain. Forbes died without a sign before I can remember, Ann Mhor, who never married, lived to be an old woman. I remember when she was lying on her death bed, hearing one old dame whisper to another, "Do you think she will confess?"; but she didn't. As to the mystery of how Tailor's body got into the pool, this still remains unsolved.

'About half a mile above Muileann a' Mhadaidh, on the north side of the old road from Auchtarsin to Struan, there is a large flat-topped rhomboid-shaped stone called "Clach na Deisdinn". Here, tradition says, some petty chief at one time held his court, with power and pit and gallows. When the evidence in a trial was inconclusive, the die was cast on this stone. If it indicated the accused was innocent, he was released, if guilty, he was led to another stone called "Clach na Ceann" a few yards to the east, and beheaded.

'There is no record or tradition of anything else that was tragic or unusual having happened there, nor any trace of a burial ground, or any of the usual concomitants of a ghostly visitation, yet people passing the spot after dark had the eerie sensation of being jammed in a seething, invisible crowd. Some were even pushed violently off the road. Nothing at all could be seen but the confused hum of a multitude could be heard, as one sufferer put it, "like a skep of bees inside your head."

'The experience left the victim very limp and very late getting home, but he had the solitary consolation of knowing that it would be accepted as an all-sufficient explanation – which was sometimes as necessary next morning as a hair from a certain dog!

'Allt Ionalais is about three miles west from Auchtarsin on the road to Kinloch. It is not wild or eerie, or even very desolate. The road runs smooth and straight from Ballin-

285

loan to the burn, and after an obtuse angle, runs smooth and straight thence to Sron an Tachair. It would be expected that a ghost associated with a burn of the name of Allt Ionalais would be considerably under-proof, but such was not the case. He was a strenuous, but discriminating ghost who clanked his chains with great vigour and chose his clients with care. The principal among these was Stewart Campbell, or "The Drover". He was the farmer of Drumchastle and a well known character in the neighbourhood for many years. After spending a few shining hours at the MacDonald Arms Inn he was apt to turn noisy and quarrelsome. At that stage the landlady Bell Craw would turn him out and he would depart for home in a state of fiery indignation against the "dry parched land of Kinloch and all its inhabitants."

'When half way along Dail aite Mhuic, the drover invariably commenced to bellow one of Dugald Buchanan's Gaelic hymns which lasted until he came to Allt Ionalais. There, if the spectre manifested himself, the drover, on his knees, made a full and vocal confession of all his misdemeanours and registered vows of eternal reformation – all of which was, singularly enough, broadcast over Rannoch the next day.

'On the whole, the Allt Ionalais ghost was less aggressive than his confreres at Eas a' Chliabhain and Muileann a' Mhadaidh, and the seasoned veterans of Auchtarsin, with few exceptions, passed freely to and from Kinloch.

'On the south side of the river, up behind Tullochcrosk, close to the foot of Sidh Chaillean, lies a little reedy sheet of water known as Lochan Doimaich. A more wild and desolate spot can scarcely be imagined. The road from Rannoch to Appin of Dull passes close to its south side, and is overhung by a fairly high cliff which is rapidly disintegrating. A few dwarfed birches and other shrubs grow about its face which makes the narrow pass between cliff and water still more gloomy.

'Here, since very ancient times, long before there was anything but a footpath through the pass, a ghost must have had its quarters. It comes not from the cliff nor from a cave, nor from anywhere on dry land, but from the Lochan, so it must be a water kelpie which is a very old form of ghost indeed. It was said to snatch solitary wayfarers from the road and dive with them into the centre of the Lochan, which was reputed to be of fabulous depth. Although its activities had considerably diminished in my time, belated travellers had still to keep a wary eye and ear on the Lochan. Many a tale was told in Auchtarsin of mysterious plungings and splashings heard in the dark pool at night.

∞

DAVID of Strathclyde remembers with fondness his dear aunt Marion who sadly died in 1982 in her 93rd year.

'I will always remember her with great affection for her joy of living, for her constant wit and for her good nature. As a young woman of 18 years of age she had a most amazing experience which she was to remember for the rest of her long life.

'It was November 1908 and the old Victorian city of Glasgow had once more awakened to another bitterly cold morning. The clip-clop of horses hooves could be heard loud and clear as they hauled their heavy loads through the city. Well wrapped figures of the city's work force could be seen hurrying along the streets making their way to their places of work. The only comfort to be found was indoors in the snug cosy little houses in the great sprawling tenement buildings.

'Marion was one of a family of five. Their home was in the Kinning Park district of Glasgow. The family had just finished breakfast. Marion's brothers and sisters had already left for work and she was just about to set off to her own job when her mother told her to go and get a heavy scarf as it was so cold.

'Marion went to her bedroom which was in semi-darkness, the only light coming in from the street lighting. As she opened her dresser drawer to take out her scarf she got a strange feeling that someone was watching her. She turned round and saw her uncle Willie standing there in the middle of her bedroom.

'This suprised her as Willie lived right across the other side of the city. Marion was just about to mention to him that she had not heard him come in the front door when he smiled at her and then just faded before her eyes. She was very shaken but was impressed by the serene look she had seen on his face. Marion ran to the living room to blurt out what she had seen to her mother. She was a very matter of fact type of woman and told the girl that she was not to be silly and that she must have been dreaming.

'Marion set off for work but found it very hard to concentrate on her job as a baking assistant, her mind being in a turmoil, remembering what she had seen that morning. Her long day ended and she made her way home. She was met at the front of the tenement by her mother who was waiting, white-faced and upset. Her mother took her by the arm and told her that she had been notified that at exactly 7.00 that morning Marion's uncle Willie had died. That was the time that Marion had seen him in her darkened bedroom.

'Even as an old lady, Marion would often talk of that morning so long ago when her favourite uncle came to say good-bye to her for the last time.'

∞

A MAN called Donald MacLeod was brought up in a small village on the island of Lewis in the Western Isles.

'My mother died when I was three years of age and I was brought up by my grandmother to whom I was very close. After national service I joined the Edinburgh City Police and although my family remained on Lewis, one uncle in particular kept in constant touch with me. In fact I was named after him.

'Uncle Donald was a great character. He was a fisherman and from the time I was a small boy he used to delight me with his sea-faring stories. When he went herring fishing in Yarmouth he always used to bring me back a big stick of Yarmouth rock.

'I got married and went to live in London where I worked for the C.I.D. Early one morning I came home from night shift very tired indeed. I went straight to bed and fell asleep but something was making me restless. I remember at one point – I wasn't quite sure whether I was asleep or awake – but I was aware that I was sweating profusely.

'I then had a dream that I was standing on the deck of a herring drifter in the Atlantic in the midst of a heavy sea. Uncle Donald was standing beside me but there was no other person in sight. We started to haul in the herring nets, just the two of us. The nets seemed to be caught in the sea by something or other and no matter how hard we hauled we could not get them over the side of the boat. Heavy waves started to crash over us and I began to feel panic inside thinking that the boat was going to be swamped by the sea any minute.

'The strange thing that I noticed then was that the boat was not sinking nor was she making any headway. I was in turmoil both mentally and physically.

'I awoke abruptly at that point to find my wife standing at the foot of the bed. She was holding a telegram in her hand. Before she said a word I sat up in bed and said, "My uncle Donald is dead." She handed me the telegram which I opened. It was from my father. It read: "REGRET YOUR UNCLE DONALD IS DEAD."

∞

WHEN Janet was a young girl she worked in Staff College House in Camberley, Surrey as a cook to Viscount Gort – later Field Marshal Gort.

'One night at a dance', says Janet, 'I met a young waiter who told me he worked at Wellington College, an establishment for young army cadet officers. His name was Albert and he was very handsome and dashing. We got to know each other and I soon found out that he was mad keen to go into the army.

'We continued to see each other at various dances and social gatherings and soon we were going out together on a steady basis. I had no doubt whatsoever in my mind that I had fallen in love with Albert and although I wasn't a

290

hundred per cent sure, I had a feeling that he felt the same way about me. In those days everything was done in a much more formal manner and so it was some time before we got around to the stage of telling each other what our real feelings were.

'I was overjoyed when one night Albert told me that he was in love with me and that I was constantly on his mind. I had secretly hoped to hear those words, sometimes hardly daring to think that he could possibly think as much of me as I did of him. Our romance blossomed and naturally I was looking forward to the day when he would ask me to become engaged to him.

'I became very good friends with Albert's mother, a delicate lovely lady who treated me like her own daughter. Albert was her only child, and she seemed delighted at the prospect of having me for a daughter-in-law. One awful day Albert's mother had a heart attack and was rushed to hospital. We both went straight away to her bedside where she lay critically ill. She had not been agreeable about him going into the army and she always told me that she was afraid for him. In fact she even tried to get me to try to talk him out of it.

'Albert's mother never recovered and he was devastated by her death. I tried to comfort him as best I could but he was in a state of deep shock. With the help of one of the footmen at Staff College House we made a beautiful wreath of flowers with a lovely ribbon tied around it. I watched helplessly as Alberta placed that wreath on his mother's grave. I felt somehow then that a part of him had died with her and it was gone from me forever.

'One afternoon we met in a park but he seemed a bit strange and unusually quiet. I asked him if anything was wrong. He told me that he had enlisted in the regular army. We were both only 22 at the time. He told me that he would love to marry me but there was an army rule (before the Second World War) which prevented soldiers marrying before they reached the age of 26.

'I was in love and starry-eyed and told him that I could easily wait. We talked it over and he felt that it would be unfair to get engaged as young soldiers were being sent out to Aden, Singapore and India for a seven year spell of duty. He was worried that he might become a casualty before he could marry me.

'The day came for him to leave; I was broken-hearted. We exchanged little tokens: he gave me his late mother's brooch and I gave him a small bible to take with him. I was overwhelmed with sadness when he finally walked away from me that day. It was as if my whole world was closing in around me.

'The first few months of separation from Albert were utter misery for me; on looking back I sometimes wonder how I got through. We wrote to each other but then suddenly the letters stopped. He did tell me in one of his letters that he was due to be sent overseas. I don't know what happened after that or if he ever tried to write to me again. All I know is that after months and months of waiting and praying that he was safe I finally heard the terrible news that I had been dreading. Albert was missing, presumed dead.

'For weeks on end I used to sit staring into space. I could hardly eat or sleep and I actually thought that I was going to die; I had no will to live. My family rallied round me and tried to make me snap out of it but they could see that it was hopeless.

'My cousin introduced me to a young Scotsman. I could see that this was just another ploy to try to get me back to normal again and I was really not interested. I'd reached the stage where I just stopped caring about everything, so when this pleasant man asked me to go out with him I agreed. In a way I felt sorry for him as I knew that I was not good company; I could not get Albert out of my mind. He seemed to like me in spite of my off-hand attitude and he asked me out more and more.

'I could have fainted when out of the blue one day the Scotsman asked me to marry him. I'd no idea that he was so serious about me. I told him that it was out of the question. He knew nothing about Albert and I just couldn't find the words to tell him. He persisted, telling me that even if I did not love him he was sure that I would grow to love him and that he so much wanted to take care of me.

'He was so dejected looking each time I refused his proposal that I started to weaken. I did not want to hurt him. In my own mind I knew that no one could ever take Albert's place in my heart, so I told myself it wouldn't make any difference who I married.

'Eventually I married my Scotsman and he took me to live in Morayshire in a little house near to his family. From the very start I knew that I had made a mistake. The marriage was shaky from the first moment. However I was far away from my own home so there was nothing for it but to try to make the best of the situation. To be fair, my husband did try to please me and he was an excellent provider. I could have no complaints really, it's just that he wasn't Albert. I knew, during those early months of married life, that I was still deeply in love with Albert and nothing on this earth would ever change that.

'One day in 1940 in the month of June, my husband answered a knock on our front door. My heart jumped as I heard Albert's voice. He distinctly told my husband that his jeep had landed in a ditch and that he needed help.

'My mind went into a panic. I was so desperately afraid that he would see I had married and that I had not waited for him after all. I did not want him to see me in that house with my husband. I ran to the living room window and looked out through the lace curtains. There he stood, tall and straight, dressed in officers' walking out uniform with a black beret, brown shoes and gloves and a silver-tipped cane. I ran back from the window in case he would spot me.

'I heard my husband tell him that he'd be out in a minute, he just wanted to put on his shoes. When he went outside in a matter of just a few moments, Albert was nowhere to be seen.

'I was weeping uncontrollably. I knew why Albert had come to Scotland. It was his way of letting me know that he understood how I felt about him. I had to run upstairs to the bathroom so that my husband would not see me crying. When I regained my composure I went back to the living room. My husband was quite baffled, saying there was no sign of the officer or a jeep anywhere. He even asked our neighbour who was out in the front garden if he'd seen where the officer had gone. Our neighbour asked, "What officer?" My husband was quite shocked by the whole business and he kept telling me over and over again that he knew he'd spoken to the soldier at our front door. He even asked me if I'd heard them talking. I just nodded, afraid that I would let my true feelings be revealed.

'Life went on and although I never ever got over Albert I had a reasonable life with my husband. Not exactly what I would call happy, but I always reminded myself that there were a lot of people worse off than me. In 1987 my husband died. Naturally I was saddened at the loss, for although our marriage was far from ideal I had been wedded to a good man who had always looked after me through the years.

'On 19 January 1988 at 9.15 in the morning, while I was sitting alone in my kitchen having breakfast, a brilliant white light spread across the ceiling. It was a cold winter morning and there was no sunshine at all. I wondered what on earth was causing this light. Then it seemed to cencentrate into an even brighter, more intense light which moved from the ceiling to a spot half-way down the kitchen wall.

'I sat staring at this strange light so bright that it almost dazzled me. I'd never seen anything like it before. I watched in stunned silence as I saw the figure of Albert appear in the centre of the light, growing clearer and bigger until there he was – right there in my kitchen – dressed in exactly the same officer's uniform as I had seen him in the day he knocked on our door.

'I remember jumping to my feet I was so thrilled to see him, but as I took a step towards the light it instantly faded and vanished. I just stood in the middle of my kitchen for ages hardly able to believe what I had just seen.

'I wondered if I had been on Albert's mind that particular day. I'll never know but I've thought about it constantly. I know in my heart that we will surely meet again some day.'

∞

SO ends our ghost stories from Scotland. In this section we have touched upon phantom soldiers, ghostly lovers, mist-shrouded kilted apparitions, murderous ministers and even a disappearing Trustee Savings Bank.

We have kept away from previously published or documented stories which is why you did not read about Tam O'Shanter's mare by Burns or the ghost of Banquo from Shakespeare's *Macbeth* (although we came near on that one). We have also avoided fairies, imps, warlocks, besoms, monsters and the legions of legendary beings which undoubtedly make for an entertaining read but do little for the credibility of the story.

All of the stories have been given to us as true accounts of real experiences and from the content it is easy to see that for most people their glimpse into the unknown has left them undoubtedly moved and often puzzled. Perhaps one of the strangest and certainly the most brief account of an unexplained event comes from Ronald Pattinson:

'While I am not sure how far I believe in ghosts, when I was a soldier in the last war I had a strange experience which I have never been able to account for.

'One morning after breakfast I left the camp and walked down to the harbour of the little island where I was in Orkney and crossed over to South Ronaldsay. Having attended to the business in hand, I returned and climbed back to the camp which was situated at the top end of the island. This was about 1.00 p.m. and I was looking forward to having my dinner so there was no question of my being sleepy or dreaming this.

'Shortly before I reached the camp I looked up and there before my eyes I saw the whole of the north of Scotland lifted up before me, from Thurso right down to Inverness. I could see all the mountains as on a map. The vision so impressed me that I retain the memory to this day. Was I somehow or another seeing a ghost of Scotland?'

Chapter Six
OVERSEAS

MR. COLE, presently living in Essex, England served in France in the last war and was stationed at Eisenhower's Advance Headquarters on arrival into the outskirts of the recently liberated Paris.

'The Command Headquarters used by the German High Command had been in outbuildings of the Palace of Versailles, mainly in the old stables, and these were speedily converted to our use. Living accommodation was very scarce for a variety of reasons, therefore temporary sleeping quarters were found in the old Satory Barracks on the hill overlooking the main palace until something better could be found. It was here, during a period in late 1944, that I experienced what could appropriately be called a proper Winter's Tale, though it was absolutely true.

'Paris proper was still out of bounds to us so we set up a makeshift Warrant Officers' and Sergeants' Mess in a disused store at the far end of the main barrack room. Since electricity was rationed for the capital to a couple of hours a night, I was forced, as Mess President, to do the stocktaking by the light of a flickering candle.

'I had just finished one night and I was awaiting the arrival of the bar steward when the lights came on earlier than expected. I became aware of the grubby condition of my hands, previously unnoticed. I went to the rear washroom which consisted of a couple of cold water basins (no toilets) apparently installed by the outgoing German Army.

'Whilst I was washing in the freezing water by the light of a bare low watt bulb, I was aware that someone else was using the other basin in the far corner. He never said a word to me but I noticed that he was wearing a dark greatcoat. With the soap in my eyes I commented over to him about the bitterly cold night – in suitable army parlance.

'Not receiving any answer, I turned to get a better view of him as I dried my face. He just continued to wash his hand and did not even think it worth his while to acknowledge my friendly chit-chat. I was just about to discuss his parentage for being so surly, when he disappeared.

'At that moment, the corporal bar steward walked in from the corridor and asked who I had been talking to. I explained as best I could that a tall bloke in a heavy coat had been washing his hands in the other basin and I'd had a few words with him. I then said the man had somehow vanished. He shrugged his shoulders and muttered something under his breath about "first signs". Then, in no uncertain terms, he pointed out to me that nobody had, or could have, passed him in the corridor without him seeing them.

'I dismissed the episode until nearly eight months later when I was the British Office Commandant of Berlin and I met a Warrant Officer of the unit that took over the barracks when we moved out. He asked me if I knew that the barrack room was reputed to be haunted by the ghost of a Colonial soldier who had committed suicide rather than join Napoleon's Army at the front.'

∞

A CANADIAN, Jean Gordon, was on holiday at her

parents' home in Buckie, Banffshire, Scotland, in 1948. She had emmigrated to Canada on her own in the year 1921 when she was only 17 years of age.

'It was a long 27 years later before I was able to get home to Scotland to see my parents and family. I was overwhelmed when I reached Buckie and saw the magnificent house which my parents had bought on dad's retirement from the railroad.

'I arrived at the house about 4.00 p.m. feeling a bit tired but very excited at seeing mother and dad and some of my family again. My bedroom was on the first floor at the right hand side of the building. Around 11.00 p.m. I went to bed and soon fell asleep.

'I felt my arm being shaken so I opened my eyes and saw that daylight was just breaking. I turned round and found a wrinkled old lady, very tall, bending over me. She wore black and had leg-of-mutton sleeves and her neck-piece was made of white lace. I was rather agitated at being awakened in such a way and I looked down at her hand, which was still shaking my arm, to see that it was very bony.

'The first moment I saw her I was in such a sleepy state that I just assumed that she must be a friend of my parents, but then as it sank through to me that the mode of her dress was so antiquated I felt a tingle of fear. The feeling that all was not normal took a hold of me and as the panic spread throughout me I let out a loud scream. She let go of me and started to back away but all the time she kept staring at my face which really unnerved me. I got myself up to a sitting position in the bed and watched as she floated backwards and then just merged into the wall and the next second she was gone.

'I was so disorientated by the woman that I wanted to

300

find out where she could have gone. I knew that I had seen her in my room and I had felt her shaking my arm so she must have gone somewhere. I got out of bed and looked all around the room and even moved a heavy dresser to see if there were any hidden exit doors behind it but there were none. I assumed that no one could have heard my scream, so in a most perplexed state, I went back to bed, wondering about the thing I'd seen.

'Next morning when I went downstairs I asked them if they had heard my scream but no one had. My mother asked me what had happened so I related everything about the old lady. I was a bit surprised to see how lightly my mother took this. She then told me with a laugh that I must have seen the ghost. I was not prepared for this and by my expression my mother must have guessed as much.

'She went on to tell me that because all of the family had become so used to living with the ghost, she had ceased to be a threat. Seemingly the fisher folk of Buckie had always referred to my parents' property as The Haunted House because there once had been a terrible lovers' quarrel in one of the rooms and the woman involved had met her death in a most mysterious manner.

'Later that day my mother took me to the nearby cemetery to see the grave of the woman who had died as a result of the quarrel. On first sight we were both amused to see that the cemetery attendants were carrying out some work on her grave and they had dug up the sods which had been covering her coffin. These where piled high up by the side of the grave. My sense of humour soon changed to a foreboding feeling as a bizarre thought occured to me: when the workmen had unearthed her coffin could she have wandered out of that grave and into my bedroom?'

∞

JANE Brewin, a lady from Cirencester in England went to Ireland to stay at a house not far from Dublin. She relates that, 'Caroline and Brigid Montgomery were cousins of my father, so they were my cousins once removed. All their lives they had lived about 12 miles outside Dublin and had made a lovely garden in what must have been an old sandpit. It was hollow-shaped, open towards the south, and looked towards the huge Sugarloaf mountain.

'The cousins died in the 1940s and the house then had a succession of owners. In the 1960s it was bought by a Mr. & Mrs. Fitzgerald. Mrs. Fitzgerald was a keen as well as learned gardener and she and her husband set about restoring the garden after its years of neglect.

'A few years ago they invited me over to see them. They wanted me to tell them about my relatives and the garden they had created. Taking tea with them on my arrival they told me about a recent visit they had made to Canada to see their married daughter. They had gone in the summer, but because there was so much unemployment in the Irish Republic they had worried about leaving the house empty. They had heard that many empty houses had been broken into so they had asked a colleague of Mr. Fitzgerald if he would stay in the house in their absence. He was delighted to do so since the house was close enough to Dublin for him to travel to work and he knew that he would enjoy being out of the city during the summer months. However, the man made one stipulation: He was no gardener and he refused to touch the garden or get involved with it in any way.

'When the Fitzgeralds returned from Canada they found

everything in order and they were pleased to find that their friend had obviously enjoyed himself. After the preliminary greetings the man asked them, "Who is the little old lady who wanders in the garden? I never managed to get near enough to speak to her."

'The Fitzgeralds could think of no old lady so they asked the old man who had lived in the next house for years and years if he had noticed any strange lady in their garden during their absence. The old man replied, "I saw her but it was only old Bridget Montgomery, fussing over her garden as usual."

∞

CHARLES from Karatina, in Kenya, Africa, tells of how his father was one of the first Indians who settled in the Nairobi area. His father had been a hard-working man and through his efforts he had built a bungalow. 'He came to like that bungalow as he liked his life. He had three sons and I was the eldest of all.

'As time went by, he became very ill and eventually died, but just before he drew his last breath he gave us all one last command; "Don't ever sell the bungalow – I built it for the family."

'Time went on and my two brothers and myself all found suitable wives and we all bought our own new modern houses and settled down to life with our own families.

'After my mother died, there was no one left living in the bungalow so my brothers and I decided that the only wise thing to do would be to sell the property and share out the money equally between the three of us.

'I started to look for a buyer and one day I met up with an

African businessman who became interested in viewing the property. I had shown him photographs of the exterior and an appointment was set up so that he could see the inside of it. The day came for me to take the businessman round the bungalow but that very same day my wife gave birth to a baby boy. The baby had not been expected for another two weeks but when it came early it upset all my plans and as you can imagine my main concern was to be with my wife and new son. With all the confusion I completely forgot about my appointment to show the man round my late parents' bungalow.

'The following day I went to see the businessman at his office hoping that he would forgive me for not turning up the previous day and that he would be understanding in view of the circumstances. We met and shook hands and I immediately started to apologise saying, "I am sorry that I could not keep the appointment yesterday because.." The man interupted me by saying, "It's okay, the man you sent showed me everything."

'I didn't know what he was talking about and asked him what he meant. I wondered for an instant if one of my brothers might have been at the bungalow without my knowledge, but then I remembered that I had the only set of keys with me all the time. In any case I knew that neither of them was in the area because they were unable to come to my home to celebrate the birth of my son. My house is quite close to the bungalow.

'I did not talk for a while as my mind was trying to work out who could have been at the bungalow to show this man around. The man, seeing how puzzled I was, tried to throw some light on the matter.

'He said that when he had approached the bungalow in

his car, he was met by an old Indian man with grey hair. The thing that he had noticed most about the old man was that there was a bit cut off his earlobe. I asked the businessman to give a full description of the Indian and he described my father down to the last detail. He then went on to give a precise description of every single room in the bungalow, all accurate in every detail, so I knew that he must have been inside the property to know these facts.

'However, although he seemed to identify my father to perfection I just could not believe that he could have seen a man who had been dead for years. I made no comment about who I thought had shown him around the house and I did not of course tell him anything about my father or the fact that he was dead.

'The businessman then said something which made my hair stand on end. He told me that although he had been treated with courtesy by the Indian who took pride in showing him all around the bungalow, the old man then told him that he was sorry but the bungalow was not for sale.

'Since my brothers and I agreed that it would be my responsibility to find a buyer for the bungalow because I was the only one living in the area, I felt that I would have to do everything I could to push the sale through. I could see that the businessman had been most impressed by what he had seen so I asked him if he would mind coming back to my own house so that we could talk over the details of the sale, and I assured him that there must have been some misunderstanding and that the bungalow was most certainly still up for sale.

'When we arrived at my house we got down to talking but the story he had told me about being shown round the

305

bungalow was still bewildering me. I went to a drawer and took out some old family photographs and showed them to the businessman. He immediately pointed to my father saying that this was the old Indian man who had shown him round the property.

'At that stage I'm afraid my expression must have given me away because instantly the man seemed to guess that there was something strange going on. I admitted to him that this old Indian man was my father and that he had died some years previously. The moment the businessman heard this he jumped up from his chair and made to leave my house saying that he was no longer interested in buying the bungalow because he knew that it would always be haunted by my father.

'I felt very odd when I had to relate the story to my brothers about how I lost the sale on the property. We gave the matter a lot of thought and between us we came to the conclusion that if father was going to scare off all our would-be purchasers like that then perhaps we'd better change our thinking. We decided then that the best thing to do would be to forget about selling the bungalow and to rent it out instead.

'Within a matter of days we found a very worthy tenant and to this day the bungalow has been rented out and over the years it has been the source of a steady income for all of our family – not a great deal, but money that we would not otherwise be receiving on a regular basis.

'My father had always been a strong-willed man and had always been able to win his way. It seems that even death had not changed him.'

∞

A STORY comes from Co. Kildare, Ireland, from Mr.

Patrick Joe Coyle: 'The following account comes from my late father who told me that a man called Mike Deeley from a village in Co. Kildare went to a fair with two young bullocks. He was unmarried and lived with his elderly parents.

'It grew late and the young man had not returned the seven miles home and his parents started to worry. They sat up till well after midnight, then went to bed trying to convince each other by various suggestions what the explanation of their son's absence might be. They had not entirely ruled out drink, and they anticipated his return the following morning showing the after effects.

'The next day when there was still no sign of the son old Mr. Deeley became quite cynical thinking that his boy had just run off with the money from the sale of the bullocks. Both parents were upset as they had never looked on their Mike as a potential thief.

'In those days many people left Ireland for America to seek their fortune so the Deeleys assumed that this must have been what had happened but they felt badly let down by the fact that they had not been informed about Mike's plans to leave the country. At the back of Mrs Deeley's mind, however, there was still a lingering doubt as she always claimed that her son would never intentionally upset her like that. On her suggestion a thorough search was made of the area, but there was no trace of Mike.

'Days passed into weeks and the weeks into months. Then, as the years passed on, the father, and later the mother, died, still without a single word from their missing son. Twenty one years went by and the name of Mike Deeley was all but forgotten except by a few of the old timers who would mention now and then, "Whatever could

307

have happened to Mike Deeley?" As is the way in rural Ireland the people are never short of an explanation and some of the old lads would say that he must have skipped it to America and that any day he would be back to the village sporting his fortune.

'Around that time several men had returned to their original homes in that part of Ireland after having done their 21 years service in some city in the States and retired on a grand pension. Always when one such man would return the stock question would be, "Did you see any sign of Tom Deeley's son in America?" as if America was just the size of our village where everyone knew each other.

'One day a number of men were cutting peat on the outskirts of our village when they came across a body which had been buried there. It had been perfectly preserved by the turf. Word went round the village like a flash for a door to be brought to the peat field. That was the normal means in Ireland at that time whereby a corpse would be carried. The body was placed on a wooden door and was left at the side of the road surrounded by locals waiting for the police to arrive.

'The village was rife with rumour and suggestion as to the identity of the body in the bog. On the way to the scene, the two policeman had picked up a returned emigrant in their horse-drawn police cart to give him a lift to his destination as they had encountered him on the road walking with two heavy suitcases. The inspector told the stranger that they would be pleased to take him the further three miles to the cottage he was aiming for but on the way they would have to stop to attend to a bit of police business that had cropped up.

'The stranger said that he quite understood the situation

as he himself had just spent 21 years in the Boston Police Force. He thanked the policemen for their kind offer of the lift to the cottage and agreed to wait in the van until they had attended to the matter in hand.

'At that moment one of the old timers came on the scene to see what all the fuss was about. He took one look at the face of the corpse and instantly recognized the features of the long lost Mike Deeley. He made his discovery known to the policemen who then made a close examination of the body and saw that foul means had brought about the death.

'Then the strangest thing happened. Whether it was a natural or an unnatural procedure I am not sure, but a gush of water spouted from the mouth of the corpse. Things have strange ways of coming to light, especially in Ireland, and the country folk around the corpse looked upon this as an omen. It might well have been the result of an accumulation of water within the body. Nevertheless, because suspicions had been aroused, some of the people began murmuring that whoever killed Mike Deeley must have scarpered off, probably to America. These remarks made the policemen think about the passenger they had in their cart.

'When they were lifting the door upon which the corpse was laid out, up onto the cart, they noticed that the stranger had gone into a severe state of shock. The inspector wondered at this since being that the stranger had been a seasoned policeman in the Boston Force he should be well used to seeing the odd dead body. There was something fishy about the way the man was staring at the face of the corpse with a look of abject fright on his face.

'Because of the stranger's reaction he was told by the inspector that due to the circumstances surrounding the identity of the corpse all people who had resided in the area at the time of Mike Deeley's disappearance 21 years earlier would be taken in to the police station for questioning. The stranger broke down on the way to the police station and admitted that he had murdered Mike and robbed him in a desperate effort to acquire the money he needed to help towards his fare to America all those years ago. He had buried him in the field not thinking that anyone would ever find the body in a million years. He had kept in touch with his relative in the village over the years and when there was no report whatsoever about the missing Mike, he assummed that his secret was secure for ever.

'The returned emigrant was charged and found guilty of murder and was later hung. Afterwards Mike Deeley's brother was asked how he felt. "It was great," he replied, "not to hear that they have hanged a man, but to know that my brother was not a thief after all." He added, "Wasn't it the pity though that the ouldfella [meaning his father] had not survived to hear the proof."

∞

MRS. Buller had an experience which, for years and years, she was afraid to discuss with anyone: 'I was very ill with a serious chest condition. The first thing I noticed was that my bedroom furniture looked as if it was leaning to the left. The next thing I remembered was being near the ceiling looking down at myself, watching myself talking to my two sons. All I could say was, "I can't see the ceiling – I can't see the ceiling," over and over again.

'I was very aware of the fact that I was hovering in mid air and I was overwhelmed by the marvellous feeling of lightness. Everything was at ease, I felt like a feather peacefully drifting and the best bit of all was that there was no pain whatsoever – just a lovely feeling of contentment. I remember thinking that I could hardly find words to describe the exquisite state that I was in. I looked down again at the other me who was stretched out on the bed and although I knew perfectly well that it was my body I just kept saying to myself, "Look at that stupid woman down there behaving like that!" I had no compassion for her at all and I felt so detatched from that body it was as if I was watching somebody else on the bed but at the same time I knew that it was me. Because I felt so fit and well and extremely alert from my vantage point I found it hard to believe that I had once been trapped inside the body of that woman on the bed.

'I don't remember much about going back into my body but I found that my husband had taken me downstairs and he was making me comfortable in front of the television saying that there was a good film on. The next thing I knew I was back up on the ceiling again and once more I could see the other me sitting there. I then became aware of watching the television again thinking that I had no idea what the film was about. With this came the realization that I was not on the ceiling any more and for some reason I began to cry. My children had never ever seen me cry before but the tears just flowed and flowed. It came to me at that point that the reason I could not see the ceiling earlier was that I was up there.

'On the following Saturday afternoon, I was sitting in my lounge at about 2.10 p.m. I know the exact time because I had looked at the clock to check, wondering if my eldest son would be home. He was married and serving with H.M. Forces in Germany where he lived with his wife and baby son. The next instant I found myself hovering near the ceiling. There was something very strange about everything though and when I looked down I did not recognize anything but suddenly I noticed that there was a photograph on the wall. It was a picture of my little grandson like the one which had been sent to me only bigger and in a frame. I remember being given a jolt as the realization swept over me that I was in Germany in my son's flat. I had never ever been to Germany in my life and had never seen any photographs of his flat but I just knew – goodness knows how – that I was there. I could see no sign of my physical body this time nor could I see any other people.

'I floated into the hall of the flat and then noticed where the bathroom door was open and I could see another door beside it which was closed. The kitchen door was open and I felt myself drift in there where I noticed that everything was neat and tidy and I took special notice of the colour scheme and the dishes. I then looked into the open lounge but there was no one in there either. I noticed that there was a clock on the wall and saw that it read 3.10 p.m.

'I floated along the corridor until I reached a child's bedroom which I knew must be where my grandson slept. There was a playpen on the floor with a pink elephant cuddly toy in it. I remember thinking that it was an unusual colour of toy to give a little boy as I would have expected it to be blue. At that I thought, "Well there's no point in phoning him if there's nobody at home", then the very next instant I found myself back in my own lounge again.

'Four hours later my son telephoned me. I asked him some questions about his flat and he was astounded to hear me describe the entire flat including the baby's bedroom. He confirmed that the playpen was indeed in the middle of

312

the floor and that there was a pink toy elephant in it. He explained that this was a present to the baby from their neighbours.

'I told him there was just one more thing I wanted to check with him; "Do you know that the clock on the wall of your lounge is fast by one hour?" He assured me that it was not fast so I must have been mistaken. It was after I put the receiver down that I realised that the time difference between Britain and Germany in the summer time is exactly one hour.'

∞

HELEN Swire was working in West Africa in the 1950s in a place called Warri on the Niger Delta. 'I lived in a company house, the gardens of which ran down to one of the tributaries of the Niger. It was the residents' custom to sit out in the evenings on the paved patio alongside the river, sipping cool drinks and chatting.

'Africa is never quiet. Even at night there is continuous music and laughter from the workers' quarters, the sound of bullfrogs and the thousands of insects which live in the bush, also the splashing of paddles from canoes which pass up and down the creeks.

'One evening I was having a drink with my neighbour, and just relaxing after a day's work in the intense heat. Suddenly, we both stopped talking and became aware of a deathly silence. There was no human voice, no rustle of insects, no movement on the river, not even a whisper, but the complete and utter absence of sound. Despite the heat of the tropical night, we both shivered and I could feel my skin break out in gooseflesh.

'After about five minutes, thankfully the normal sounds of the African night began to return. I heaved a deep sigh of relief. My neighbour, a Geordie, and a most practical and down-to-earth young man, admitted to me that the hair on his scalp had risen during the silence as had mine. We saw nothing but we were both overwhelmed by an indescribable atmosphere of evil which had descended on the place.

'Next morning when I mentioned the matter to my African houseboy he was very subdued and informed me that very bad ju-ju was about last night. Ju-ju is a kind of curse. Africans are very superstitious and if a person has a ju-ju put upon them they become very frightened and in extreme cases people have literally been frightened to death.

'The particular area where the incident took place is believed to be subject to hauntings by spirits which are said to be present in the river. The natives always used to sing in a loud chanting fashion as they came up the river and its tributaries in their canoes in an attempt to scare off these spirits. There was a fish festival every year when all the local tribesmen would travel up the river in their canoes, their bodies highly decorated by certain paints, colours and dyes which were meant to neutralize the power of the spirits.'

∞

HAROLD Hampson is a man who never had any time for what he calls 'spooks' and has always dismissed stories about anything unexplained as codswallop, but now he's not so sure. 'Last year my wife, daughter and myself all went to New Zealand to visit my son and his family.

'He had only recently immigrated and had purchased

eight-and-a-half acres of land in a very isolated spot. It was six miles to the nearest village, a place called Takaka, near Golden Bay on the northern tip of South Island. My son had cleared all the scrub and trees, and had cultivated the land to grow vegetables and fruit.

'My son had almost finished building a house for his family on the grounds and had completed two bedrooms by the time we arrived there. As he had a lot of work to get through on the building side, my wife, daughter and myself agreed to take the burden of the cultivation work away from him so each day we used to busy ourselves with tilling the land and planting all sorts of vegetables – sweetcorn, fruit, etc.

'We had been working on the land one particular morning and even though it was fairly early it was stifling hot. I was not quite acclimatized and felt a bit tired so I told my wife that I was just going into the house to have a lie down for a while.

'I drew the curtains to keep out the brilliant sunlight, settled down and closed my eyes to have a cat-nap. After no more than a few moments something made me open my eyes. From up in the corner of the shaded room near the ceiling a wicked looking face zoomed down to within a few feet of me. It was the most wicked looking face I had ever seen. He had dark skin like dried prunes, black rotted teeth and a fuzzy matted beard and long bushy hair. He gave me a sneering grin then shrank back into the corner of the room where he had come from. Three times this awful face zoomed down on me and then it disappeared. I went out of the house into the sunshine again but I decided not to mention my experience to anyone in case they became alarmed.

'A few days later my son told me that over 100 years ago the land he had bought had been a Mauri settlement and there was supposed to be a burial ground on the land. I could not get that face out of my mind and it struck me that it must have been a Mauri tribesman. I kept wondering why I should see such a thing and got the impression that I was being given some kind of warning.

'Within that week my wife took ill. I was very worried about her, so worried in fact that I arranged to return to England straight away. Before we had gone to New Zealand she had been perfectly fit and well. Very shortly after we got home she died.'

∞

AN ex-Singapore resident tells of the night a friend came into her house looking as white as a sheet. 'He was a big brawny R.A.F. policeman but he was reduced to a quivering jelly.

'He told us that he'd just come off duty and had got to the bottom of the hill which led to our houses when he saw a Malay girl standing at the corner. As it was a very dark night, he stopped and asked her if she wanted a lift. She said nothing, but got into his car. She was dressed in a sarang and had a flower in her hair, the perfume of which filled his car.

'When they got to the top of the hill our policeman friend turned round to ask the girl where she wanted to go to but she had vanished. He jammed on his brakes and sat there stunned. He then noticed that a frangipani flower was on the passenger seat.

'You can imagine how he felt. It took a long time for him

to get over it and he swore us to secrecy as he knew the ribbing he would receive if his mates got word of the incident. Needless to say he never gave anyone else a lift at night. He never even told his wife about the incident.

'We learnt later that just before our houses had been built, a Malay girl had been killed on the spot where he had picked up the stranger.'

∞

EILEEN, an English lady, had travelled to India one year to visit the family of her husband who had come to Britain several years earlier. Eileen was particularly looking forward to meeting her Indian mother-in-law as the woman had always begged her son, in her many letters, to bring his wife out to see her.

'We were not all that well off at the time so the only way we would ever manage the trip would be to go overland in our battered old blue van, taking ferry boats where necessary, and hopefully working our way when funds ran scarce. We set off with just the minimum of belongings and soon we were on our way.

'Everything went well considering our mode of travel, and apart from the expected inconveniences we were quite happy with our progress. After many weeks we reached the Khyber Pass with 500 miles still to travel. We were running very low on petrol so we pulled up to try to buy some. We were asked to produce a ration book. We had no idea what this meant, then the horror of horrors hit us when we were informed quite officially that because petrol was in such short supply there was no chance of us being sold any without a ration book. Even the people with ration books were being severely restricted.

'We sat in our old van quite devastated knowing that our tank was almost empty. We did not even have anything like enough to go back to the border and it looked like we would not be allowed to progress. We felt utterly helpless.

'Suddenly a strange wave of energy seemed to devour me. I ran out of the van up towards the official who was guarding the petrol. I started screaming at this man at the top of my voice telling him that he just had to give us some petrol. My husband came running up behind me wondering what the commotion was. I truly do not know what got into me that day as it was so unlike me to cause a fuss. My husband just stood and stared in disbelief at my irregular behaviour.

'The official started speaking loudly back to me but because I did not understand his language I had no idea what he was saying, having always relied on my husband to be my interpreter. I thought, by the tone of his voice, that he was arguing with me. This made me go into an absolute frenzy and I screamed and yelled blue murder into his face, bellowing at him to let me have some petrol.

'He suddenly stopped talking and stretched out his arm towards me. He then gestured for us both to follow him and he led us into a little building and told us to wait. He went into a back room and a few seconds later he came out carrying a can which he handed to us, explaining to my husband that it was enough petrol to at least get us on our way. I'm sure he only wanted to get rid of me screaming and yelling at him. We were overjoyed at receiving the petrol and thanked him and I must admit that I felt deeply ashamed of the way I had behaved.

'My husband poured the petrol into the tank and noticed that it could not have filled more than about half the tank. We had no idea how far this would take us but at least we could try to make it to the next petrol station and then see what could be done.

'It was very heavy going over that territory as the road was nothing more than a dirt track which made driving quite arduous. However, we plodded on hoping for the best. We reached the next petrol point but because the van seemed to be going fairly well we felt that maybe we should keep going while we could, and the petrol gauge reading was just under the half way mark.

'We travelled on without stopping for several hours and we both began to wonder at the petrol gauge being still just under the half-way mark. We assumed that it must be broken and we expected to run out of fuel any minute but since it was beginning to get dark we agreed that we would just keep driving until the petrol ran out then we would have a sleep in the car and wait for help. There was little else we could do as we were travelling down an endless road which was totally deserted of any towns or villages. The funny thing was that the old van showed no signs of struggling and just kept going.

'My husband drove all through the night while I slept, and in the early morning as dawn broke I woke up absolutely amazed to find that my husband was still driving and the petrol mark was still just under half full. Leaving the engine running we quickly changed seats so that he could have a sleep and I took over. Later on we changed places again just before we approached my husband's village.

'It was with great joy that he ushered me into his parents'

home but our joy quickly turned to sadness when we were informed that my Indian mother-in-law had been taken seriously ill. Within minutes of being introduced to her she died.

'A bit later that day, amidst the upheaval caused by the death in the family, with relatives and friends pouring into the house, my husband whispered to me that he would take me out to purchase a few items. In his sudden grief, I think he just needed to get away from the house for a little while.

'Without thinking, we got into our blue van but no matter how many times we tried we could not get that van to start. We just sat there in tears.'

∞

PATRICK Joy brings yet another story from Ireland and relates: 'I was born in Co. Kerry in 1934, taught at the national school in Killorglin, and that was about the sum of it till I started work. Like my brothers, I worked for my father who was the town blacksmith.

'The story begins when my brother Seamus took to the drink in an attempt to brow-beat my father who always drank too much. At least that was Seamus's excuse. A card game was played most nights at the local pub, but it was well known that these games were usually fixed by a gang of lads we called the bright boys. They used to wait until the unsuspecting players were well and truly sozzled when they would raise the stakes and of course they always came out winning.

'At that time there were two routes to our home which was only a mile away. We could take the main road which was fairly well lit until we got to the outskirts of the town when we had to rely on the lights from the odd cottages scattered along the way. The other way home was along the railway track which we usually joined at the nearest point to the pub which was by the exit to the local cinema.

'Nearly every night Seamus and I walked along the railway and our conversation would inevitably revolve around the fact that each night poor Seamus always seemed to lose money at the cards. We concluded between us that the only way he could hope to beat the bright boys would be for him to cut down on the drink. We also drummed it up between us that we would try to beat them at their own game by using their kind of tactics. The idea was to rig up some of his pals to join in the game with fixed cards. We put our plan into practice the next night and of course Seamus won every game. Then he sportingly bought every one of the bright boys a drink, taking care just to have coke ourselves.

That night we decided to go home by the main road. We were both cold sober as we had purposely kept off the booze so that we could concentrate on the cards and get one over on the bright boys. As we approached Carter's Shed which had once been a stable for the horses of the gentry, a huge black dog raced out from a doorway and stood right in front of us.

'Seamus was well used to animals and had a great way with them so he attempted to persuade the dog to move so that we could get past. We walked forward but the creature reared up on its hind legs and appeared more like a horse than a dog. It was then that we got really scared and I could feel my hair stand on end. Seamus looked over at me and whispered that this thing was no ordinary dog. We edged over a bit to see if we could slip past but there was no way that the beast was going to let us pass.

'We looked at each other and then very slowly started to move backwards, too frightened to turn our backs on the thing. We walked backwards for quite a time until we could see that the thing was not going to follow us. Then we turned round and ran as fast as we could back to the town without stopping once for breath. We got to the railway and made our way home by that route.

'We told the rest of the family about the dog the minute we got home but of course they all roared and laughed at us and none of them believed us, except for my mother. She was very serious about what had happened and told us that it was a warning for us and that we should not be gallavanting around the town at that hour anyway.

'I just did not know what to think about it and tried to put it out of my head but Seamus was so affected that he took to asking the priest for advice and also one of his old teachers who he was still very friendly with. From that day on we never ever went near Carter's Shed again.

'The years went by, Seamus got married and then took his family out to America. One night I received a telephone call from him. He told me that he had just finished doing some work for nuns at the local convent and he had just got into his car to drive home when suddenly the same black dog rushed out in front of him to prevent him taking his normal route home. He was petrified as he recognized the same creature by the way it reared up on its hind legs just like a horse, and he knew that the nuns did not keep any dogs so there was no mistaking the beast. He naturally tried to drive past but the animal kept leaping up on to the bonnet of his car making it impossible for him to proceed.

'He remembered my mother's words about it being some kind of warning so he did what we had done all those years earlier – he turned the car round on the roadway and drove home by a different route.

'He had only been home about ten minutes when news came to the house that there had been a terrible crash on the road and there was a big pile up of cars. This was the road that he would surely have been on had the dog not prevented him.'

∞

MR. JOHNSON M. ARAN from Kagumo in Kenya, Africa, is a schoolteacher by profession having started teaching in 1982. He has travelled extensively in Africa and has remained great friends with one of his tutors who related to him the following experience: 'One time my tutor went from Mombasa to Pakistan for further studies where he stayed for two years. Before he left Africa he had left his car with a friend who agreed to keep it in good condition and check it for rusting, etc. His two years' course completed, on the night he was due to leave Pakistan he telephoned his friend to inform him that he would be back shortly and to make sure the car would be ready for him.

'He arrived back in Mombasa and went straight to his friend's place to collect his car. They had only a soda together as my tutor was longing to see his own family and did not want to spend too much time before going home.

'His house was on the mainland Kilifi, and therefore he had to cross the old Nyali pontoon bridge. Before he crossed over onto the bridge a girl waved him down for a lift. By this time it was quite dark and he hesitated, but feeling a bit sorry for the stranded girl he stopped and opened the door of his car for her. She got in and he drove off but just as the car was halfway over the bridge the girl opened his car door while the vehicle was still moving and jumped out. He jammed on his brakes as he was sure she must have been very badly injured, and got out of his car expecting to find her stretched out on the road.

'Instead of that he saw the girl step up onto the safety bars of the bridge. He was terrified that she was about to commit suicide so he rushed up to her calling out not to jump.

'As he reached her, she just stepped off the bridge. He looked over and saw that she was gently floating downwards towards the water. He then watched her walk across the surface of the water as if it was a solid road. He just stared and stared, hardly able to believe his eyes as the girl walked further and further down mid-stream until she disappeared into the darkness. My tutor stood on that bridge for ages in a state of shock just staring down at the water. The loud bleeping of other motorists eventually brought his attention back to the fact that his car was holding up a long line of traffic on the bridge. He got back into his car and to this day he still doesn't know how he managed to drive himself home as his hands shook so much.

'On his arrival at his house he could not say one single word to his family, who were all convinced that he had become deaf and dumb. His wife went into a state of hysterics and some of the neighbours, hearing her loud screaming, came in to see if they could help. They arranged for my tutor to be taken to hospital where he was thoroughly checked over and it was found that he was in deep shock. He was kept in hospital that night for observation and thankfully the next day he had recovered sufficiently to tell the doctors what had happened.'

∞

A FISHING lady named Lorna was once on a holiday in Norway with some friends. 'They stayed at a large house in the mountains which we used as a base for our fishing trips. The house was owned by the uncle of one of my friends who normally travelled with us on these trips but that year he had suddenly been taken ill and was unable to leave his home in London.

'One day I had been out walking on the mountains and returned to find the house empty so I sat down in the dining room to have my supper. The window looked out onto a verandah where there was an assortment of chairs where we all used to sit out in the sun. My host always used to sit in one particular rocking chair out on the porch every day when he was staying in the mountain house. While I was having my supper I saw the rocking chair begin to rock back and forwards. This went on for some time so I went outside to see if a sudden high wind could have sprung up but outside all was calm and still except for the chair which kept rocking back and forwards with no one sitting in it.

'After supper I went down to the river to find my friend who was fishing as I had not seen her since breakfast that morning. When I reached her she had just caught a fish but she seemed very depressed. I asked her what was wrong and she told me that there had been a telephone call from London earlier that day to inform her that her uncle, my host, had just died.'

PETER and his wife Doreen went to stay at a friend's house just outside Sydney in Australia. The first night they went to bed in the comfortable guest bedroom on the ground floor. 'We fell asleep but I was wakened in the middle of the night by heavy footsteps trudging up and down the staircase, the foot of which started just along the corridor outside our bedroom. The next morning I asked Doreen if she had slept well and she told me she had. I was waiting for her to tell me that she too had heard the footsteps but she never mentioned it so, not wishing to frighten her, I kept quiet about what I had heard. Being that I was a guest in the house I did not like to say anything to my host so I just kept my mouth shut about the footsteps.

'I settled down to sleep the following night trying not to think too much about the previous night's activity and after reading for a while I drifted off to sleep. A thundering thumping noise wakened me up once more. It went on and on up and down the stairs, up and down, for ages. I was nearly out of my mind with the noise but what really amazed me was the way my wife continued to sleep right through this pandemonium as if nothing was happening.

'This went on for about half an hour and it took every ounce of self-control not to roar out to anyone who might be listening to stop the din. I eventually got to sleep again and in the morning, just like the morning before, my wife made no remark to show she had heard anything unusual. Something still prevented me from reporting the tramping footsteps to my host.

'On the night before we were due to leave, I was again wakened but this time I heard not a sound but I could feel icy fingertips running up and down my back. I turned round quickly to see if my wife had touched me but she was fast asleep beside me and I could still feel the freezing cold fingers on my back. I broke out in a cold sweat and lay down on my back and pulled the bedcover right over my head to try to block out whatever was touching me.

'As soon as I did this the fingers left my back. I had just heaved an enormous sigh of relief when suddenly I felt almost winded as something thumped me on my ribs. Once more I felt a tremendous punch in the ribs but by this time I'd had enough. I just screamed out telling whatever it was to clear off and leave me alone except my actual terminology was somewhat more forceful than that.

'My wife sprang up in the bed with fright wondering who I was shouting at. I told her not to worry. From that moment I had no further trouble but I got the distinct impression that the entity had made its point by getting me to recognize its existence and would now be happy to let things be.'

Watch out for

II

by
**Peter and Mary
Harrison**

ISBN 1–872149–04–9

THE CHILDREN THAT TIME FORGOT

"The most unusual book of the year"

– Derek Naylor, Yorkshire Evening Post

Peter and Mary Harrison

MYSTIC FORCES

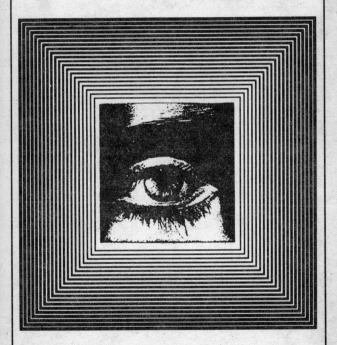

Peter and Mary Harrison

ISBN 1–872149–00–6

IF YOU HAVE HAD AN EXPERIENCE WHICH YOU CANNOT EXPLAIN IN ORDINARY LOGICAL TERMS WE WOULD BE VERY PLEASED TO HEAR FROM YOU. PLEASE WRITE DOWN THE DETAILS AND SEND THEM TO:

> PETER & MARY HARRISON
> c/o SINCLAIR PUBLISHING LTD
> 26 SILVER STREET
> WELLINGBOROUGH
> NORTHANTS NN8 1AY

WITCHCRAFT CONSPIRACY

Graham St. John-Willey

The Mystique of Love

BY
PETER & MARY
HARRISON

OUT SOON